Political Asylum Deceptions

Carol Bohmer • Amy Shuman

Political Asylum Deceptions

The Culture of Suspicion

Carol Bohmer
Department of Government
Dartmouth College
Hanover, USA

Department of War Studies
King's College
London, UK

Amy Shuman
Department of English
The Ohio State University
Columbus, USA

ISBN 978-3-319-67403-2   ISBN 978-3-319-67404-9   (eBook)
https://doi.org/10.1007/978-3-319-67404-9

Library of Congress Control Number: 2017963263

Cover Image - RichardBakerHeathrow / Alamy Stock Photo

Printed on acid-free paper

This Palgrave Macmillan imprint is published by Springer Nature
The registered company is Springer International Publishing AG
The registered company address is: Gewerbestrasse 11, 6330 Cham, Switzerland

Carol dedicates this book to the memory of Ian Borrin: kind employer, wonderful friend, and irreplaceable clipping service.

Amy dedicates the book in memory of her mother, Noni Shuman.

ENDORSEMENTS

Political Asylum Deceptions is a timely and well-argued book that addresses head-on the most fundamental, yet vexing questions in asylum law and policy, especially those relating to the ambiguous boundaries between lying and truth-telling. The authors' combined expertise in law and policy and narrative and textual analysis provides the perfect combination for decoding the flaws in our current approaches to differentiating between legitimate and fraudulent claims for asylum. This original and provocative book will become an essential resource for everyone involved in the asylum process.
—Iris Berger, *University at Albany, State University of New York, USA*

This sequel to Bohmer and Shuman's ground-breaking volume *Rejecting Refugees* (2007) does not disappoint: their analysis of asylum cases is brilliant and their empathy for asylum seekers is, as always, admirable. But it is their discussion of the link between truth and deception that makes this book mandatory reading not only for scholars but also for asylum lawyers, judges, and refugee advocates.
—Marco Jacquemet, *Professor of Communication and Culture, University of San Francisco, USA*

Millions of refugees desperately need humanitarian protection, yet today asylum seekers are increasingly labeled liars, criminals, and even terrorists. How did we get to the point where society's most vulnerable are enveloped by a cloud of hostile suspicion? In this rigorous and highly readable book Bohmer and Shuman resume their highly productive collaboration to highlight the relentless governmental focus on pseudo-science, evidence, truth, credibility, and proof, and examine real malfeasance stories. Illicit activities and complex webs of transnational mobility ultimately contribute to claims of fraud, corruption, and deceit, trapping countless numbers and further eroding compassion and understanding.
—Benjamin N. Lawrance, *Editor-in-Chief, African Studies Review*

In grappling with the issue of 'deception' in the asylum process, Bohmer and Shuman tackle some of the most important and difficult questions facing both advocates and decision makers. What counts as evidence? Is it enough to 'tell your story'? When is it okay to lie? And do the deceptions that are an inevitable consequence of the complex and messy situations from which people flee invalidate their claims for protection? Sharply observed and carefully written, this is a 'must read' for anyone who believes that 'truth' is almost always more complex than it seems.
—Heaven Crawley, *Chair in International Migration at the Centre for Trust, Peace and Social Relations, Coventry University, UK*

From stories through 'facts', evidence and 'having a case', to being a subject in a world of restrictions and deception: this is the journey described in this book, and it is the journey of large numbers of asylum seekers in the 21st century. Richly documented and carefully argued, Bohmer and Shuman's book must be placed among the handful of studies that take our understanding of the contemporary asylum system genuinely forward.
—Jan Blommaert, *Professor and Director of Babylon, Center for the Study of Multicultural Societies, Tilburg University, the Netherlands*

Acknowledgments

We would like to thank the following people who have made it possible to write this book. They include those who gave their valuable time to be interviewed, as well as those who provided ideas and information. Their help was immeasurable. Those wonderful people include Navtej Ahluwalia, Dan Berger, Katia Bianchini, Ana Cara, Christina Corbaci, Kathleen Dickey, Sophie Feal, Jane Herlihy, Jean Pierre Gauci, Guy Goodwin-Gill, Alison Harvey, Shannon Hurd, Erin Jacobsen, Megan Kludt, Matthew Kolken, David Lebow, Rachel Lewis, Jess McIntyre, Michael Marszalkowski, Sonali Naik, Mark Nesbit, Peter Patrick, Angie Plummer, Tuesday Reitano, Catherine Robinson, David Ruoff, Charles Rutonesha, Helene Sigmond, Farzad Siman, James Sinclair, Sarah Singer, Solange Valdez-Symonds, Guglielmo Verdirame, Peter Verney, Wendy Hesford, and Stephen Yale-Loehr. The Mershon Center for International Security provided funds for us to do our collaborative work. We are grateful to Universal Uclick, a Division of Andrews McMeel Universal, for permission to reproduce the *Doonsbury* cartoon. We deeply apologize if there is anyone we have left out in error.

ABOUT THE BOOK

This book explores the legitimacy of political asylum applications in the US and UK through an examination of the varieties of evidence, narratives, and documentation with which they are assessed. Credibility is the central issue in determining the legitimacy of political asylum seekers, but the line between truth and lies is often elusive, partly because desperate people often have to use deception to escape persecution.

The vetting process has become infused with a climate of suspicion that not only assesses the credibility of an applicant's story and differentiates between the economic migrant and the person fleeing persecution, but also attempts to determine whether an applicant represents a future threat to the receiving country. This innovative text approaches the problem of deception from several angles, including increased demand for evidence, uses of new technologies to examine applicants' narratives, assessments of forged documents, attempts to differentiate between victims and persecutors, and ways that cultural misunderstandings can compromise the process. Essential reading for researchers and students of Political Science, International Studies, Refugee and Migration Studies, Human Rights, Anthropology, Sociology, Law, Public Policy, and Narrative Studies.

CONTENTS

Author Bios

Carol Bohmer is a visiting scholar in the Government Department at Dartmouth College, and a teaching fellow at King's College, London. She has worked in the area of law and society, examining the way legal and social institutions interact. Her most recent book is *Rejecting Refugees: Political Asylum in the 21st Century*, (2007) with Amy Shuman.

Amy Shuman is a professor at the Ohio State University where she is the recipient of the Distinguished Scholar and Distinguished Teaching awards. She is a Guggenheim Fellow. Her publications include *Storytelling Rights: The Uses of Oral and Written Texts Among Urban Adolescents*, *Other People's Stories: Entitlement Claims and the Critique of Empathy*, and, with Carol Bohmer, *Rejecting Refugees: Political Asylum in the 21st Century*.

CHAPTER 1

Introduction

Hugo Bohmer (Carol's father) grew up in what was then Czechoslovakia. As a young man, he worked in Germany in the 1930s, but his employer was forced to fire him because he was a Jew. He spent a lot of time in the late 1930s looking for a visa to get out of Europe. For someone without assets, connections, or family living outside Europe, this was a difficult proposition, more so as the 1930s progressed.

In the end, he was able to get a visa to New Zealand. He did this by telling the government that he was a farmer, because New Zealand was giving visas to farmers. In fact, although he had grown up on a farm, he was a textile engineer and had never had any intention of being a farmer. To obtain the visa, he also had to show the New Zealand government that he had some assets, so he borrowed the money from an acquaintance for a fee, put it in his bank account, and then having provided the bank statement to the New Zealand visa authorities, gave it back to the person he had borrowed it from. Visa in hand, he and his wife, Augusta (Carol's mother), left Europe in May 1939. All the other members of their families subsequently died in the Holocaust. Hugo's visa was obtained on the basis of two lies, without which Carol would not be around to write this book.

Hugo Bohmer did not obtain a visa as a refugee because such visas did not exist at the time. He would have had a valid claim as a refugee who fled because he feared persecution as a Jew. Not until after the Holocaust, which showed the tragedy of not providing a safe haven for those who were persecuted, did the international community come together and pass an international convention, called the Convention on the Status of

© The Author(s) 2018
C. Bohmer, A. Shuman, *Political Asylum Deceptions*,
https://doi.org/10.1007/978-3-319-67404-9_1

Refugees, in 1951. That Convention defines a refugee as someone who, "owing to a well-founded fear of being persecuted for reasons of race, religion, nationality, membership of a particular social group or political opinion, is outside the country of his nationality, and is unable to, or owing to such fear, is unwilling to avail himself of the protection of that country." This definition is the basis for all asylum claims in the 148 countries that have signed on to the Convention or the Protocol, an expansion agreed to in 1967. The Convention was seen as a way of ensuring that should there be crises in future, countries would not stand by as they did in the Holocaust, but rather provide a home for genuine refugees.

Fast-forward to the twenty-first century, and the decision about who is a genuine refugee is the central concern in asylum law and policy. How do we know that an applicant for asylum is telling the truth? What evidence is enough for us to make that decision? The word "credibility" is used constantly as the holy grail to differentiate the truth tellers from the liars. But as Hugo's story shows, it is often necessary to lie, or at the very least to shade the truth. Was Hugo, the son of a farmer, who had been required to spend time working on his father's farm, a "farmer" as defined by the New Zealand government? Or was his claim an outright lie? The story of Jews using deceptive means to cross borders in the early days of the Holocaust are by now familiar and include lying to border guards and lying about financial means to gain a sponsor (Stapinski 2017). Our book is based on the premise that there is an important difference between the lies desperate people tell so they can escape persecution to find a safe haven and the lies told by people attempting to game the system. Lying is widespread, but the lies vary greatly, from small, insignificant lies, to the use of forged documents, to lies that are central to the asylum claim, for example, people who claim to be victims of persecution, but who are in fact the perpetrators. In this book, we identify the methods used by the officials to differentiate between different kinds of lies, and we discuss how the climate of suspicion influences officials' decision. By failing to differentiate among the varieties of deception, officials sometimes disregard the difference between lies that count and those that do not (or should not) in the assessment of the legitimacy of asylum claims.

We're writing at a time when asylum policy has resulted in proportionately fewer and fewer acceptances each year, and increasing numbers of applicants are overwhelming the system. However, as we will argue, the numbers do not tell the whole story of what could be an impending breakdown in political policy practice. Understanding how the system

conceptualizes deception is an important key that exposes often unarticulated attitudes toward particular groups of asylum seekers.[1]

Our book, focusing primarily on the UK and the US, also examines
what the asylum authorities do about lying. Are any lies acceptable? If so,
which ones? The tendency in host countries nowadays is to take a very
tough line with any lie, however small and insignificant, as a way of limiting the numbers of people who successfully claim asylum. In this book, we
also discuss methods used by the authorities in their attempts to decide
whether someone is lying or not. How can we tell if someone is lying? In
fact, research shows that we are generally not very good at telling if someone is lying (Gray 2011). This includes those whose job it is to assess the
veracity of narratives, like judges and police officers (see, e.g. Vrij 2008;
Ekman et al. 1999; Stromwall and Granhag 2003; Hartwig et al. 2004).

The book is also about evidence. What counts as evidence? Is an applicant's narrative enough? What about the veracity of documents? We also
examine how the requirements for evidence have changed over the last
couple of decades, as asylum has become harder and harder to obtain. The
law generally says that an asylum seeker's narrative should be enough, but
the reality is that without some supporting documentation and other evidence, an application is often doomed to fail.

We also discuss the possible motivations for lying. For some applicants,
the necessity of deception may be self-evident. Carol's father lied about
being a farmer and having some assets without which he would not have
been granted a visa. But the motivation to deceive is not always so clear.
Our research has found that often people lie even when the truth would
have been more likely to result in a successful asylum claim. We assume
they do so because they do not know what evidence is likely to support
their claim and make assumptions, often unfounded, about what the
authorities want to hear. We have also heard about people who get stuck
in their lies when the strategic thing to do would be to accept that they
had made a mistake and explain how that had happened. As we discuss,
facing the challenge of relating unimaginable atrocities, legitimate asylum
seekers sometimes embellish or exaggerate their accounts, perhaps, as
some scholars explain, because the inconceivable "had to be described as
greater in scope in every retelling" (Gessen 2017). Are these exaggerations
evidence of suffering (thus confirming the applicant's legitimacy) or of
deception (justifying a denial)?

Over the last decade, many political asylum scholars and policy makers
have pointed to the issue of credibility as a fundamental feature of the

success or failure of asylum claims. The literature includes extensive discussion about how we can determine whether the applicant is telling the truth or not (Shaw and Witkin 2004: Herlihy et al. 2012; Granhag et al. 2005), which is something we can never know. We have no idea of how many people get asylum based on false information, or how many are denied because they are thought not to be credible when, in fact, they are telling the truth. Many in the field assert that there is a "culture of disbelief" in which the authorities assume that everyone is lying. As Didier Fassin points out, "There was a time, not so long ago, when the relationship between the administration and the claimants was one of trust. It has reversed into mistrust" (2013: 48). We challenge two faulty assumptions prevalent in asylum discourses in the media, both those who assume that everyone is lying and those who assume that asylum applicants never lie. We acknowledge that some applicants lie, attempt to game the system, and/or use deceptive means to gain asylum. However, the current practices for differentiating between legitimate and fraudulent applicants are seriously flawed and require careful scrutiny of what counts as evidence, how evidence is evaluated, and what forms of supporting evidence is useful.

One of the problems lies in the origin of the system, created to address issues post-World War II, as embodied in the 1951 Convention relating to the Status of Refugees, and the 1967 Protocol, which removed previous temporal and geographical restrictions. The Convention was focused on issues that were seen as important at the time and was originally designed by European states for European refugees. During the Cold War, the system worked reasonably well, when refugee-producing states and those providing asylum were ideological opponents who welcomed refugees for political reasons (Hathaway 1990). The officials just assumed that those fleeing the communist bloc to the West were fleeing communism, which made them perfect candidates for asylum, especially in the anti-communist USA. Since the end of the Cold War, for the most part, the political benefits no longer exist, and refugee-producing countries may just as easily be political or economic "friends" as enemies. At particular moments of conflict, groups of people fleeing violence in failed states (or communism, in the case of Cuba) have been admitted without proving individually targeted persecution. Examples include Somalia, Afghanistan, Iran, and Syria. These exceptions are temporary, and as we will discuss, asylum seekers sometimes attempt to pass as a member of a group more likely to be approved. Additionally, Brad Blitz argues that these shifts in political alignments have produced the current contradictions between border protection and the humanitarian goals underlying asylum (2017: 383). Some argue that preference is still given to people from particular countries facing particular forms of persecution. Chang and Lithicum report:

> Statistics show that an immigrant's chance of winning asylum depends largely on where he or she is from. In 2012, more than 10,000 people from China were granted asylum, compared with just 126 Mexicans and 234 Hondurans, according to federal data. Immigration court figures, which do not include cases approved in an initial hearing by an asylum officer, show a success rate of nearly 50% for Chinese versus 1% for Mexicans (2013, np).

Claimants today have to take into consideration how their cases will be viewed within current political circumstances and changing global attitudes toward those circumstances. Except for the few exceptions of those fleeing extensive civil war mentioned earlier, people have to prove that they personally have been persecuted and that this persecution was because they were part of a recognized persecuted group. Someone who flees civil war and arrives in another country where they apply for asylum must prove not only the existence of general persecution but also that they were at risk as individuals because of one of the listed bases of persecution, which include race, nationality, religion, political opinion, and membership in a particular social group. It is not enough to claim that they fled because the situation was violent, and therefore anyone in the area could be in danger. Immigration authorities question whether all of the people who flee *en masse* to neighboring countries are at risk of persecution.

Some scholars argue that the Convention is no longer fit for purpose and should be expanded to those fleeing from such things as environmental degradation or civil war generally (e.g. Betts 2013; McAdam 2014). Given the political climate and the fears generated by the recent refugee crisis on both sides of the Atlantic, this argument is a nonstarter. In fact, political leaders are more interested in limiting the possibility of asylum in various ways in Europe and North America rather than expanding its reach. One of many examples can be found in the EU plan to send refugees who arrive in Greece to Turkey to be processed there, in a deal with Turkey which involved payments of up to 3 billion Euros and "reenergising" talks on Turkey's future EU membership (Rankin 2016). This current enthusiasm for outsourcing the refugee problem away from Europe is an illustration of the need to make policy that serves the immediate needs of the EU, despite questions raised by NGOs and others about the ethical and human rights implications of such a policy. Some of the justification for this policy stems from the current conflating of the refugee crisis with the security crisis felt in Europe after recent terrorist attacks in several countries in Europe. Relocation arrangements between particular countries are central to restrictive asylum policies. Brad Blitz writes, the condition in which "states are granted aid in exchange for receiving refugees (e.g., Turkey, Ethiopia, Morocco)—explicitly reframes humanitarian policy as another facet of security policy and harkens back to a Cold War logic" (2017: 395).

Asylum law is based on the idea of protecting people from persecution, but it has turned into a discourse about protecting the receiving country from potentially dangerous migrants. As we complete this book, the discourses of anxiety about admitting economic migrants who purport to be victims of persecution has shifted into a discourse about international security and the fear of terrorism. Calling it a security problem is a way of justifying what could be a violation of international law (see also Blitz 2017: 395). Intensified by 9/11, the fear of terrorism is sufficiently widespread and deeply rooted as to make other concerns about rights and obligations seem less important.

The legal system is designed to identify deception of economic migrants masquerading as asylum seekers. Using the same methods, they are now trying to identify terrorists. The methods of identifying minor contradictions to catch deceptive economic migrants were faulty and somewhat ineffective, but these methods are even more useless and inappropriate for detecting terrorists. We examine the efforts that are being made, including increasingly "scientific" measures, a response to anxiety about terrorism that is being applied to all asylum seekers, regardless of any indication that they are connected to a terrorist group.

What we are *not* saying in this book is that asylum seekers are frauds. Rather, we examine the fault lines in determining fraud. We suggest that the current methods used by immigration authorities are not effective for determining fraud, who, instead, sometimes disqualify legitimate applicants. We recognize that some people who claim asylum do not satisfy the legal standards of the 1951 Convention, but they are not the serious criminals they are portrayed to be. The asylum system now has extensive requirements designed to assess the validity of elements of the claim. For example, many immigration offices attempt to use modern scientific methods to decide whether someone is telling the truth and check documents to determine whether they are forged. Someone whose passport is found to be false can be charged with a criminal offence and then labeled a criminal for what may have been a legitimate effort to use the necessary and available means to escape persecution. The law requires a high standard to prove that an applicant suffered persecution rather than discrimination. Some groups, such as the Roma, who suffer many difficulties in their homelands, may not be able to prove that these difficulties reached the level of persecution rather than the more mundane discrimination suffered by many minority groups. The Roma are also vulnerable to being portrayed as criminals, because, historically living on the fringes of communities, they have been characterized as dangerous.[2]

But the world has come full circle. Instead of welcoming those fleeing persecution, as was the intention of the Convention when it was passed in 1951, the immigration officials and policy makers now devote time and attention to finding ways of preventing people from finding a refuge in another country. If refugees do manage the increasingly difficult journey to a safe place, the receiving countries work hard to find ways of denying that they are legitimate refugees and sending them back, or if that is not possible, of forcing them to live in limbo and in miserable circumstances.

One current framing of asylum seekers is that some of them are terrorists, and therefore all should be denied asylum. This is particularly popular in the USA, where more than half the states have said they will not accept Syrian refugees (Fantz and Brumfield 2015). The extreme version of this is Donald Trump Junior's comparison of Syrian refugees to a bowl of Skittles. He said, "If I had a bowl of Skittles and I told you just three would kill you. Would you take a handful?" (Hauser 2016). The implication, which is factually incorrect, is that a significant percentage of the Syrian refugees who would come to the USA as refugees are terrorists, and therefore all refugees should be rejected. Such an attitude has become more widespread recently, partly because the occasional perpetrator of terror attacks has been a refugee, and partly because states are reeling from the huge influx of refugees into Europe from the Syrian civil war and other problem areas.

Until recently, the American public has been largely ignorant of the category of refugee. With a short break after 9/11, refugee admissions of up to 80,000 per year have taken place largely out of the public eye. However, anti-refugee sentiments have been fueled in the USA by recent cases of terrorism by refugees, including the Boston Marathon bombers who were the children of refugees and the Somali-born refugee student in the Ohio State rampage in November 2016. Perhaps the most significant in terms of impact on the public consciousness were the recent attacks in San Bernardino in December 2015 (Nagourney et al. 2015). Home-grown Islamic extremists engaged in a planned attack at a holiday party in the Inland Regional Center that killed 14 people and injured 24. Despite the fact that neither of the perpetrators (a husband and wife couple) were refugees, the fears generated by this attack increased public concern about Muslim immigration in general. The current concern about Syrian refu-gees can be seen to be the result of such terrorism by Islamist jihadists. This concern flies in the face of the fact that the Syrians are often fleeing jihadists in Syria, rather than being among their number.

In contrast to these portrayals of popular sentiment of not welcoming refugees, an Amnesty International survey of public opinions regarding refugees reveals that "government refugee policies [are] out of touch with public opinion" (Amnesty International 2016). Policy makers may be developing obstacles for asylum seekers, but the general public remains sympathetic to their plight. Brad Blitz argues "that there has been a marked divide between public attitudes towards the treatment of refugees and asylum seekers and official policies regarding asylum and humanitar-ian assistance" (2017: 381).

In this book, we document the different means used by immigration officials to identify fraud, and we note that the methods used to identify economic migrants are often the same as those used to identify other opportunists, terrorists, or persecutors masquerading as victims. We sug-gest that more accurate assessments of legitimacy require better under-standing of the different kinds of deception applicants deploy, and especially we argue for the importance of understanding the strategic uses of decep-tion used by legitimate asylum seekers. As we discuss in the following chap-ters, the system is not particularly effective in its efforts to identify fraudulent applicants, and, often, legitimate applicants are refused asylum.

In the USA, many fraudulent applicants are presumed to be economic migrants. However, economic migrants and refugees are not necessarily dichotomous categories, but more often represent a continuum. All asy-lum seekers fleeing persecution hope for a better life, including economi-cally. Also, in reality, many asylum seekers had professional careers in their home countries and take on much more menial positions when they receive asylum, thus defying the assumption that they are actually eco-nomic migrants.[3]

The asylum process must wrestle with the larger issues of who deserves asylum and who should be prevented from gaining asylum (Blitz 2017: 381).

Much of that decision is dependent on how asylum seekers frame their claims, which is a matter of strategic presentation and emphasis, and might include strategic uses of deception.

Although asylum seekers and refugees always have been accused of potentially having nefarious motives, for example, as spies during World War II, in the current climate, the grounds of suspicion have shifted and intensified. Despite statistical evidence to the contrary, asylum seekers currently are suspected of being terrorists.

In some well-documented cases, some individuals who received asylum were later discovered to have lied on their applications, and in some cases, persecutors successfully presented themselves as victims. Differentiating between a perpetrator and a victim may require different methods than the current efforts, which focus on finding discrepancies and inconsistencies in an application. One of our arguments, which we return to in the conclusion of the book, is that careful vetting of applicants requires better understanding of the ways that claimants rely on strategic presentations of the truth to frame their experiences in terms acceptable to the authorities. The strategic presentations of the truth that applicants need to survive to escape violence do not always translate into a coherent narrative recognized by the asylum officials. As we have observed elsewhere, the interchange between an applicant and her legal representative is all about developing ways of developing a coherent narrative that will enhance the claim (Shuman and Bohmer 2004). For this reason (among others), claimants who are legally represented are much more likely to be granted asylum (Ramji-Nogales et al. 2009).

Ironically, at the very time when the asylum system is intent on rooting out those whose claims are not credible, we make heroes of those who in the past lied to help people escape persecution. Sir Nicholas Winton, who died recently, was celebrated for his efforts to help 669 children escape the Nazis. He is reported to have forged documents because the Home Office documents were too slow to arrive. As Colin Yeo points out, "Today's politicians like to claim that Britain has a 'proud tradition of providing refuge at times of crisis'. The words are carefully chosen. What is not said is that the tradition is a bygone one that has ended. A modern day Sir Winton would risk prosecution by the UK authorities" (Yeo 2015). He could be prosecuted both under the Immigration Act of 1971 and the Forgery and Counterfeiting Act of 1981 (ibid.). Another case recently came to light involving Adolfo Kaminsky, who, as a teenager, saved thousands of lives by helping children escape the Nazis (Druckerman 2016).

He subsequently devoted his life to helping others flee persecution by forging documents for them. He is viewed with respect, rather than prosecuted, for his efforts to make flight possible when it would otherwise have been impossible.

The larger question underlying our inquiry is the culture of suspicion that motivates political asylum decisions. Liisa Malkki suggests that the "fake" asylum seekers are quite possibly victims of "life-threatening postcolonial poverty" who find no solution other than to claim that they are asylum seekers. She writes, "We should be ready to consider the possibility, at least, that contemporary asylum seekers and immigrants are de facto being forced to convert the psychic trauma of impoverishment and hopelessness into a performed psychic trauma of formulaic political violence" (2007: 341). In this book, we consider three connected practices and discourses that help to illuminate the culture of suspicion in the political asylum process. First, expanding Malkki's observation, we ask, if asylum seekers *are* imposters, then who are they in actuality? Are they economic migrants, opportunists, terrorists, or people who don't fit in the current asylum categories? We argue that who they are *presumed* to be matters for how their cases are evaluated. Second, we consider the technologies and methods used to assess asylum cases and observe that these methods, often faulty or imprecise, might give the illusion of greater scrutiny, but they are often motivated by the desire to control borders rather than by an interest in more comprehensive understanding of the complex situations the applicants describe. Third, we offer an in-depth account of the varieties of deception used in the political asylum system, including both the applicants' strategies and the immigration officials' assessments. Although asylum applicants have had actual, documentable experiences, and although we live in a world of increasingly available knowledge about all areas in the world, violence is usually accompanied by restricted information; further, the immigration officials deploy their available knowledge strategically. Exposing the contradictions, strategies, and forms of deception does not necessarily change the system, but it might provide a clearer picture of how it works.

ORGANIZATION OF THE BOOK

The book begins with a discussion of the nature of evidence and its connections to strategic deceptions, fabrications, and lies in the asylum process, as well as the various ways the authorities attempt to determine whether the applicant is telling the "truth." We look at what counts as evidence and how fraudulence is evaluated. We ask what are the kinds of evidence that are needed, disregarded, or overlooked in asylum claims? What kinds of discrepancies arouse suspicion? In Chapter 2, we examine the role of narrative in the asylum-hearing process. In the absence of documentation, these narratives of what happened are a primary form of evidence and, thus, a focal point for suspicion. As Caroline Moorehead (2005: 165) notes describing asylum applicants, "Their story is their only real passport." Narrative is a culturally specific form; how much description is given, and when it is given, whether at the beginning or in the middle of an account, differ according to cultural conventions. Some cultural conventions for telling personal accounts rely more on dialogue; some provide more meta-commentary. In some cases, asylum applicants fail to offer enough contextual information to explain what might otherwise look like a discrepancy. Some applicants fail to report a significant event because they do not remember, are too humiliated, or are too traumatized. And the contrary is also possible; some applicants fabricate traumatic events in their narratives. In addition, some applicants use scripted narratives that they have been told, or that they imagine, will be more convincing to the hearing officer. Although it is impossible to know with any certainty that a narrative is fraudulent, it is possible to identify some of the dimensions of narrative that are helpful in understanding discrepancies.

We use discourse analysis to better understand the complexities of testimony, and the ways in which "truth" and "lies" are framed and perceived.

In Chapter 3, we describe the increasing demand for documentation to support a claimant's narrative. In legal procedures, documents are often considered to be neutral and given more credibility than oral accounts, when, in fact, like narratives, they are dependent on the conditions of their production. Documents function very differently in asylum cases than in other areas of law. There is very little standardization, predictability, or reliability in the evaluation of and use of documents in political asylum hearings. Applying Western legal methods to understand these documents (or absence of documents) only exacerbates a situation already complicated by this lack of standardization, the risk applicants take in acquiring or traveling with documents, and the motivation to use fraudulent documents in life-or-death situations.

Chapter 4 examines the efforts by many immigration officials to quantify what is in fact soft data. The authorities, especially in the UK, try to find what they consider to be more "scientific" evidence to question asylum narratives, by using such tools as language analysis, bone age tests, DNA, medical exams, as well as supporting evidence from experts. Many of these "scientific" tools have been discredited as unworkable or inappropriate in asylum claims. The authority-granted supporting evidence may work in favor of the claimant or against them. In either case, this approach moves the focus from the narrative to the body of the asylum applicant. Evidence on the body, for example, scars resulting from torture increasingly require additional documentation, and the requirement for additional certificates or other authoritative expertise has served to shift what counts as truth and evidence in the asylum process (Fassin and d'Hulluin 2005: 598).

Chapter 5 addresses evidentiary issues in claims based on membership in a particular social group, a category that is increasingly used in asylum cases. While this is one of the original Convention grounds, the category has been expanded recently to include new types of claims to accommodate the recognition that people are persecuted for a broader range of reasons than was anticipated in the original plan, especially as a basis for claims on the basis of gender and LGBT persecution.

We focus on the category of social group because it has generated significant challenges to assessing deception. First, determining what constitutes a social group is difficult; second, determining whether an individual applicant belongs to that group proves problematic. The authorities have used standard techniques that are often unhelpful for assessing credibility to make these determinations. Our discussion of these measures as well as new measures of credibility addresses these problems.

In the second half of the book, we examine cases of corruption in the lives of asylum seekers and show how cultural differences can factor into different perceptions of appropriate behavior. We also examine known cases of evidence in which the claimant has lied, to learn more about the effect the known lies has on the system. The most extreme version of this is the determination of whether someone is a victim of persecution or a perpetrator of it, a distinction that is surprisingly quite difficult to make.

Asylum applicants' participation in corrupt practices, including bribery, the purchase of false identity documents, and payment to smugglers, is not necessarily a sign that their applications are fraudulent. On the contrary, refugees in general find themselves navigating many forms of underground and illegal operations in their efforts to survive (Tinti and Reitano 2016: 254). Further, refugees often utilize the same routes as those used in drug trade, illicit exports, and sexual trafficking (Hibou 1999: 79). The most legitimate asylum seekers are sometimes criminalized as a result of these associations.

Chapter 6 focuses on cultural assessments to illustrate the difficulty in evaluating evidence cross-culturally. We examine the use of bribery and corruption; bribery falls into the category of things that are "illegal" and therefore make the officials suspicious. They assume this is something only people from asylum-sending countries do, although, in fact, we all do it but we consider it perfectly acceptable and call it "networking" or "making use of contacts." We show that certain kinds of fraudulence are considered offensive and reprehensible (and not credible) even though they are business as usual in the society from which the applicant is fleeing, and especially so for someone fleeing persecution.

In Chapter 7, we examine cases in which it is clear that an asylum claim was fraudulent, either because a court has made such a decision or for other reasons such as a confession by the claimant that s/he lied. By using cases in which the "proof" is as good as can be obtained, we can learn more about the nature of lying in the asylum process and the working of the process itself.

Chapter 8 examines the difficulty in differentiating between a victim and a perpetrator in some cases. There's no question that there are legitimate asylum seekers in great numbers fleeing violence, but the violence itself, especially in contemporary civil wars, makes it difficult to sharply divide perpetrators and victims. This complicated question of whether someone is a victim or a perpetrator illustrates the high stakes involved in the assessment of asylum claims in the current security environment. We examine cases in which aggressors self-identify as hero or as victims, while members of the victim group, in particular in the diaspora, identify them as perpetrators. Our goal is not to provide a panacea or easy solution (we argue there is none) but to elucidate the complexity. In cases where an applicant may be a perpetrator, the authorities are caught between admitting someone who may turn out to be a criminal or a security risk, or not admitting someone who is genuinely fleeing persecution. Because the stakes are so high, the system may treat all fraudulent cases as dangerous, especially in the current climate of security concern.

In the conclusion, we return to the complex current situation in which the policy of providing safe haven for people fleeing persecution is often at odds with the interests in controlling borders, limiting migration, and identifying potential terrorists. We discuss how the fear of admitting unwanted asylum seekers drives the system. Instead of saying that too many people are coming in, and we can't cope, the system finds them fraudulent. We ask, if asylum seekers are masquerading, what are their true identities? If they are economic migrants, is it possible that the description of oneself as persecuted and the description of oneself as suffering are inseparable? Further, we consider how the current climate of suspicion turns victims of persecution into possible liars, opportunists, or criminals. The process has become transformed from its interest in protection to its focus on border control, resulting not only in the reduction of numbers of accepted applicants but also in a culture of suspicion in which individuals who have endured horrible atrocities are positioned not as victims but as accused.[4]

We review how immigration officials use narratives, documentary evidence, and new technologies to assess the legitimacy of claims and suggest that greater attention to these measures could yield more accurate results. In particular, we observe how the attention to minor contradictions and/or inaccuracies in an applicant's claim is not necessarily an indication of fraudulence.

We don't presume to offer solutions to the problems we describe, but we hope that our discussion of the kinds and degree of deception used by asylum seekers provides a guide for a more complex and nuanced examination of the claims.

NOTES

1. See Brad Blitz' review of the comparison between policies and public attitudes toward particular groups of refugees and asylum seekers (2017).
2. Silverman, 2012, p. 297. Note 21.
3. "Most refugees unable to get recognition of their domestic qualifications have neither the money nor the language skills to re-qualify in their host country and are forced to take unskilled jobs in order to feed their families" Van Wassenhove and Boufaied, 2015.
4. See Susan Coutin's discussion of how victims become suspects (2001) and Didier Fassin's discussion of dialectics of criminalization and humanitarianism in the political asylum process (2005: 52).

CHAPTER 2

Telling the True Story

To be successful in the political asylum process, applicants need to be able to tell a coherent, credible narrative about their experiences of persecution in their home country. This is rarely an easy task, not only because their experiences are often so complex, leading to a noncoherent narrative, but also because the immigration officials, who assess the narratives, make many assumptions about what is credible and what seems deceptive.

In their narratives, the applicants recount the experiences that prompted them to flee their home countries (including, as relevant, the larger political historical circumstances of their home country), the obstacles they faced to escape and to journey to the place they are seeking refuge, and their fear of returning to their homeland. As needed, the applicant's narrative is translated into the language of the receiving country. The narratives are told multiple times, both orally and in writing, from the applicants' initial arrival to their formal immigration hearings, and the multiple versions are scrutinized for consistency, coherence, and credibility.[1] In this chapter, we review how narrative is used as a form of evidence in the political asylum process, the ways that applicants' credibility is challenged, and the multiple additional communicative strategies and difficulties endemic to the process. Building on our earlier work on political asylum narratives (Bohmer and Shuman 2007, 2013; Shuman and Bohmer 2004, 2007), in this chapter we focus on the difficulties asylum applicants face in telling the "true story," on particular narrative problems that raise suspicions for the immigration officials, and on some of the

© The Author(s) 2018
C. Bohmer, A. Shuman, *Political Asylum Deceptions*,
https://doi.org/10.1007/978-3-319-67404-9_2

deceptive strategies used by applicants. As we will discuss, in some cases, the most legitimate asylum seekers are deemed not credible, and in other cases, identified fraudulent applicants have been able to pass as credible. We argue that closer attention to how narrative works in the political asylum process could contribute to more accurate decisions.

The simplest version of a political asylum narrative is contained in the definition of the UN policy: A person with a well-founded fear of persecution for reasons of race, religion, nationality, membership of a particular social group or political opinion is outside his country of nationality and unable to avail himself of protection from that country. The narratives told by political asylum seekers are never so simple; nor are they even similar to each other. Instead, political asylum seekers tell stories about vastly different forms of persecution and suffering, different moments when they realized they could no longer stay in their homes, different means of escape, and different dangers they might face if they were to return.

Narrative is the center of a political asylum hearing. As we discuss in Chaps. 3, 4, and 5, the hearing process relies increasingly on other forms of evidence, but the narrative remains crucial for assessing the legitimacy of a political asylum claim.[2] We began our research on political asylum with a narrative question. In 1999, Carol, a lawyer, was offering her services *pro bono* at Community Refugee Immigration Services in Columbus, Ohio, and told Amy, a narrative scholar, about the difficulty in and significance of getting an accurate and thorough story for political asylum applications and hearings. Together, we wrote our first publication on political asylum narratives (Shuman and Bohmer 2004), and since then, we have had many opportunities to learn more about cultural dimensions of political asylum narratives including the obstacles, cultural and psychological, and narrating trauma and the problem of inconsistencies among narrative versions.

Political asylum narratives are told by refugees themselves and also by immigration officers, journalists, advocates, politicians, and scholars such as ourselves. Each kind of narrator has a different investment in the political asylum process, for example, as an applicant relying on the narrative to convince an immigration official, as an immigration official assessing the validity of the account, or as an observer evaluating the historical and/or contemporary process.[3] Political asylum narratives are part of larger institutional frameworks of expectations about legitimacy and deception and of the sometimes conflicting discourses of personal suffering, political violence, human rights, economies of migration, and border control.[4]

Political asylum narratives are part of multiple, often competing, usually unfinished, narratives. People apply for asylum in the midst of ongoing conflict, and their stories are part of larger stories that appear in the media or are documented by various bureaucratic entities. The media stories can *[Influence of Media]* be quite influential in determining which asylum-seeking groups get attention and how they are considered. In the middle of a conflict, or even shortly after, differentiating among persecutors, victims, bystanders, politically targeted individuals, and legitimate refugees can be difficult. The story of Alan Kurdi, the two-year-old Turkish boy who drowned, galvanized sympathy (Homans 2015). The story of the San Bernardino terrorists (a US-born man and his Pakistani wife) prompted increased suspicion of asylum seekers, though the Cato Institute's report following the attack points out that only "four asylum seekers … of the 700,522 admitted from 1975–2015 turned out to be terrorists" (Nowrasteh 2016). These facts notwithstanding, media accounts influence how political asylum narratives are assessed for credibility. As Garry Trudeau's comic illustrates, the idea that asylum seekers are would-be terrorists can prevail even though the asylum and refugee vetting processes would be the least effective means for terrorists to enter the country.

Trudeau's cartoon is itself a narrative about political asylum, offering a counter-narrative to the idea that seeking asylum would be a path taken by terrorists. The cartoon features a character, possibly President Trump, asking, "Who **ARE** the terrorists?" and answering, "They could be anywhere." The scene then shifts to an "ISIS Recruitment Drive" in which a would-be martyr asks how he would get to America to "wage Jihad." The masked interviewer responds that there are two ways, a tourist visa or as a refugee in which "You have to apply to the UNHCR. If you get by them, you'll be vetted by the national counterterrorism center, the FBI, and the Departments of Defense, State and Homeland Security. Then you go through the enhanced review process. It all takes about two years." When the prospective terrorist describes the choice as a "tough call," the interviewer says, "Okay, so we're looking for someone a little brighter."[5]

Trudeau's cartoon points to the difficult and lengthy process for gaining asylum as an explanation for why it is unlikely for a terrorist to choose asylum as the route to enter the USA. The terrorist recruiter is positioned as intelligent—more intelligent than the would-be recruit—who, like the Trump-like character in the first frame, fails to understand that claiming to be a refugee is probably the least effective means for terrorism. The recruiter implies that a terrorist masquerading as a fraudulent asylum seeker would be too likely to be caught in the process. Nonetheless, the fear that asylum seekers could be terrorists persists, and the burden of proof is placed upon the applicants who must persuade the immigration officials that they are legitimate. Their primary means for doing this is through their narratives. In this chapter we examine the role of narrative in the political asylum process, the strategies used to identify fraudulence, and the methods of deceit used in identified cases of asylum fraud.

We are not arguing that all asylum seekers are legitimate, or that their narratives are entirely truthful. Neither are we arguing that terrorists never claim to be refugees. Very few cases of terrorists hiding among refugees have been documented, and yet these narratives can dominate public discourse, often superseding the narrative told by Trudeau and others, that masquerading as a refugee is more often an ineffective means of entering another country. For example, several news sources reported that ISIS fighters were "hiding among the flood of refugees" (Thiessen 2016); another source described the Paris terrorists who "masquerade[d] as migrants all the way to Paris" (Faiola and Mekhennet 2016).

The narrative of hidden terrorists is not new, and it has been deployed for different purposes, toward different ends, either countering or supporting a climate of suspicion. Historian Max Paul Friedman documents the suspicion that during World War II, Jewish refugees either were themselves "subversive" or were spies or dangerous individuals hidden among other refugees, similar to what President Trump has described as "bad dudes." Friedman writes,

> At a press conference on June 5, 1940, FDR himself warned that "among the refugees there are some spies, as has been found in other countries," explaining that "especially Jewish refugees" could be coerced to report to German agents under the threat that if they did not do so, "we are frightfully sorry, but your old father and mother will be taken out and shot." Roosevelt said this applied to "a very, very small percentage of refugees coming out of Germany," but that "it is something we have got to watch." (2003: 214)

Friedman asks, "Was the threat real? For all the concern about alien subversives, fewer than one-half of one percent of all refugees arriving from Nazi or Soviet territory in 1940 were ever taken into custody for questioning" (2003: 215).[6]

The narrative of the Jewish refugees denied entry to the USA at the beginning of the Holocaust has been used for radically different arguments, either as a call for compassion in the present or as a reference to the possibility that terrorists hide among refugees. For example, as part of a rationale for the idea that terrorists are entering Europe along with refugees, the Belgian Interior Minister Jan Jambon compared hidden terrorists to Jews who hid during the Nazi occupation. He said, "There are Jewish people who went into hiding for years ... and (the Nazi) regime never found them" (CUFI 2016).

Discourses of fear about potentially illegitimate asylum seekers are fueled by such allegations as well as by identified cases of fraud. For example, Kellyanne Conway, counselor to President Trump, referred to Iraqis who "were the masterminds behind the 'Bowling Green massacre,'" which she said, was not covered by mainstream media. It hadn't been covered because it never occurred, a fact that resulted in ridicule (Chappell 2017). Commenting on what Conway described as an "honest mistake," National Public Radio reporter Bill Chappell said, "That statement highlights a dilemma in today's America: When public officials become known for promoting inaccuracies—and fake news is blamed for misinforming people—the task of distinguishing honest mistakes from calculated misstatements becomes more complex" (Chappell 2017).

The political asylum process depends on "distinguishing honest mistakes from calculated misstatements," an effort that is made difficult not only by the absence of means of verification in many cases but also by ideological discourses that pre-judge credibility without attention to what we can know about the production of a credible story and its corollary, the fabrication of a deceptive one.

In this chapter, we discuss the primary reasons given by immigration officials for denying asylum cases. We also discuss one of the most prominent cases of identified fraud. In this as in many highly publicized cases, discrepancies often were discovered *after* the person received asylum. The highly publicized cases have potentially significant influence on public sentiment, and possibly on political asylum policy, but they bear only marginal resemblance to the ordinary refusals we discuss here. Here we examine the variety of narratives that are part of the asylum process, including the stories told by asylum seekers at official hearings, the stories told about asylum seekers in summaries of those hearings, and stories about asylum seekers in the media. We are interested in how credibility is established and questioned in each of these narrative forms and occasions.

As we will argue in this chapter, the indicators of deception used most often by the immigration officials are not necessarily accurate. In Chapter 7, we return to cases of asylum seekers whose narratives were initially considered truthful but later were found to contain deception or fraud.

Political asylum inquiries into the credibility of an individual applicant's narrative have never been based only on assessments of a singular story. In each case, government-issued country reports and other sources of information supplemented the assessment. However, before 9/11 and before the terrorist attacks in the West, applicants were suspected primarily of being economic migrants rather than political refugees. Applicants came from war-torn places, but the assumption was that they left violence behind; whether their motives for leaving were political, or economic, or both, the assumption was that they wanted to build a peaceful, possible prosperous life in the West and that their continued contact with their homelands would be primarily in the form of remittances sent to support family left behind. In the current climate, although few asylum seekers have committed terrorist acts, they are under suspicion of being not only economic migrants but also terrorists. Further, and more important for our understanding of how political asylum narratives are assessed, not only is fleeing a failed state no longer sufficient for an asylum claim, but, as we complete this book, people from those states face increased suspicion. Thus, whereas formerly, the discrepancies in applicants' narratives might have cast doubt on their credibility, creating suspicion that they might be economic migrants, today, those discrepancies create suspicion that the applicant might be a terrorist.

In the political asylum process, narratives are used as evidence and are assessed for their credibility (Knudsen 1995; Jacquemet 2005). Although this use of narrative is necessary, especially in the absence of other forms of evidence, narrative is a cultural form that is shaped as much or more by cultural conventions, expectations, and constraints as it is by adherence to factual representation.[7] To describe narrative as informed by cultural conventions is not to say that narrative is a less true or less accurate account of events. Put bluntly, narrative is not the same as fiction, and to say that a narrative is culturally constructed is not to say that it is a lie. As historian Hayden White pointed out in1973, narrative histories are governed by formal narrative properties, the knowledge of which helps us understand how those histories are constructed, but that does not deny that the events they report actually occurred. However, narrative places listeners in a position to be positively or negatively disposed toward what they hear and, of particular importance for political asylum hearings, to position themselves as suspicious and to regard narratives with disbelief. Further, belief and disbelief are not only directed toward particular facts; in addition, the listeners' expectations and assumptions inform their assessments of what is credible.

In our earlier work (Shuman and Bohmer 2004; Bohmer and Shuman, 2007), we outlined some of the ways that expectations about narrative influence political asylum decisions. We pointed to the constraints faced by the applicants, including the difficulty of even talking about trauma, sometimes because the asylum hearing re-traumatized the applicants or placed them in a situation of describing humiliating experiences; the possibility of not remembering significant details; and cultural conventions for demeanor (being unemotional) that might make an applicant seem less credible. Several other scholars have made similar observations (Berger et al. 2015; Ramji-Nogales et al. 2009). These considerations of narrative constraints are significant, but they aren't sufficient to account for the culture of suspicion in political asylum hearings. As we discuss later in the examples, some of what might look like deceit in applicants' narratives can be attributed to cultural differences in the production of narrative. In some cases, applicants embellish a story to bolster a claim, but the claim is substantially legitimate. Sarah Goodman argues that genuine applications more often have the kinds of errors, inconsistencies, and failures of logic that target an applicant as not credible. She writes, "The fraudulent applicant is more likely to survive impeachment than the genuine applicant for two reasons: first, by telling a consistent, rehearsed story, the fraudulent applicant leaves herself less open to charges of inconsistency; and second, the same factors that can make a genuine applicant appear evasive during her direct testimony—cultural norms, PTSD, and negative experiences with officials—can make it even more difficult for her to respond to a surprise attack on her truthfulness" (2013: 1087).

Many immigration lawyers and officials believe that they are able to detect one of the most willful forms of deceit, the use of a borrowed script, a stock story. In other words, some forms of deceit are easier to detect than others. Probably the biggest obstacle facing the applicants is an immigration official's stance of incredulity, often based not on identifiable significant discrepancies but on assumptions based on insufficient knowledge. Katrijn Maryns and Jan Bloomaert argue that interviews between immigration officials and asylum seekers require more attention to different understandings of the contexts of communication. They observe that an interview "offers very little space for interactional negotiation. Although the contextualization and negotiation of what they want to convey is indispensable for the applicants in order to make themselves understood, it is not picked up as such by the officials" (2001: 179).[8] To better understand the culture of suspicion governing the asylum process, and to offer some alternative means for assessing narrative credibility, we have categorized the grounds of suspicion represented in hearing officers' letters of denial as (1) failures of logic (regarded as too unfamiliar); (2) inconsistencies and discrepancies (regarded as suspiciously incomplete); (3) embellishments (regarded as excessive); and (4) scripted, borrowed stories (regarded as too familiar). We observe that the discourses of credibility in political asylum hearings and in the media are often overly general and insufficiently attentive to how narrative works, generally, and how deception is understood, more specifically. We will return to a more extensive discussion of these issues in Chapter 7.

FAILURES OF LOGIC

The category we're calling failures of logic refers to assessments that an applicant's narrative does not correspond to, or is missing, a part of the expected narrative template, according to the immigration officer's sense of logic. The applicant provides a copy of the narrative in the application, but the hearing itself is an interrogation, that not only examines possible discrepancies and/or missing pieces of information, but often produces gaps in logic.

Narrative scholars understand narrative logic to refer to the way that a narrative is organized (Bremond 1980; Herman 2004; Shuman 1986). Importantly, the chronology of the events described is not the same as the presentation in a narrative. Each juncture of a narrative presents possibilities, alternative consequences for an action. For example, a problem is solved; a situation deteriorates; or there is an interruption in a crisis (Bremond 1980: 381). Political asylum hearings are interview-based, and applicants rarely, if ever, have the opportunity to recount their experiences as complete narratives (Jacquemet 2005). Nonetheless, the asylum hearing references narratives, including not only the narratives provided in the application but also the immigration officials' preconceptions about what constitutes a credible narrative about persecution and escape. Here we consider asylum denials that refute the logic of the applicant's account.

In the first example, from a UK Home Office asylum denial letter, the gap is produced because the immigration official doesn't believe an escape story. We found many instances in which escape was the fault line for suspicion.

> You state that the men drove you to a place one and a half hours away and told you to run before they opened fire on you. The Secretary of State … considers that if the men had intended to kill you they would have done so straight away rather than give you a chance to escape. (Asylum Aid 1999: 1)

In this excerpt, a man who describes himself as targeted for persecution for his political activities is denied asylum because the events recounted do not make sense to the immigration official. The applicant describes the moment of his escape when either he would be killed as he ran away or he would escape, which he did. The officials refuse the logic of that moment, and their refusal hinges on the unexplained motivation of the persecutors. The applicant is perceived to be less credible because he does not know or does not fully explain his persecutor's intentions. Victims of persecution do not always know the motives or intentions of their oppressors. In particular, many stories of escape describe moments in which the guards were negligent or in which one could have been killed or caught. In other work, we describe the case of a Cameroonian woman who had difficulty persuading the immigration officials that she had bribed her way out of prison (Bohmer and Shuman 2015). This issue is also discussed in Chapter 6.

Similarly, a Colombian described moving to a new house after witnessing a killing and receiving death threats. His refusal letter said:

> You also stated that you started to receive threats at your new address and when asked how the perpetrators knew where you lived you stated that they were probably following you. The Secretary of State took the view that it was incredible that someone who is allegedly receiving written threats should not know that they were being followed at anytime. (Asylum Aid 1999: 26)

According to the immigration official's template for a logical narrative, someone who receives written threats would expect to be followed. Logical gaps such as these are common in applicants' narratives, but the failure to explain the motivations of the persecutor might not be an effective means of assessing credibility.

Both of these examples are the officials' restatements of the applicants' narratives. The restatement reframes the narrative and focuses attention on a detail that, from the officials' perspective, warrants further explanation. However, instead of exploring that explanation, the gap becomes a warrant for regarding the applicant's case as not credible.

Peter Margulies describes growing up hearing about his parents' experiences in the Holocaust and the "recurrent refrain ... 'No one would ever believe this if they did not know it already to be true'" (1993: 135). As a director of a law school clinic in Haiti, Margulies reports that similarly "disbelief is a pervasive reaction to Haitian refugee narratives" (1993: 136). He considers three factors that provoke disbelief: first, narratives about flight, for example, narratives in which individuals describe taking "precious time to saying goodbye to loved ones" (1993: 137) or the failure to depart at the first signs of dangers (or failure to see those *as* signs of danger); the inexact account of one's political involvement; and deception. It is the third category that interests us here. Margulies reports that "mythic events and apocryphal stories get mixed in with the truth in refugee narratives" (1993: 141). As we ourselves have found in other cases, he found that the Haitians often had to use deception to survive: "The practice of deception is a necessary art for the refugee; without craft and guile, as well as luck, no refugee can survive" (1993: 142).

Inconsistencies and Discrepancies

Sarah Goodman writes, "Differences in interpretation may also result in apparent inconsistencies. One applicant, for example, testified before the IJ: 'They took my husband and they put chains on him, and they searched the house, and they took some documents from the bedroom.'" The ICE attorney sought to impeach the applicant for inconsistency, relying on the AO's Assessment to Refer, according to which the applicant said: "[The soldiers] came into the living room and spoke to my husband. ... They took him to the car and drove him away." The applicant explained that she said the same thing both times; she did not see a conflict between the two statements; and the different interpreters may have conveyed her story differently. Although the interpreters were not questioned about the discrepancy, the IJ concluded that the applicant's "'inconsistencies and overall vagueness' merited an adverse credibility finding" (2013: 1088; see also Einhorn 2009: 190). In our earlier work, we describe many cases in which asylum authorities determine that the claimant is not credible based on small inconsistencies and discrepancies in their descriptions of events (Bohmer and Shuman 2007: 134ff).

Unlike failures of logic, which refer to the structure and organization of the narrative, inconsistencies and discrepancies refer to details within the narrative, often details of time and place.[9] Several asylum lawyers have argued that attention to inconsistencies and discrepancies is probably not the most effective means for identifying a fraudulent application. For example, Marisa Cianciarulo writes, "Most Courts of Appeals have held that discrepancies and omissions that do not go to the heart of the claim are not an appropriate basis for an adverse credibility determination" (2006: 133). Further, "The focus on minor inconsistencies would be an ineffective means" of improving the asylum process. "A terrorist bent on gaining access to lawful immigration status will likely not make mistakes on his or her asylum proceedings, but rather will be well-rehearsed and thoroughly coached" (135–136).

In one case of a Falun Gong practitioner we observed in London, there was much attention paid to whether she began practicing Falun Gong at the beginning or the end of April 2005. She was asked in court when she began to practice, and she replied in the end of April. After inquiring whether she was sure, the Home Office representative told her that in her witness statement she had said it was early April, a difference which the Home Office representative called a "key discrepancy" in his final submissions to the court, despite the fact that it was hardly central to her claim, and that there was some evidence that this was a translation problem. In any event, it was hardly the most effective way of determining the validity of her claim.

Sociologist Olga Jubany reports that asylum officers are trained to identify discrepancies: "New recruits are not taught about refugees in terms of their rights and options, but through techniques to 'identify the lies' in asylum seekers' narratives: 'If you find inconsistencies you are less likely to believe and so to give them entry. Some people think that exaggerating makes the story more credible and in fact it is the opposite, because then they mix lies with truths and create inconsistencies'" (2011: 82). Jubany reports that immigration officers believe that they can instinctually differentiate between truth and lies. "Officer's 'instinct' is a main source of information, an indicator of the credibility of applicants, but always carrying a deterrence message: 'You feel it, you feel it perfectly, I could be wrong but, in case of doubt, I would say it [the narrative] is false'" (2011: 87). As someone, who until recently worked as an asylum case worker in the UK, put it: "A great deal of my initial training was about establishing 'credibility'—largely, how to explain that you disbelieve someone's story. We would use example claims as case studies and practice writing refusal letters" (Anonymous 2017).

Although targeting inconsistencies is one of the main means for challenging an applicant's account, several lawyers and experts argue against this practice and point out that truly fraudulent applicants are less likely to make such mistakes. An Asylum Aid report argues, "The more traumatic (or 'genuine') the asylum-seekers' experiences, the less he or she is likely to have all the details neatly arranged, ready for interrogation. Yet men and women who have seen their family killed, who have been detained, or lived for months in hiding, are expected to arrive in Britain with the perfect recall that many people cannot achieve with all the props of a modern office" (Asylum Aid 1999). According to Asylum Aid, the discrepancies used to discount the credibility of applicants included many instances of incorrect or vague dates (saying "summer" rather than specifying a month) or an applicant who first said he was abducted by the police and later used the word "soldiers." The Asylum Aid reporters argue that attention to these minor inconsistencies often replaces attention to the substantive claim.

> The most common complaint, by men as well as women, is that they never got a chance to tell the full story. In answer to the accusation that they did not divulge a relevant piece of information during the interview, the answer is: "but he never asked." These omissions cannot be put down to individual immigration officers disregarding official policy. The immigration officers who conduct interviews at the port of entry do not operate in a cultural vacuum. Their approach echoes the culture of disbelief that runs from top to bottom. The Home Office subverts its own instructions with the ever-present reminders of "alleged" victims of torture, and so on. The message is clear: "they're probably liars." (Asylum Aid 1999: 65)

EMBELLISHMENTS DESIGNED TO BOLSTER A CLAIM

Refusals of asylum applicants sometimes accuse the applicant of fabricating signs of torture and of inflicting harm on themselves to strengthen a claim. In one report, the officials wrote, "You have embellished, altered, or invented this part of your account in order to enhance your chances of being granted asylum" (Asylum Aid 1999). Medical records and other documents are suspected of being forged. In one letter of denial, the officials write,

> The Secretary of State is aware of fake newspaper articles and police wanted notices being produced. In your case the Secretary of State feels unable to place any reliance on any of the evidence without other independent corroborating evidence. (Asylum Aid 1999: 26)

This letter accuses the applicant of fabricating evidence. As we discuss in subsequent chapters, in some cases even false publicity can support a case. Attorney Katia Bianchini described a case of a man who said he was a guerrilla, though his sister later corrected the story to say he was in the army; he thought that saying he was a guerrilla would bolster his case. Bianchini says,

> It is my experience that even those who have a strong case exaggerate something, or forget something. They often lie about when they commit a crime—this is relevant to exclude you from protection. They try to minimize past crimes. I had a man from Algeria, he had spent time in Germany and Sweden, applied in Germany and then Sweden. He was always refused. He said he'd committed a crime, and it was theft. I asked the German authorities to send me the record of his conviction. It turned out he had a conviction for kidnapping and robbery. He went to a club in Germany, pretended to be interested in a man, went to his room, stole his wallet, tied him up, used his card at an ATM machine. He lied, but I didn't withdraw from representing him. I told him I knew; I tried to tell him in a way that kept his dignity. (Bianchini 2016)

Several lawyers we consulted described similar situations in which they believed it likely that a client was embellishing a tale. In some cases, the clients offered explanations for withholding information. For example, one lawyer reported that a gay couple from Honduras, "an older gentleman and a younger man" pretended to be father and son. The lawyer asked them, "How come you said he was your son, now you say partner?" The lawyer regarded the case based on persecution of a gay couple to be "a better case than extortion in Honduras." He reports that the younger man said, "'I didn't want to tell the officer he was my partner.' The older gentleman is still married, has three kids. The question is: did they have a relationship? The younger partner now dating a US citizen, he is going to come to testify" (Siman 2016).

In these cases and others, asylum applicants select the truths they tell in their narratives, and selective reporting can look like deception. We return to a discussion of embellishment in Chapter 7.

SCRIPTED STORIES

Scripted stories have received extensive attention in the press, perhaps most notably Suketu Metha's *New Yorker* article, which we discuss in Chapter 7. The article refers to Andrew Johnson, an immigration lawyer in Manhattan, who says, "When there's a problem anywhere, a horrible slaughter in Somalia, wherever, the first couple of years of those cases are very real. Then the next four or five years, they just mimic those stories (Metha 2011). According to a government lawyer, Stan Weber, interviewed for the article, the immigration officials learn how to detect stock stories. The immigrants' words mirror the language in the written application. The applicants do not know basic information about their country or church. "They sound scripted," he said (Dolnick 2011).

Many lawyers and immigration officers believe that they can recognize particular kinds of lies told by people from particular countries. For example, Jubany, who conducted interviews with asylum officials, reports:

> Applicants arriving from Turkey are classified as being cunning and exaggerated in presenting their stories: "It's like all the Turks who've been beaten up so many times, you know? or not so much the women, but the men, every time they go out they seem to have been beaten by the police. I don't believe it. You know? I just don't believe it happens quite that much. If they didn't guild the lily." (Jubany 2011: 84)

Immigration officials told Jubany, "I think particularly when you get into African cases you can sense that, you know that they are lying" (P12-746:747). The immigration officials believe that young African applicants have rehearsed scripted stories. "Youngsters from Africa do not present a very articulate story because it is the one they have been provided with. Maybe if they presented their real story, although it would be much more incredible, well, I don't know" (P6-785:792). The officials regard many stories as scripted: "Everyone tells the same story from a particular country, like in Sri Lanka they would say we fled because the army invaded and they thought we were sympathizers of the Tamil Tigers, something like that" (UK4-AR00-9). And also, "If you take Tamils from Sri Lanka they'll all tell you the same story with minor variations. Always the same basic story, but the beauty of their story is the fact that it's so vague. It can't be proven but equally it can't be disproved" (2011: 83–84).

In contrast to a narrative that is regarded as not credible, not corresponding to expected narrative logics, or containing inconsistencies, both cases in which the narrative lacks some form of coherence, narratives deemed to be scripted, rehearsed, or borrowed, are regarded as *too* coherent. As we will see in the case that follows, and in cases we discuss in Chapter 7, sometimes the errors in these cases are discovered retrospectively, as a result of some later investigation that exposes a fraudulent case. The highly publicized cases of coherent, perhaps scripted, fraudulent cases are quite different from the assessments Jubany describes, in which applicants appear to conform to a recognizable stereotype and fail to convince the immigration officials that the accounts they present are theirs.

The Case of Beatrice Munyenyezi

All of these dimensions of deception—logics, inconsistencies, scripted stories, and narratives about how the present might rectify the past—come to bear in the case of Beatrice Munyenyezi, a Rwandan refugee who received asylum in the USA in 1995. Munyenyezi was convicted of lying on her asylum application in 2013, and as a result is currently serving a ten-year sentence. After she completes her sentence, she will be deported to Rwanda (McPhee 2015).

We are interested in several narratives here, including not only Beatrice's narratives (as told to her lawyer and to the court) but also the lawyer's narrative, and the narratives told by witnesses in the court. All of these narratives are part of both local cultural conventions for representing events and larger discourses of truth-telling, deception, and the possibilities for credibility in the political asylum process. Munyenyezi occupies several different subject positions in the different narratives. Her neighbors in New Hampshire initially described her as "just Bea," and later as "the monster next door."

We begin with the narratives told by Munyenyezi's lawyer, David Ruoff. His story is intertwined with that of the prosecutors, part of ICE, whom he describes as tenacious in their efforts to convict her.

Munyenyezi had been living in New Hampshire for ten years when ICE indicted her for participating in the Rwandan genocide and then lying about it on her citizenship application. She was identified as part of the ICTR (International Criminal Tribunal for Rwanda) case against her husband, who was described in the book *Leave None to Tell the Story: Genocide in Rwanda* as a perpetrator (Des Forges 1999). However, Munyenyezi was not prosecuted for genocide but for lying by answering "no" to the following question on her political asylum application:

> Have you or your family members ever belonged to or been associated with any organizations or groups in your home country, such as, but not limited to, a political party, student group, labor union, religious organization, military or paramilitary group, civil patrol, guerrilla organization, ethnic group, human rights group, or the press or media?

Again, after receiving asylum, on her application for citizenship form, Munyenyezi was asked "have you ever made any misrepresentation on an application form? Have you ever committed a crime?" (Ruoff 2014).

In the lawyer's words, "They nicked her." In other words, they were able to prosecute her for lying on the form. The lawyer, David Ruoff, says,

> Her claim is that she had nothing to do with it, she didn't lie. ... Her mother-in-law was a Minister, her father-in-law the Provost of the University. She never lied about her identity; it would have been easy for her to make up another name, identity. She disclosed that her mother-in-law and husband were part of the genocide.

Munyenyezi is not the only protagonist of her narrative. The lengthy account of her arrest and trials also includes the story of Brian Andersen, the federal agent who prosecuted the case, and who "blamed himself" (McPhee 2015) for the failure to convict her in the first trial. Andersen is described as certain that she had committed genocide. His goal was to prove "that Munyenyezi was not just a hapless housewife but an active member of the Hutu-led MRND government" (McPhee 2015).

The narratives about Munyenyezi, like other accounts of refugees later found to be persecutors, depend on several other characters, including the prosecuting federal agent (Andersen) and the former victims.

> At trial, the U.S. attorney had what seemed like a solid strategy: The prosecution looked to Munyenyezi's co-conspirators and underlings to rat on their boss. It was an approach that seemed straight out of the playbook the feds have been using, for decades, to dismantle organized crime. During 11 days of testimony, the government called 22 witnesses. Several admitted killers from Butare took the stand and testified to taking orders from "the Commander" and killing the "Inyenzi," or "cockroaches," which referred to the Tutsis. (Ruoff 2014)

Although scripted narratives are cause for suspicion when produced by asylum seekers, the prosecutors themselves use a script, or playbook, to uncover fraud. However, in the second trial, the prosecutors chose a different strategy. Rather than depending on the reports by survivors of the genocide, they relied on the account of a doctor from Doctors Without Borders. Describing the prosecutors' strategy, Ruoff reports,

> Instead of overwhelming the jury with a barrage of horrific images from the mouths of killers, prosecutors let the doctor, an authority, recount the mayhem. The secret to convincing the jury was to downplay the carnage, which was too much for them to believe. Prosecutors spent most of their efforts proving that Munyenyezi had lied on her application to become a U.S. citizen, which, after all, was the technicality for which she was being prosecuted. (Ruoff 2014)

In the first trial, according to Ruoff, the description of atrocities defied the narrative logics of believability for the jurors. Perhaps the disjuncture between Munyenyezi's exemplary life as a refugee was too great a contrast with the depiction of her as a killer. Her neighbors in New Hampshire described her as "Just Bea," or as "a single mom who had fled a war-torn nation" (McPhee 2015). Her lawyers noted that she had never been arrested in the USA. Following the trial, extensive newspaper coverage described her as "the monster next door" who had allegedly "participated, committed, ordered, oversaw, conspired and aided and abetted, assisted in and directed the persecution, kidnapping, rape and murder of numerous individuals at the roadblock in front of the Ihuriro Hotel in Butare" (McPhee 2015).

Other individuals granted asylum also have had their asylum revoked because of a similar error on their application, as we will discuss further in Chapter 8. Ibrahim Parlak, a Kurdish restaurant owner in Michigan, failed to list his membership in the Partiya Karkerên Kurdistanê (PKK), the Kurdistan Workers' Party, in his original application. As in the case of Munyenyezi, media headlines present a succinct version of the contrasting possibilities of his character. For example, "A Friendly Café Owner in Michigan … Or a Militant from Turkey" (Emmanuel 2016). The Department of Homeland Security accused Mr. Parlak of lying on his green card application by checking a box saying he had never been arrested or supported a terrorist organization. The agency said he covered up the fact he had been arrested after being involved in a 1987 border gunfight in which the PKK killed two Turkish soldiers. Mr. Parlak said he had disclosed the arrest and his PKK affiliation on a previous asylum application.

Unlike the Munyenyezi case, resulting in her 10-year prison sentence, as of this writing, Parlak has been protected from deportation by a personal bill introduced in the Senate and renewed each year (Lewin 2015). Also unlike Munyenyezi, Mr. Parlak's deception has been regarded by many as insignificant. For example,

"Ibrahim has been a wonderful citizen, a lovely person with this wonderful business," said Geoffrey Stone, interim dean at the University of Chicago Law School and a friend and supporter of Mr. Parlak. "He's a Kurd who many years ago challenged Turkey, but I do not for the life of me understand what rational justification the Department of Homeland Security has for continuing to persecute him." (Emmanuel 2016)

At the same time, the narratives of Mr. Parlak and Ms. Munyenyezi are similar in many respects. Both were living rather unremarkable lives in the USA when their possible connections to terrorism were discovered. Parlak disputes any connection to terrorism. The NPR report first gives his side of the story:

During high school, Parlak became a Kurdish activist. That's when he was jailed by the Turkish government and, he says, tortured.
"No food, holding [me] in a small box, spraying [me] with cold water," Parlak says. "I mean, anything you can imagine (Emmanuel 2016)."
After Parlak was released, he continued his activism and spent a second stint in prison. Eventually, Parlak fled to the U.S. with a fake passport and a suitcase packed with documents showing he had been tortured. (ibid.)

NPR continues with the Turkish Embassy's version,

"After meeting with the chief of the PKK, Abdullah Ocalan, Ibrahim Parlak obtained training in PKK camps," reads a strongly worded statement from the Turkish embassy spokesman, Fatih Oke. "On May 21 1988, his heavily armed unit illegally crossed over to Turkey from Syria."

The Turkish Embassy says Parlak was involved in an attack that left two Turkish soldiers dead and they've asked for Parlak to be sent back to Turkey.

Parlak says he was crossing the border at the time, but was not part of the fighting that broke out. "We went over a hill and then the fighting started behind us," Parlak says. (Emmanuel 2016)

The narrative then turns to Parlak's life in the USA,

In Parlak's Michigan community, his supporters say what counts is the life he's lived here for the past quarter-century.

"He's led an exemplary life," says U.S. Rep. Fred Upton, a Republican who represents the district where Parlak lives. (Emmanuel 2016)

Since this story appeared on NPR, American immigration policy is undergoing changes under the Trump administration. Parlak's only crime in the USA was his failure to check a box on his application for citizenship (even though the PKK was not a terrorist organization when he filled out his initial form). That may be enough for him to be deported when his deferred action expires and when the fact of the life he's lived in the USA has less bearing on the decision.

NARRATIVE AS DOCUMENTATION

Documents and narratives do very different kinds of work in terms of establishing identity and proof of the events recounted. Obviously, establishing one's identity is crucial in an asylum hearing. And on the surface, documents can establish identity in a particular group or nation. Narratives, in contrast, establish identity by accounting for familial or community relationships. Identity cards confirm that a person is a member of a nation, tribe, or political organization. Narratives might report how one became a member or what one knows about being a member.

The asylum interview creates "narrative inequality" and a one-sided interview, which, when transposed into a written record, can create serious difficulties for an asylum applicant. (Campbell 2017: 6)

People seeking asylum face the double problem of, first, trying to narrate unspeakable events and, second, translating those personal stories into a different sort of narrative that conveys the information needed by the asylum officials (Shuman and Bohmer 2004). The stories people told us when we first met them in the central Ohio immigration agency often focused more on the trauma of loss and the struggle to survive than on the details of persecution. However, it is these details about the persecutors and their interrogations, incarcerations, and torture, as well as the individual's role in a larger political, religious, or social conflict, that interest the asylum officials. Asylum law and the expectations of the adjudicators who are hearing the claims have narrowed the range of possible narratives that can result in a grant of asylum. They have also injected the need for claimants to prove their claims through the use of documents, a process that is alien to them. It is often necessary to explain to an applicant how and why documents are valued above the narrative. The claimant must walk a narrow line to fit his or her story into the confines of a suitable narrative, as well as support it with material he or she may not be able to obtain.

Documentation and narrative are intimately connected in political asylum cases. Applicants need to prove that they are who they say they are and that their stories are true. In the absence of documentation, applicants rely on their narratives of what happened as the primary form of evidence. The narratives people tell are, in a sense, stand-ins for missing or suspicious documents (and the officials cast suspicion on many documents). As we discuss in Chapter 3, documents are no more neutral than personal stories. Asylum officials might acknowledge the subjectivity of narrative but sometimes imagine documents to be neutral, when, in fact, like narratives, they are dependent on the conditions of their production. Documents function very differently in asylum cases than in other areas of law. There is very little standardization, predictability, or reliability in the evaluation of and use of documents in political asylum hearings. Further, applying Western legal methods to understand the political asylum documents (or absence of documents) only exacerbates a situation already complicated by the lack of standardization of documents, the risk applicants take in acquiring or traveling with documents, and the motivation to use fraudulent documents in life-or-death situations. Ethnographers further complicate our understanding of the production and use of documents as cultural artifacts not only with no singular meaning but, importantly, variable in their significance and use (Riles 2006). Here, we suggest that paying attention to this complexity would be a means of creating more accurate assessments of asylum applications.

CONCLUSION: NARRATIVE AND DECEPTION

When lawyer Heather Yvonne Axford, who works for CALA, a legal assistance organization in Brooklyn, was asked by journalist Francisco Goldman, "how she can tell if a potential client is being truthful," she answered, "I think that's something that requires both experience and an intimate knowledge of country conditions. We talk to prospective clients in great detail about their claims, and, to be frank, it's usually very obvious when someone is not telling the truth because—unless they are some master storyteller—the story starts to fall apart pretty quickly when you get into the nitty-gritty of it" (Goldman 2016). One of the lawyers we interviewed told us, "As for lying clients, if someone says they are afraid to return, and they can't say why in detail...if there is not detail, they can't articulate the case, they don't retain me, I tell them that they don't have a case" (Kolken 2016).

Similarly, Katia Bianchini describes her efforts to differentiate between legitimate and deceptive claims. She reports that many stories sounded similar and says that fabrication about the journey to the UK was common.

> They don't want to identify the smugglers, maybe because they are scared for their family. ... You shouldn't refuse a case because of a small lie, which doesn't go to the heart of the case, but the HO does. They say if you lie about one small thing, you are not truthful and deny the case. (2016)

In this chapter, we have observed that some of the ways that deception is manifested in political asylum narratives do not necessarily constitute either fraud or deception. Instead, what look like inconsistencies can be attributed to the complexity of the situation described and to the difficulty of producing a coherent narrative about it. In some cases, applicants who embellish their accounts actually have a legitimate claim but were persuaded to tell what they were told would be a more persuasive story. As we have discussed, we spoke with many lawyers and advocates who argued that more polished, coherent accounts are not necessarily less deceptive.

The immigration officials' assessment of the legitimacy of asylum narratives depends on many extraneous factors. The assessment that a narrative is too scripted can be based on the immigration officials' familiarity with country circumstances or previous applicants' accounts. The officials' lack of familiarity can result in what we have called a failure to recognize the narrative logic of the applicant's account. Assessing what counts as deception requires understanding both the larger political circumstances and the applicant's particular cultural conventions for relating an account of their experiences.

Many of the lawyers and advocates we spoke with offered distinctions between what Robert Beneduce calls "innocent lies," "revealing lies," and "strategic lies" (2015: 557). With Beneduce, we are interested in the conditions that result in what are considered by the immigration authorities to be compromised narratives. Most legitimate asylum seekers have experienced the shattering of their "trust in the world" (Amery 1980: 28)[10] in which the world as they knew it has been completely destroyed. A successful asylum claim depends on being able to produce a coherent, logically credible, consistent narrative, despite the asylum seeker's mental state or sense of loss of both coherence and trust in the world.[11] Beneduce writes, "The perception that the right to asylum depends on the oratory ability (the narrative capital) of the appellant, on his or her greater or lesser ability to persuade the committee" (2015: 448). Individuals who cannot prove who they are, or who cannot convey the truth of their experience are rendered illegible in their own lives (Bohmer and Shuman 2010: 9).

As we discuss in the chapters that follow, the narrative tactics that might help to produce a credible story are part of larger tactics of legibility and legitimacy, including not only the forms that Munyenyezi and Parlak filled out erroneously, but also passports, fingerprints, and many other technologies that are part of the culture of suspicion of asylum applicants.

NOTES

1. See Baker's distinction between material and characterological coherence in narratives 2006: 146–152.
2. Berg and Millbank write that the reliance on narrative is even more pronounced for applicants who claim asylum based on sexual persecution (2009: 196).
3. See Johnson's discussion of the role of translators and legal assistants in asylum courts and also her discussion of the strategic role of silence (2011: 65).

4. See Susan Coutin's discussion of disjunctions between human rights discourses and the experiences of Salvadoran asylum applicants (2001: 65).

5. See Sidonie Smith's discussion of the way comics in Human Rights Campaigns manage subjectivities. She writes, "They contribute to the global "social work" of producing and disseminating the subject positions of "victim," "perpetrator," and "rescuer" managed by the rights regime" (2017, np).

6. For a journalistic account, see Ahmed, 2015.

7. See Jacquemet's discussion of the policy of reliance of "facts" and rejection of narratives in UNHCR asylum interviews (2005: 202).

8. Describing a particular case, Bloomaert further describes a case in which immigration officials pay more attention to an applicant's errors in speaking than to the import of what he says. "The narrative structure and the salience of what the man tells us are over-shadowed by the code in which he tells it: a variety of colloquial and informally acquired French in which grammatical, syntactic and lexical errors are frequent when measured against normative standard French" (1981: 420).

9. For a discussion of interrogations about place, see Maryns, 2006.

10. Amery writes, "Trust in the world includes all sorts of things: the irrational and logically unjustifiable belief in absolute causality perhaps, or the likewise blind belief in the validity of the inductive inference. But more important … is the certainty that by reason of written or unwritten social contracts the other person will spare me … will respect my physical and with it also my metaphysical being" (1980: 28).

11. As Eastmond (2007; Showler 2006; Macklin 1998, 2006) have discussed, producing the coherent narrative is not always possible.

CHAPTER 3

Documentary Evidence

Facing challenges in their efforts to differentiate between legitimate and fraudulent political asylum seekers, immigration officials increasingly expect and even demand documentation. Documentary evidence can include passports, birth certificates, drivers' licenses, marriage or death certificates, and records issued by hospitals, prisons, schools, or other institutions. The increased demand for documents has intensified the already extensive production of fakes.[1] In this chapter, we review the difficulties faced both by the asylum seekers, attempting to obtain documents, and by the immigration officials, attempting to determine whether a document is legitimate. Obtaining documents can put people at risk, whether vulnerable to the forgers or to the possibility that the home country will harm family members when they aid someone attempting to obtain a document. The immigration officials have new methods to identify fakes but the system is nonetheless quite limited. Beyond the question of the meaning of the term credibility, and its confusion with proof, we are interested in how particular kinds of fraudulence receive attention and how others are overlooked.

The hearing system is burdened by a lack of documentary evidence. In theory, asylum law does not require evidence other than the narrative of the applicant, but in practice, current applicants are rarely granted asylum with only their stories. Other evidence is always hard to come by, and the credibility of the story is always under suspicion.

Building on our discussion of the examination of consistent representation of facts and narrative credibility in the last chapter, here we focus on

© The Author(s) 2018
C. Bohmer, A. Shuman, *Political Asylum Deceptions*,
https://doi.org/10.1007/978-3-319-67404-9_3

how documents confirm or raise suspicion in asylum hearings. Documents are, for the most part, supplementary in a narrative hearing, but they are often given more weight. Narratives are personal, connected to experience, and documents are the opposite, connected more to the bureaucratic institutions that produce them.

Like narratives, documents are subject to being challenged as fraudulent; both are scrutinized for inconsistencies and missing pieces. Documents and narratives do very different kinds of work to establish identity and provide proof of the events recounted. Obviously, establishing one's identity is crucial in an asylum hearing. And on the surface, documents can establish identity in a particular group or nation. Narratives, in contrast, establish identity by accounting for familial or community relationships. Identity cards confirm that a person is a member of a nation, tribe, or political organization. Narratives might report how one became a member or what one knows about being a member.

Questioning an applicant's lack of documents often shows the same absence of cultural awareness as questioning the applicant's failure to recount a particular incident. However, both the legitimate and the fraudulent production of documents is specific to cultural and national institutions. So much is written about the fact that asylum seekers frequently lack documents or rely on smugglers to provide them with false documents that we might fail to understand the cultural, historical, and political relationships to documents. The officials do not always consider how cultural attitudes toward documents contribute to the use of fakes. For example, Gaston Gordillo describes how the acquisition of identity cards changed an indigenous Argentine group's legally ambiguous status, and although people in that group cannot read the cards, they regard them as significant possessions, displayed with reverence (2006: 162). Identity documents can also be regarded as a source of affliction (in the case of Holocaust era requirements that Jews display a yellow star of David) or friction. According to most accounts, the Belgian colonizers' creation of identity documents set the stage for what became the Rwandan genocide by clearly identifying who was Tutsi and who was Hutu. The attachment of a person to a particular identity card is both cultural and historical. If identity documents have value, then they can be bought and sold. Heath Cabot's ethnographic discussion of the *roz carta*, the pink identity card given to asylum seekers in Greece, demonstrates how a document is used not as a neutral source of information but as a variable, manipulated, form of regulation (2012:

12). A pink card is necessary for immigrants who want to work in Greece. It also provides access to health care. Documents have a life of their own (2012: 13) that responds to particular relationships, and establishes different bureaucratic circumstances, depending on the situation and the people involved.

THE CULTURAL, INSTITUTIONAL PRODUCTION OF DOCUMENTS

Assessing documents in political asylum cases requires attention to political, historical, and cultural contexts of production and use. Documents cannot be assumed to be uniform in their production, use, or accessibility. In most countries from which asylum seekers come, there is also less emphasis on the identity documents we take for granted in the West.

The lack of uniformity of birth certificates in the USA is a small example of a much greater lack of consistency in documents from birth, death, and marriage records to police and detention records. Even in the USA, where reliance is greatest on documents, and it is assumed that everyone has a birth certificate, birth certificates are contentious documents prompting arguments about race and ethnicity data, birth defect data, and parents' education and occupation data. A 2003 group recommended that sex be indicated by male, female or not yet determined as is the case elsewhere (Report of the panel to evaluate the US Standard Certificates, National Center for Health Certificates 2000, 2001).

The uniformity of documents for travel, including visas and passports, also makes these documents more available to fraud. What might be called "scientific" records, including medical records or DNA tests, differ in their accessibility if not in how information is recorded. Personal records, such as correspondence, and media records, such as newspaper articles, are not expected to be uniform. The most personal records, such as personal diaries, carry little bureaucratic weight unless they are used as confessions. Each of these kinds of document is granted a different status in a political asylum hearing, and each is subject to different lines of inquiry regarding their validity. The US State Department is aware of this problem. The State Department notes the potential for fraud with the use of birth certificates, which, like social security cards and identification documents issued by foreign consulates (Consular Identification Cards), can be used as what are sometimes described as "breeder documents," that is documents used to fraudulently gain other identity documents, for example driver's licenses and passports.

PASSPORTS, IDENTITY DOCUMENTS, AND BIRTH CERTIFICATES AS DOCUMENTARY EVIDENCE

The discovery that one of the terrorists in the Paris terrorist assaults in 2015 used a false passport led to a wider investigation about the production of false Syrian passports by ISIS. Initial reports by Agence France-Presse said that a passport found near the body of one of the suicide bombers "was either taken or fabricated based on a real identity" (NY Times 2015). This report was followed by news reports that ISIS may have a passport-printing machine that was used to help its followers infiltrate American borders with fake passports (McPhee and Ross 2015).

As Susan Coutin writes, in bureaucratic encounters, "status inheres in papers not persons" (2003: 55). The asylum process places increasing dependence on documents to prove identity, but the information may be more complex than a face-value determination reveals. For example, immigration officials might assume that an identity card stating one's ethnicity is accurate. There are, however, many examples of multiple identities produced by changing contexts, often the very civil unrest which caused a person to flee his homeland. Longman describes a young Rwandan woman whom he calls Claudette, who grew up as a Hutu (2001). During the Rwandan genocide, it was discovered that her grandfather had been known as a Tutsi before he moved to the area where Claudette had been raised. He had received an identity card stating his ethnicity as Hutu, which he passed down to his descendants. As a result of this becoming public knowledge, Claudette's family was the target of ethnic violence, and several family members were killed. Her "new" identity as a Tutsi became suspect, as she and her family had enjoyed the benefits of being Hutu before the genocide. Now she says, "I do not really know what I am. I do not know what it means to be Tutsi" (346).

The possibility of laundering one's identity has a long history. Carol recently discovered that her "non-Jewish" great uncle was, in fact, Jewish. Foreseeing the possible disaster which might come from being Jewish in the 1930s, he used his connections and knowledge as a lawyer to change his identity label, and acquire a non-Jewish identity document. As a result, he was one of the few in Carol's family to survive the Holocaust and was also able to protect his Jewish wife (Carol's great-aunt) from being sent to the camps.

In some places, most notably Somalia, even such basic documents as birth certificates are not available because of the turmoil that has existed in that country for so long or because people never had them in the first place. In Somalia and other African countries, people born or married in rural areas are unlikely to have birth certificates; many of them do not even know their date of birth. Only half of the children under five years old in the developing world have their births registered. In sub-Saharan Africa 59% of births go unregistered, and in South Asia 29% of all births go unregistered (UNICEF 2016). Even in Mexico, more than seven million people currently lack a birth certificate (Asencio 2012). Similarly, many children born in the border area between Myanmar and China have no birth certificates; this provides the loophole through which militias recruit child soldiers. And in Egypt, "Baha'is and certain other nationals have been unable to obtain birth certificates, identity cards, marriage certificates, death certificates and other vital records because the government requires all such documents to list religious affiliation and restricts the choice of religion to the three officially recognized religions: Islam, Christianity and Judaism. Many persons have been unable to obtain identification papers because they refuse to lie about their religious affiliation and have been denied the possibility of leaving the entry about religious affiliation blank" (Massey 2010). In the USA, many refugees have been given January 1 as their birth date by the authorities to provide a detail that is important in the USA but not in the country they fled.

Recently, the problem of obtaining a birth certificate began to spread to the USA, where unauthorized immigrants in Texas had difficulty registering the births of their children, because the state of Texas demanded that parents provide identification of the kind they do not have.[2] They began to require that foreign passports presented by parents include a valid US visa, which of course, undocumented immigrants cannot provide. Texas officials also stopped accepting photo identity cards, known as matrículas, that Mexicans obtain from their consulates in the USA. This issue was the subject of a lawsuit on behalf of a number of children and adults from Mexico, Honduras, and Guatemala filed by Texas Rio Grand Legal Aid (Fernandez 2015). Without a birth certificate, children have problems getting access to public education, the ability to travel, and eligibility for assistance programs, although the state of Texas denied these problems in the initial court hearing (Preston 2016). In a settlement in July 2016, the parties agreed that Texas would accept Mexican voter identification cards. Under a recent change by Mexico, its citizens can now obtain those cards from consulates in the USA (Preston 2016).

Even having a birth certificate may not be enough to counter the pressure of the authorities who, for strategic reasons, claim that a person is a national of a country other than their own. In Mexico, apparently as a result of a crackdown to prevent Central Americans entering the USA, funded by the USA, indigenous Mexicans migrating internally for work have been picked up by the police and pressured to sign a document stating that they are Guatemalan (Lakhani 2016). Ultimately the women described in the Guardian article were able, with legal help, to prove they were Mexicans from Chiapas, though one wonders about what happens to those who are not lucky enough to get legal assistance (ibid).

THE USE OF FALSE DOCUMENTS

The exigencies of escape often require deceptive or concealed identities. Asylum seekers routinely use false passports because they are afraid to apply for their own, because they know they will not be given one, or because they need to flee using someone else's identity so as not to be detained at the border.

There is evidence that Syrians fleeing Syria in the latest refugee crisis are, ironically, using fake Syrian passports. A spokesperson for Frontex, the EU border control agency, described the reasons Syrians might need fake passports: "Well, they are coming from a war-torn country. Probably many had to leave their homes rather quickly. Maybe some didn't have passports, and obtaining a Syrian passport right now – it's probably extremely difficult. Many Syrians whom we are seeing in – for example, in Greece right now have been living in - either in Syria but also in camps in Turkey, Lebanon or Jordan, and they are coming from these camps. These are people who've been on the move, sometimes for several years. These are people who some of their children were born outside Syria. And this is how long the conflict has been going on" (Moncure 2015).

Other research examines the production of fake passports more generally: "It has been found that the largest number of passports that are procured fraudulently are Swedish. The Swedish government has detected criminal networks arranging marriages of convenience, false adoptions and fraudulent work permits to bring people illegally into Sweden" (Tinti and Reitano 2016: 7).

There are a variety of ways in which forged passports are obtained. In some cases, consular officers sell them to forgers who then insert the relevant details; in a variant of that, a consular officer sells just one passport that becomes a template for counterfeiters to copy (Tinti and Reitano 2016). Despite recent efforts of governments to make passports counterfeit-proof, there are some forgers who can make very good counterfeit passports which can pass muster at borders. Examining officers may be in a rush and not be paying sufficient attention to flag every forged passport.

Many people who flee persecution use agents to help them, and often, the same people who help genuine asylum seekers flee persecution also provide the means whereby others can enter the country illegally. They provide sets of false documents on which the asylum seekers enter the country, which they often take back immediately to reuse; the applicants are kept ignorant of whose passports are being used. Because of this ignorance, anything the applicants may tell the authorities about their identity or about details of their arrival is simply more of their uncorroborated story and becomes a major barrier to their asylum claims. In the most recent refugee crisis, the borrowing of passports is big business. Tinti and Reitano report that criminals from the Eastern European diaspora buy, rent, or steal passports (2016: 76). Though the exact sum is unknown, the rental of a passport from a "good" country can net the holder of a passport from that country thousands of dollars.

The "imposter method" in which the user closely resembles the photograph in the passport can be particularly difficult to detect. Tinti and Reitano report that Turkish authorities acknowledge the difficulty of differentiating among sub-African applicants who use the passport of a similar-looking relative or friend (2016: 77).

They also describe what is called the "double-check" method in which someone checks in at the airport for a flight to a country that does not require a visa (such as Ecuador) and then, after passing through passport control, meets someone who provides a fake passport with fake entry stamps and flight tickets that can be used to board a plane to a different country. "The last passport scan before boarding the plane is usually the most cursory" (2016: 77).

Not all agents who provide false documents exploit refugees. Many stories from the Holocaust describe people who used a variety of illegal means to extricate Jews and others from the Nazis. Nicholas Winton, recently honored for his work saving 669 children, mostly Jewish, from Czechoslovakia, used "dangers, bribes, forgery, secret contacts with the Gestapo, nine railroad trains, an avalanche of paperwork and a lot of money" in his efforts to transport the children to safety in the UK (McFadden 2015)

THE RISKS OF OBTAINING DOCUMENTS

Documents in the asylum process are treated as neutral, decontextualized objects. They become less reliable as evidence when they are lifted from their context of production and examined without regard to the circumstances that constrained political asylum applicants from acquiring them. Even without the constraints of war or the upheaval of governments, practices for issuing documents differ widely. When used in the asylum process, documents are used for a purpose other than that for which they were produced.

Some time ago, Audrey Macklin, a former member of the Immigration and Refugee Board of Canada, described the cycle of suspicion about documents in the asylum process. She wrote, "Claimants are rejected because they are unable to furnish sufficient identity documents or documents proving residence in a refugee camp, etc. Some claimants protest that they are unable to obtain documents and are met with the reply that other claimants managed to do so. Of course, decision makers have no idea early on whether or how many of those earlier documents were genuine and thus how easy or difficult it is to obtain genuine documents from one's country of origin. Soon, all claimants show up with the requisite documents, having learned through the grapevine that failure to produce documents will lead to rejection" (1998: 136).

Obtaining a document for an asylum hearing can not only be difficult, but dangerous. Even obtaining a passport legitimately can be dangerous, as it alerts the authorities to the possibility that someone is planning to leave. As Sarah Goodman observes, "Often, however, the applicant does not have such supporting evidence because 'a genuine refugee does not flee her native country armed with affidavits, expert witnesses, and extensive documentation'" (Goodman 2013: 1083).[3] Obtaining documents from a refugee camp is usually a difficult and lengthy process.

In the USA, there is a complex process of checking the validity of documents in general, including those presented by asylum seekers, which is fraught with difficulties and dangers. Such checking requires a basis for comparison, and often those who are involved in authenticating documents do not have such a benchmark. In addition, one of the ways documents are authenticated is by sending them back to the country of origin, for the Embassy there to check on their validity. The Embassy usually has their local employees do the job, on the ground that they attract less attention. While it may be true that a local attracts less attention than a consular officer would, the risk of disclosure and resultant danger to the applicant's family remains a serious problem. The Embassy attempts to keep information confidential but they cannot provide guarantees, especially when the name of the person is essential to the verification of the document. In addition, asking a government which tortures its citizens to authenticate documents supporting a claim of persecution is unlikely to result in reliable evidence (Wiebe and Parker 2001–2). By contrast, the UK Home Office is specifically prohibited from making checks in the country and releasing the name of the person because they recognize it is such a risk. As one UK lawyer we interviewed told us: "We try to get around the problems in serving expert representatives, or contacting the lawyer who represented them (in their country). It's often easier to get lawyer to lawyer contact with the witness statement." He gives an example: "There was a lawyer who was a well respected advocate in Turkey, had taken a number of cases to Strasbourg. The lawyer's position in Turkey was to set out in detail the number of times he'd been to prison to secure the person's release, he was never able to see him. When someone has standing he is less likely to lie in the account" (Ahluwalia 2008).

Authorities use written documents as a basis for opening up inquiry into an applicant's contacts and networks. Applicants are asked how they obtained a particular document, who sent it, and when it was received, and often this information is used to corroborate other information the applicant has provided about contact with relatives or others. For example, in the following case, the officials question the legitimacy of a letter received by a Tamil applicant by asking who sent it, from where, and whether it was handwritten or typed. They ask for the envelope, and they question the sender's location in order to evaluate the truthfulness of the applicant's testimony. Letters provide written evidence, but at the same time, the officials are aware that the senders are not always in a position to use postal services. The letter can create more problems than it resolves.

Tamil case October 27, 2008:

(R is the applicant's representative, HO is the representative of the Home Office, AP is the applicant, J is the judge)

R: OK, moving on then to the Gangatharan solicitors' letter. I'm just going to show you this letter, can you explain to me how you received this letter?

AP: I contacted an uncle of mine there and he posted it.

R: And that's the second letter dated 31 March 2008, and the first letter dated 19 July 2007. I wanted to ask you about that letter. It was submitted in the HO interview. How was this letter received?

AP: Again the uncle faxed it to us.

R: You referred to an uncle you've been in touch with, p.34, March 08, and so that we are clear, you said your uncle contacted Mr. Gangatharan. Would you mind just giving us the uncle's name?

AP: Easwarakumar

R: Thank you. The original of either letter, do you know where they are now?

AP: These letters were faxed; we did not receive them otherwise.

HO: You have submitted a letter that you say is from your mother. Was that letter typed or handwritten?

AP: It was a handwritten letter

HO: When was the last time you had verbal contact with your parents?

AP: I don't understand

HO: The last time you had verbal contact

AP: A month ago

HO: Where were they a month ago?

AP: They are in India

HO: When you spoke to them how long had they been in India for?

AP: I believe they moved during December last year

HO: This letter was actually written from India?

AP: Yes

HO: You say this letter from your mother and father was handwritten, can I see the letter please?

AP: It should be in the court's file

HO: We have a copy of something that looks like this. How did you receive the letter from your mother?

AP: By post

HO: Do you have the actual copy you received yourself?

AP: It would be in the court's file

J: Give me a moment to have a look (lots of scrabbling through all the documents).

J: Let's carry on and you can ask her what she did with the letter if she remembers

HO: What have you done with the original copy of the letter from your mother?

AP: I gave it to my solicitor and I believe they gave it to the court

J: (to interpreter) You must not explain the question. Tell her exactly what we say.

HO: When did you give the original to the lawyer?

AP: I believe it was in March this year

HO: Did you receive the letter from your parents in 2007.

AP: I received it in January 2008

HO: Do you have the original envelope the letter came in?

AP: Again, I gave that to my lawyer

This is a typical inquiry into the means by which a document was acquired and what the applicant did with it. It demonstrates some of the scrutiny directed at documents and the ways that having documents can raise further suspicion about the case. The Home Office representative was skeptical about the letter in his submissions to the court: "The parents' letter from India. We know there has been verbal contact. There is nothing to show that this letter was not submitted to the court-very little weight can be placed on the translation or a Tamil handwritten copy we do have. I can't say what the solicitors' should have submitted to produce original hard copies on which she relies."

In the following case, an Iraqi woman is asked how she obtained a document. The officials are aware that acquiring a document after they have departed can be dangerous to the family or friends who are asked to obtain it. It can be a source of additional, unwanted information, for the persecutors. Asylum applicants are typically very aware of the politics of obtaining documents, even if they are unaware of the import or usefulness of these documents for the asylum officials. In this case, the way the documents were acquired provides another basis to question the credibility of the applicant.

HO: Within the bundle of papers you supplied, you supplied an Iraqi nationality certificate.

AP: Yes

HO: How did you obtain that document?

AP: I contacted my sister in Jordan one week before my interview at the Home Office. She never replied. I could not get an answer because of her problem with her husband so I was compelled to contact her in Jordan so she could respond to me. Through my solicitors she was able to call me and I obtained the document because I only came with a passport and a copy of the passport and at that time the circumstances surrounding obtaining the document, they had a lot of problems because they had only one week to leave Jordan because they were staying there illegally and on the ... just before the interview they sent them to me.

HO: You submitted your degree certificate?

AP: That was among the documents they sent me because it is an important document which is my degree certificate and then the certificate of my employment with the Ministry. I took them home with me before the war and when I left to travel to Jordan I took them with me

HO: So they were sent by your sister as well?

AP: Yes

HO: Did you take your degree certificate with you to Jordan?

AP: During the era of Saddam....

J: The question was did you take them with you to Jordan?

AP: I had a friend with me, she attended the university, I asked her to send them to me

J: The answer is no. You say your friend got them and sent them to you

AP: Yes

HO: What friend was this?

AP: She was the same year as me at university and the same course

HO: What was her name?

AP: Sahar Al Shama

HO: How did she remain in contact with you in Jordan?

AP: There was no contact with her in Jordan. When I needed the certificate, because I was looking for a job in Amman, so I could have it as part of the documents required.

HO: When you were in Jordan, how did you contact her?

AP: I made a contact to her mobile

HO: You supplied some translated text messages. How did Yusef get your telephone number in the UK?

AP: Because I was in contact with him, because he was my husband, that's how he was able to get my number.

R: You referred to your friend sending you your degree certificate, do you know how she obtained your degree certificate?

AP: She went to the university herself, to the registration desk. I asked her to get mine as well, and get it confirmed by the Ministry. She did all the procedures and she sent it to me.

J: The evidence you've given, that you were able to contact your ex-husband, and he was able to get your mobile phone number in this country...

AP: When I came here I was still in contact normally with my husband and family, they didn't know about that issue.

J: What issue is that?

AP: Because I needed some papers sent to me from Iraq, needed by Iraq Embassy here. That is the way they came to find we were married, they found the marriage certificate.

J: They found the marriage certificate and then the balloon went up?

AP: Because when I left Jordan I left all the documents behind in Amman.

The applicant testifies that the Iraqi government discovered that she was married when she requested documents from the Iraq Embassy in Britain. When the official asks her "They found the marriage certificate and then the balloon went up?" he is asking if the request for documents put her husband and family in danger. At the beginning of this section of questioning, she says, "I contacted my sister in Jordan one week before my interview at the Home Office. She never replied. I could not get an answer because of her problem with her husband so I was compelled to contact her in Jordan so she could respond to me. Through my solicitors she was able to call me and I obtained the document because I only came with a passport and a copy of the passport and at that time the circumstances surrounding obtaining the document, they had a lot of problems because they had only one week to leave Jordan because they were staying there illegally and on the ... just before the interview they sent them to me" (Court hearing, London, November 11, 2016).

THE ABSENCE OF DOCUMENTS

Just as the presence of documents can provide the hearing authorities with material to question an applicant's credibility, so, too, can the absence of documents. In the following case, the officer is asking for documents relating to the applicant's medical treatment.

Tamil Case October 13, 2008

HO: Between April 2006 and November 2007, this period of sustained beatings, did you ever visit the hospital or a medical doctor?

AP: Yes, I did attend a private hospital for bruises and the pain I had due to the beatings I sustained.

HO: And you haven't provided any medical evidence or documents or evidence relevant to these visits?

AP: They used to give me slips of prescriptions that I obtained but I didn't bother to keep them.

AP: And the military policeman who secured your release on each and every occasion, you have no evidence from him about these arrests?

AP: He would have had documents to that effect, but he was shot dead so there was no way I could get evidence.

Here the Home Office representative is asking for the kind of documents that patients in the West would expect to receive, but in this case, the only paper the applicant received was prescriptions. The representative seems to lack cultural awareness that the documents he seeks simply are not produced in the context of the medical treatment obtained by the applicant. He is using this lack of document as evidence of a lack of credibility of the applicant's narrative.

Using False Documents as a Criminal Act

When asylum seekers use forged passports, they face the risk of being charged with fraud, even though, for many, this was the only means of escape. Using a false passport was not previously a particular problem either in the USA or the UK as the authorities recognized its necessity, but now, with the widespread securitization measures implemented after the attacks of 9/11, it has become a bigger issue. If someone enters the USA on a false passport, the case is immediately referred to the Immigration Court, without the more informal hearing with an asylum officer. In 2004, UK legislation made it a crime to enter the country without a passport or with a false passport, unless the person had a "reasonable excuse" for doing so (Asylum and Immigration [Treatment of Claimants, etc.] Act 2004, sec. 8). This move was intended to prevent people from deliberately destroying their passports before arriving; it was also intended to be a response to those who claim to come from a country other than their real country of origin, as part of a false claim (Neumayer 2006). The authorities, especially in the UK, argue that many applicants claim to be from a different country of origin—one where persecution is more common—in the hope that this deception will go unnoticed. In reality, however, many people are charged with the offense and have no idea of the possible defense, and end up pleading guilty, even though there is a defense available to those who have a good reason for using a false document. If the applicant is represented by a criminal lawyer, the lawyer may also have no idea that such a plea can have negative immigration consequences later on (Right to Remain 2017). When the time later comes for the person to apply for naturalization, the Home Office denies the application on the ground that the applicant has a criminal record. These cases can be resolved with good legal representation, but not everyone is lucky enough to find it.

The paradox here is that although it is supposed to be acceptable for someone to seek asylum even if it means using a false passport (and it is even acknowledged in the law that it might be necessary to do), in practice a false passport is a barrier to asylum. As C. Peter Erlinder (2008: 228) reports, though the 1967 UN Protocol Relating to the Status of Refugees stipulates that an asylum applicant who declares the use of false documents cannot be prosecuted, the fact is that in the USA, applicants can be indicted and detained and face felony criminal prosecution for the use of false documents under a law which is designed to address all those who use false documents whether they are asylum claimants or not (18 US Code Title 18 › Part I › Chapter 75 › § 1546).

The difficulty stems, in part, from the undoubted fact that some people do destroy their passports so that the adjudicators cannot find proof of their country of origin. They may use false documents to claim they are from a country more favored at the moment in the asylum system. In January 2016, "There was enormous demand for Syrian passports ... and nearly every European state was offering expedited asylum processing for Syrian refugees. For the enterprising or desperate Palestinian or Lebanese, a fake Syrian passport could prove the ticket to a new life in Europe" (Tinti and Reitano 2016: 80). The general rule is that a person can only be sent back to his or her own country when that is known and as long as he or she would not be at risk of persecution (the principle of nonrefoulement). At present, some countries seem to be willing to violate both of these rules when a person is suspected of using false documents, assuming they can persuade a country to receive him (Human Rights Watch 2005).

There is often a class bias here. People with more education and greater resources are more likely to own passports, so they need not risk the exposure when applying for one. They are also more likely to be able to find ways of getting to the USA or the UK on their own passports and a visitor's visa, a student visa, or a short-term business visa. Those with fewer resources have to fall back on illegal means to enter a country before applying for asylum. We assume that persecution knows no class boundaries, but the process of seeking asylum is easier for more sophisticated and better-off applicants.

The Difficulty of Assessing False Documents

The production of fake passports is a global industry. According to Tinti and Reitano, Lebanon is the regional hub for fake passports in the Middle East, and Thailand is the global hub (2016: 80). Immigration authorities are aware of the different methods used to produce fake passports, and in some cases have been successful in identifying a major source. A February 2016 raid on a Turkish site yielded thousands of passports (Tinti and Reitano 2016: 81). The sources for fake passports include those purchased or stolen from the original bearer, those manufactured to look like official passports, and those that use actual blank official passports.

The final category, the use of blank, official, passports, is the most difficult to identify as fraudulent. It is no longer as easy as it once was to obtain a blank passport from an embassy (Tinti and Reitano 2016: 78). However, During World War II, some sympathetic government officials and private citizens surreptitiously issued passports and identity documents to individuals escaping the Nazis. For example, Frank Foley, director of the British passport office in Berlin during the 1930s, was recently honored for giving visas to German Jews (Lipman 2012). And, famously, Raoul Wallenberg created Swedish Protective Passports that enabled 20,000 Jews to escape the Nazis.

Today, immigration officials in the West often know which countries currently have loose or unregulated passport production, and this is also often known by people trying to acquire passports. Those passports are far less expensive and more subject to scrutiny. A country's reputation for corruption or honesty is directly tied to its production, management, and control of documents.

Immigration authorities face many challenges in identifying false passports. Tinti and Reitano report, "Identifying a fake that has been printed on a real Syrian passport is very difficult" (2016: 75). Further, they write that it is almost impossible to detect the false use of an authentic passport, unless the person traveling makes a mistake filling it out or it appears as stolen on a data base (2016: 79). The NBC show *Dateline* exposed the ease with which individuals procure false passports that are virtually impossible to detect (Greenberg et al. 2007).

Assessing the validity of documents is not necessarily straightforward. Lawyer Navtej Ahluwalia reports the following discussion of documents in an asylum case:

> In one case from Iran (a classic venue for arrest warrants) the applicant had a document—"we were arrested in the past, were wanted," this tallied with the account. We went to an expert, "can you evaluate this?" "Yes, the stamp is right, the seal is right, official is correct, the language it is written is consistent with that coming to a judge." The HO sent the document to the British Embassy in Tehran, who used an unnamed person, from the Constitutional court, to evaluate it. He said it was defective; it used the wrong provision; the case started ten years ago, and there were no such delays. We went back to our expert who said it was total baloney that there were not such delays, and it is a question of judicial interpretation which section we use. The judge will properly evaluate this. This is a rare exceptional scenario. Usually they say—"we just don't believe" (in the validity of the document) in the country of origin scribes can craft your document, same in Pakistan (Ahluwalia 2008).

The view of the authorities that forged documents are readily obtainable in Pakistan, and elsewhere, is corroborated by Sadiq's work, in which he describes what he calls "networks of complicity" involving officials in a range of institutions who facilitate the manipulation and theft of passports and other documents (2009: 187–190).

CONCLUSION

As documents increasingly become a kind of currency, the artifact necessary for being regarded as a legitimate asylum seeker, they are, ironically, part of an industry that produces counterfeit identities. Although increasingly expected, documents do not necessarily support a case, and in any case, they are compromised by different cultural and historical attitudes toward them, the corruption of the place where they are produced, the ease of obtaining fakes, and the difficulty of identifying counterfeits. As

John Torpey writes, "Ultimately, passports and identity documents reveal a massive illiberality, a presumption of their bearers' guilt when called upon to identify themselves. The use of such documents by states indicates their fundamental suspicion that people will lie when asked who or what they are, and that some independent means of confirming these must be available if states are to sustain themselves as going concerns" (2000: 166).

Documents function very differently in asylum cases than in other areas of law. There is very little standardization, predictability, or reliability in the evaluation of and use of documents in political asylum hearings. Further, applying Western legal methods to understand the political asylum documents, or absence of documents, only exacerbates a situation already complicated by the lack of standardization of documents, the risk applicants take in acquiring or traveling with documents, and the motivation to use fraudulent documents in life or death situations.

In the West, we assume a correspondence among identities, events, and documents. Further, we regard documents as a relatively neutral representation of identities and events, and we therefore give greater credibility to a document than to a personal account. Also, along the same lines, forged or fraudulent documents are considered to taint the character of anyone using them, no matter how legitimate the reason.

In the absence of any means to determine the truth, political asylum officials are in the untenable position of claiming authority based on evidence, faulty evidence, and silences. They have to determine whether the evidence is sufficient, whether the faulty evidence is motivated by legitimate fears.

In *Discipline and Punish*, Michel Foucault demonstrates how documentation can be understood as part of a history of institutionalization and control of bodies as part of regulatory practices (1977). The documents that asylum officials seek are far from neutral but rather are at the core of the persecution asylum applicants face. Denying access to travel documents is a primary means of controlling people, and requiring documents of people who have not had that access is also discriminatory. Subjecting documents to scrutiny to determine their authenticity, and thus the authenticity of the applicant, is a way of bureaucratizing the political asylum experience and thus denying applications as bureaucratically, rather than substantially, flawed. In *The Archaeology of Knowledge*, Foucault writes, "The document is not the fortunate tool of a history that is primarily and fundamentally memory; history is one way in which a society recognizes a mass of documentation with which it is inextricably linked" (2012: 7).

A reconsideration of the role of documents in the political asylum process requires rethinking the relationship among history, memory, and documentation for ordinary individuals. The experiences of individuals in political events are rarely documented, and then only by oral historians who assert the value of an alternative, on the ground, everyday experience (Portelli 1991). Political asylum applicants' ordinary lives have been disrupted; not only are they are being asked to produce documentation of lives not ordinarily documented, they are being asked to produce the part of life experience that is outside the purview of historical records.

The demand for documents is part of a constant effort by all those involved in the asylum process to quantify what is in fact soft data. The authorities depend on documents and other forms of "scientific" evidence in their effort to evaluate the evidence contained in the applicants' narratives. In the next chapter, we review the scientific methods used to evaluate both narratives and documents.

NOTES

1. In his study of the history of the passport, John Torpey reviews the concomitant production of legitimate and fraudulent documents. Writing about the introduction of passports in eighteenth-century France, Torpey writes, "It is axiomatic that fraud and forgery are more or less automatic responses to the imposition by states of documentary requirements of this time" (2000: 49).
2. In the case of *Perales Serna* et al. *vs. Texas Department of State Health Services (DSHS)* the judge refused to grant an injunction against the state of Texas and there was to be a full evidentiary hearing to decide whether the failure to obtain a birth certificate unconstitutionally curtails rights of US citizenship or whether the state's interest in protecting against fraud outweighs those interests. The case was settled before going to a full hearing.
3. Goodman cites Abankwah v. INS, 185 F.3d 18, 26 (2d Cir. 1999).

CHAPTER 4

Science and Technology as a Way of Determining Credibility

As a response to the difficulty of relying on identity documents to determine the credibility of an application and the increasing pressure to identify fraudulent documents (discussed in Chapter 3), asylum officials have turned to more scientific methods of assessing the validity of an application. As we discuss in this chapter, these efforts only partially confirm truths or identify falsehoods on an application answer. Technologically based methods are used to supplement both narratives and other forms of documentary proof, especially to assess whether either documents or other evidence are fraudulent. Some of these methods have been appropriated from other parts of the legal system, some of which, such as assessments of language dialects have more specific relevance to asylum cases. As discussed elsewhere in the book, the increased reliance on technologies is an illustration of the change in the way asylum is perceived, with the focus having shifted from a concern about providing safe haven to a focus on preventing false claimants from gaining protection. Here we discuss the use of DNA to determine identity, age assessments, use of voice recognition, language assessments, fingerprinting, use of lie detection technologies, medical evidence, digital technologies, the body as a form of evidence, and other uses of expert technological evidence.

The enthusiasm for science as a solution to credibility problems is more predominant in the UK, although others, for example, Italians, also rely on language assessment tools (Jacquemet 2005), and fingerprint records are used throughout Europe for border control (Van der Ploeg 2003).

© The Author(s) 2018
C. Bohmer, A. Shuman, *Political Asylum Deceptions*,
https://doi.org/10.1007/978-3-319-67404-9_4

As of this writing, biometrics have limited use in asylum hearings (Liberatore 2007; Roeper 1998; Van der Ploeg 2003; Ajana 2013). Our informants in the USA have told us that hearing officers and judges make the credibility decision without resorting to these scientific methods. They do use the Internet to check on some reported information, but methods such as DNA testing, age assessment, and language analysis are not widely used by the authorities in the USA. One lawyer told us that even DVDs and videos, which might provide evidence in support of a claimant's narrative about, for example, attending demonstrations, are not used in US immigration courts. "No one has a drive anymore" (Kolken 2016).

DNA Testing

DNA testing, pioneered in the UK in 1985, is sometimes used by immigration authorities to try to verify the identity of applicants or their family members in asylum and refugee cases (McKie 2009). The question of whether people are related to each other, as they claim, can be an important element of an asylum claim. It is now mostly used in cases of family reunification of refugees who are permitted to bring in members of their family after they are accepted as refugees in the host country. In this context, and in the current climate of skepticism, it can be a helpful tool for refugees and others who want to have their family members join them but who do not have sufficient documentary proof to satisfy the authorities. In 1998, the German government approved the use of DNA testing for family members of Kurds already in Germany (Roeper 1998).

The UKBA (United Kingdom Border Agency) tried to take DNA testing a step further in 2009 when they set up a pilot project for testing ancestry and geographical origins. The project, called the Human Provenance Pilot Project (HPPP), was set up to test the utility of genetic and isotope testing as a way of corroborating asylum seekers' accounts of their nationality. The authorities hoped that these scientific tests would be able to determine the nationality of refugees, particularly whether they were from Somalia or Kenya or another neighboring country. The project came at a time when there were many asylum seekers who said they were from Somalia, and the UKBA thought they were lying and were in fact from elsewhere. It was subject to a huge amount of professional and academic criticism, was reduced from a 12-month to a three-month project, and was changed from a live study of actual applications to a research study only. The results of the study do not appear ever to have been made public (Tutton et al. 2014). The criticism was on both scientific and ethical grounds, although the policy makers argued that the "ethical issues at stake are far less critical than those related to medical genetics" (2014: 744).[1] The project also illustrates the "uncritical way in which technologies that had yet to establish their validity and utility in the context of forensic science and criminal investigation were nonetheless adopted into the asylum context—initially, at least, on the assumption that they could be useful in evaluating 'live' asylum applications" (ibid.: 743). DNA testing using databases collected in recent years can determine that some of that individual's ancestors were members "of a particular biogeographical population" (ibid.), but cannot determine either where that person has lived recently or his or her nationality. Nationality is a complex legal construct that is by no means synonymous with geographical origin. These limitations significantly undermined the validity of the project. The DNA project also purported to provide protections for the asylum applicants involved; they were given the option to refuse to participate and told that their refusal would not jeopardize their claim. However, such "protections" did not constitute genuine informed consent. In particular, departing from standards for informed consent, applicants also were told that their refusal would be recorded and made known to the hearing officers and judges responsible for deciding their claim. As Tutton, Hauskeller, and Sturdy reported, these procedures were "entirely contrary to the normal tenets of biomedical ethics, which apply to criminals as much as to other human subjects" (2014: 739).

DNA testing of family membership in refugee reunification is more acceptable scientifically, but is nonetheless problematic, both as a scientific endeavor and in terms of its significance. First, the underlying assumption is that genetic relationships are the only ones possible to identify membership in a family, thereby excluding the various other definitions used, especially in non-Western cultures. In addition, some countries regard DNA testing as a necessary but not sufficient condition for a successful family reunion application. In Finland, for example, a recent study showed that some cases were turned down even though the DNA showed a biological relationship, because the applicants did not show a "genuine family life." Underpinning this sort of approach are arguments by the Finnish authorities that the relationship was no longer one of a genuine family because of the lapse of time. This argument was used even when the person had humanitarian protection, showing that their departure from their homeland was not voluntary. In some cases, the authorities made this argument even when the delays had been caused by the state's own difficulties in reaching a conclusion about whether the case qualified for humanitarian protection. So DNA is useful to the authorities if it denies a relationship, as a rationale for denying asylum, but less so if it supports claims, for example, for family reunification (Helen and Tapaninen 2013).

AGE ASSESSMENT

One of the important distinctions in asylum policy (and immigration more generally) is the determination of whether someone is a minor or an adult. Countries have an obligation toward minors in general, and this also includes minors who arrive unaccompanied, seeking asylum. Age assessment is an issue in many asylum-receiving countries but seems to be handled differently in the UK, perhaps because the authorities in the UK have been especially interested in using what they regard to be "scientific" evidence as a justification for denying applicants in the absence of other documentation about their age (see Age Assessment Practice in Europe 2013). Many of these young people do not have birth certificates, so the only evidence is their word about how old they are. They are then treated like adults and go through the asylum process without the support they would have had as minors. The situation has also become more acute recently because of the increase in the number of unaccompanied minors arriving in Europe without documents, who may not know their birth dates. The United Nations Children's Fund reported "that approximately 41 percent of all births each year in the developing world (excluding China) go unregistered" (Asencio 2012). In 2015, record numbers of unaccompanied minors came to Europe, mostly from Afghanistan, Eritrea, and Somalia, and the numbers have been increasing in recent years (Migrantionsverket 2015). This increase in numbers has a significant effect on the way asylum applicants are managed, because according to the law, minors must be protected and treated differently from adults. Recently, the USA has also seen a huge influx of people fleeing violence in Central America, many of whom are women and children. Thus, accurate determinations of age have become even more important. Additionally, some asylum officials believe that asylum seekers lie about their age so that they can be dealt with as minors. A recent report by the Coram Children's Legal Centre recognized the problem: "Organisations supporting young people in the immigration system would not deny that there may be occasional cases of people claiming to be younger than they are. Nor can it be ignored that some unaccompanied children may have been briefed by the people-smugglers who facilitate their journey, providing them with information on what they should say when they reach the UK" (2013: 7). But they go on to point out that the existence of a few people who lie about their age is not a reason to use these exceptional cases to shape the entire system.

These efforts to determine age can be seen, like so much else in this area, as either a legitimate need to know whether to treat someone as a minor or an adult or as a political tool used by the asylum authorities as a way of limiting the rights of young asylum seekers. Applicants' claims to be minors are frequently in conflict with the government's response that they are adults. The problem is made more acute by the fact that a careful collection of evidence and its evaluation is an expensive option, so the authorities may not be willing to undertake it and instead rely on a superficial examination. The case of Gulwali Passarlay provides a chilling example. He arrived in the UK at the age of 13 after a horrendous year-long journey from Afghanistan. "Three weeks after all this was finally over, I found myself in front of five strangers who were tasked with assessing my age. They were so careless they didn't bother to spell my name right or get the month and day of my birth correct on their form.... They asked me questions about my family background, my journey—even silly questions about the province I came from in Afghanistan. After three or four hours they announced I was not 13 but 16-and-a-half....They said I couldn't have travelled so far when I was still so young, and that I was too smart to be 13. I know I looked older than I was—I still do, but I grew up in a harsh, mountain environment and had been through a long, hard journey. They tried to give me a new date of birth" (Passarlay and Khaleeli 2016).

A recent report has found that one quarter of all unaccompanied minors who claim asylum have their age disputed (Coram Children's Legal Centre 2013: 3). The authorities use various techniques in an effort to determine a person's age, using such tools as X-rays that help in measuring bone age, dental records, medical opinion, and psychological evaluation. Professionals agree that this is not an exact science, especially for applicants aged between 15 and 18, the ages of most of the minors in question. The margin of error can sometimes be as much as 5 years on either side (Royal College of Paediatrics and Child Health 1999). They argue that assessments of age aids in measuring maturity rather than chronological age; it is, of course, the latter information that the asylum authorities need to make the decision about treatment of an asylum seeker.

In the USA, unaccompanied minors are initially dealt with by the asylum office (Kludt 2015). A settlement agreement made in 1997, known as the Flores settlement, governs how minors under 18 are treated in custody if they are unaccompanied. Clause 13 of that agreement states:

> If a reasonable person would conclude that an alien detained by the INS is an adult despite his claims to be a minor, the INS shall treat the person as an adult for all purposes.... The INS may require the alien to submit to a medical or dental examination conducted by a medical professional or submit to other appropriate procedures to verify his or her age. (Flores v Reno 1997)

These procedures are used occasionally; more commonly, the authorities ask the minor to contact family in the country of origin to obtain a birth certificate (Corbaci 2016). This is more likely for minors from Central America than with young people from, for example, Afghanistan, who make up a large percentage of minors who come to the UK, many of whom don't have birth certificates.

As mentioned earlier, the question of whether someone is an unaccompanied minor is significant for receiving countries in Europe. Norway, for example, has made serious efforts to make such assessments as fairly and ethically as possible. The evaluation is conducted by medical doctors who write reports assessing the probability that someone is a particular age. The report is handed on to the hearing officers in the Norwegian Directorate, who make the decision depending on how certain the doctor is (Sigmond 2017).

The inadequacy and appropriate use of supposedly scientific methods can be illustrated by the case of dental X-rays, which have been called into question more than once in the UK. In 2012, the UKBA was forced to discontinue its program that required minor asylum applicants to submit to dental X-rays without ethical approval from the NHS (Meikle 2012). The issue resurfaced again in 2015, prompting the British Dental Association to publish a statement that X-rays for child asylum seekers are unethical and inaccurate (British Dental Association 2015). The statement followed evidence from the Refugee Council (which has been hired by the UKBA to provide support to child migrants) that the practice was on the rise and that children were having dental X-Rays without providing informed consent. While the Home Office no longer orders X-Rays, "Some local authority social workers have been keen to use them as part of multi-agency assessments of age, perhaps mistakenly believing that this is appropriate and accurate" (Refugee Council 2016). The Home Office finally may be revising X-ray practices. In October 2016, David Davies, a Conservative Member of Parliament, proposed once again the use of dental X-rays to assess the ages of the children who were arriving in the UK under a special program for unaccompanied minors. The tabloids snapped up the suggestion with such headlines as "Tell us the Tooth." This time, the Home Office was quick to dismiss the idea as unethical (Muir 2016).

A body of law has developed on this subject as a result of the judicial reviews of a number of age-disputed cases. In such cases, it is now up to the court to decide the age of the applicant, and the results of the recent cases show both acceptance and rejection of the Home Office's claims. In the 23 cases examined by the Coram Children's Legal Centre, eight were declared to be the age claimed by the Home Office; in four cases, the court decided the child's age was as he had claimed; and in the remaining cases, a completely different age was determined, which was between the age claimed by the child and the Home Office (2013: 24–28). Judges fulfill their role as arbiters of such disputes, despite the fact that they may feel it is beyond their abilities. As one judge put it, "What is my experience of judging the age of teenagers in Afghanistan or those who have lived in Afghanistan and have lived in this country for a year or two?" (R (A) v Camden [2010] EWHC 2882 (Admin), para 46).

A particular problem for our purposes is that the information a minor provides to the Home Office about his or her age may be used to discredit the asylum claim, despite guidelines from the Home Office that this should not be the case. Children may lie about their age or about their asylum claim for unconnected reasons, yet the authorities have in some cases conflated the two narratives to the detriment of the claim (Coram Children's Legal Centre Report 2013: 29).

The Home Office's policy of judging the age of unaccompanied minors seeking asylum based on their appearance was recently ruled unlawful by the High Court (R (AA) v The Secretary of State for the Home Department 2016). The court held that age assessment was a matter of "objective fact," so the Home Office could no longer conduct subjective assessments of age. AA, the boy involved in the court case, later had an age assessment carried out by social workers, which confirmed his age as 16. Before this result was communicated to the Home Office, they had detained the boy, and locked him up in an adult immigration removal center, from where he was not released for two weeks (Refugee Council 2016).

Errors in which a minor has been classified by authorities as an adult have reached such proportions that in the UK, the government has been forced to compensate those it wrongly classified as adults. Recent figures show that the total legal costs of losing the 262 age-disputed cases since 2010–11 amounted to £4,437,410 (Yeung 2017). These classifications of age are conducted by local councils who have an incentive for social services agencies deciding someone is an adult rather than a child; as one lawyer told us: "these people are expensive, so they want them off their books" (Robinson 2016).

LANGUAGE ASSESSMENT

Immigration officials use LADO (language assessment for the determination of origin) to determine whether claimants are lying about their place of origin. The premise of these assessments is that by using speech analysis, an expert can determine where individuals come from by analyzing their language patterns. The use of language assessment is rationalized as a way of filling in the gap for the many asylum seekers who do not have documents to prove their country of origin. Although framed in the neutral objective language of science, language assessment is, in fact, a political tool most often used when the authorities do not believe the asylum seeker's claim of nationality (Campbell 2013). UKBA policy has used LADO since 2000, that until recently has been provided by the Swedish firm, Sprakab, in a number of different situations in which they questioned an applicant's credibility. The evaluation is conducted by a 20–30-minute phone interview, which is recorded for subsequent analysis, by a commercial firm who, the UKBA claim, has "qualified" linguists in their employ, who are native speakers of the language in question, and who can determine the origin of the applicant. Sprakab does not reveal the identity of their analysts, apparently out of fear of reprisals should their names be revealed. Like all agencies that conduct this kind of analysis, they are very secretive about their methods and about the examiners (Fraser 2009: 129). Many linguists dispute the ability of such experts to come to a firm conclusion in such a short interview and also dispute the ability of someone who is a native speaker rather than a linguist (or preferably both in consultation) to make such a complex judgment (Patrick 2016; Campbell 2013). There are many reasons why someone's speech patterns may not clearly indicate where they are from, and without details of a person's history, the determination of geographical origin is at least partly guesswork.

Marco Jacquemet has documented some of the incorrect cross-cultural assumptions about language, resulting in erroneous assessments in asylum cases. As he points out, most asylum cases are multilingual, often involving more than one dialect. In his observations of Italian assessments of applicants claiming to be Kosovar, Jacquemet found that rather than asking for narratives about what the applicants had experienced, the officials asked questions about places in Kosovo, including the location of mosques or about significant geographic locations, such as important bridges. When a translator didn't know a word, he looked it up online. However, as Jacquemet points out, Internet-based translation tools often offer several choices for the translation of a word, and none of them may make sense. In some cases, the translator turned to a third language for a likely translation. "The digitalization of the workspace has allowed the asylum courts to become 'smart courtrooms,' fully wired offering access to the digital information infrastructure 24/7" (2016a: 26).

In some cases, confirming an applicant's identity is not just a matter of determining the country of origin. Many Somali applicants, for example, base their claims on membership in a minority clan, for which the adjudicators are always seeking proof. They often use language and cultural knowledge as ways of proving nationality or clan membership, both of which are often considered strong evidence in support of the claim.

For some time, policy makers, lawyers, and others have expressed serious concern about the accuracy of these assessments, and the matter has been litigated in the UK and Scottish courts, initially with different results. The English case decided that if a Sprakab report concluded that the person's native language was "with certainty not" that of the claimed country of origin, Somalia, then "little more" than that opinion was required to conclude that the person was not Somali (*R.B. [Somalia] v. S.S.H.D.* 2012). The Scottish cases, by contrast, disapproved of the use of anonymity for those who make the assessments, as being in violation of normal practice with experts in court cases (*M.A.B.N. and K.A.S.Y. v. Adv. Gen. for Scotland* 2013). The Home Office appealed this decision and a similar one, but lost in the Supreme Court; the case has been sent back to the Upper Tribunal for interpretation of the judgment (*Secretary of State for the Home Department (Appellant) v MN and KY (Respondent)* [2014] UKSC 30).

Like so many issues, assessing the value of the language programs is, at least in part, a matter of money. Because of the reluctance of the UKBA to pay for highly specialized services, Sprakab and other similar companies employ people who are often insufficiently qualified as linguists to undertake the careful analysis required in such cases. The integrity of language analysis is further compromised by using anonymous evaluators (not the norm in expert testimony) and occasions in which the language evaluators went beyond linguistic evaluation to make adamant statements about the credibility of the asylum seeker's claim. The UK Supreme Court in the case of *Secretary of State for the Home Department (Appellant) v MN and KY (Respondent)* [2014] (UKSC30) recommended caution, and even skepticism, on the part of the Upper Tribunal (the immigration court which deals with appeals from the Lower Tribunal) in the general guidance they gave. They argued that courts should evaluate each report on its merits, rather than accepting their reports on face value. They also said that some of the statements went beyond that appropriate for a witness.

A few months later, without publicity, the Home Office stopped using Sprakab (Green 2014, but see Campbell 2013, who states that this happened in 2010). The issue did come to public attention shortly thereafter when it was reported that one of Sprakab's key analysts was a convicted drug dealer, who, it was claimed, sent hundreds of asylum seekers back to war-torn Somalia (Green 2014). This man was apparently the analyst who conducted the interview of one of the respondent in the case of the aforementioned MN and KY, whose evidence was described by the Court as inappropriately offering an opinion about the applicant's credibility, beyond the analysis of a where he came from.

LADO is used all over the world, for the most part by governments trying to determine credibility. But such is the fear of airlines of being found responsible for allowing someone not permitted to enter a destination country that Aer Lingus at one point took it upon itself to use language analysis. According to the Associated Press, "(a)pparently hundreds, if not thousands, of Greek passport holders had been required to fill out forms demonstrating their fluency in Greek before they could board Aer Lingus flights from Spain and Portugal to Ireland" (Pogatchnik 2012). After a Greek businesswoman complained, Aer Lingus was forced to back down and compensate her.

Sprakab apparently has conducted 40,000 linguistic analyses (LA) for governments all over the world, including Canada, Sweden, Australia, the Netherlands, and the UK (Green 2014). Other organizations also conduct LA, for example, De Taalstudio in the Netherlands, which uses only expert linguists (rather than those who are native speakers and not linguists) who are identified by name, unlike the Sprakab policy. The Home Office now has a contract with another Swedish firm, called Verified, though they continue to use Sprakab occasionally (Gov.uk 2014). Some countries mostly use their own resources (e.g. the Swiss, Germans), though sometimes even they buy in from companies or other government bureaus; others depend on companies like Verified (e.g. Norway) (Patrick 2016). One of the important differences in country practices is the extent to which the process is contracted out to the firm conducting LADO; the UK Home Office contracts out the entire process, including quality control, whereas the Swiss and the Dutch, for example, keep significant control in-house (Patrick 2016: 351). Some of the problems discussed in the cases about the use of Sprakab by the Home Office stemmed from outsourcing all control of the process.

The US employs less formal use of language analysis. One lawyer we spoke to thought it was because judges in the USA are "so overworked that they do not have time for this (Yale-Loehr 2016)." Another lawyer described his experience of such cases as "People from one country say they are from another. Immigration has become diligent—what dialect does he speak, if that dialect is not native to that place…Unless a person has good English, he speaks in his native language, they get him an interpreter, who needs to speak that dialect. It used to be that you brought your own interpreter; now they have someone on the line" (Siman 2016). In some cases, the interpreter acts not only as a language analyst but also in the capacity of an immigration authority who questions the asylum seeker in an effort to determine whether she is indeed from the place she says she is from. Sometimes this results in an outcome that flies in the face of reality. One lawyer described an applicant who had fled the DRC for Angola and managed to get (false) papers there. The judge couldn't be convinced that he was Congolese, even though he spoke French rather than the Portuguese he would have spoken had he been Angolan (Marszalkowski 2016).

Anthropologist John Haviland, who has been called upon to translate for Tzotzil speakers from Chiapas, Mexico, reports that immigration officials often try to restrict their communication with the immigrants. They request "denotational transparency," a word-for-word translation that is often impossible due to the absence of semantic equivalents for particular words, especially legal terms (forthcoming).

The burden to prove positively where someone comes from can fall on the lawyer representing the applicant in the USA. In one case a lawyer described a Tibetan client who had a fake Nepali passport, and the asylum officer asked in his interview how he could determine that the applicant was in fact Tibetan as he alleged. The lawyer contacted the Tibetan Office (the equivalent of the consul, as there are no diplomatic relations), where he was interviewed extensively in Tibetan. They were convinced he was Tibetan and wrote a letter accordingly, which was accepted by the asylum office (Berger 2016). In many cases, this might not have worked because many Tibetans moved to Nepal decades ago, but have recently had to leave because of ethnic cleansing. Accordingly, the question of who is a Tibetan and who is Nepalese is a problematic one.

Voice Recognition

As far as we know, voice recognition technology has not been used in asylum applications yet. But it has been used in other immigration cases in the UK and is testament to the increasing reliance on science and technology to supplement evidence in immigration hearings. The most recent and egregious example is the use of voice recognition as justification for the deportation of many students whom the Home Office concluded had cheated in a required English test. Thousands were determined to be liars, arrested in dawn raids, detained, and then deported, based, as it was subsequently found in a court ruling, on unscientific hearsay evidence. The project was the result of a 2014 BBC program, *Panorama*, which investigated fraudulent tests in one English language school in London (Merrill 2016). The Home Office response was to claim that everyone who had taken the particular language test, written and conducted by an American firm, ETS, had committed fraud. The licenses of about 60 educational institutions were revoked, though there was no evidence that any fraud was involved at any other language schools. ETS was apparently hired by the Home Office because they claimed that they had special new voice recognition software, which had already detected thousands of fraudulent language tests. ETS alleged these must have been done by test surrogates, and it also claimed that humans had verified these software results. All this became public when two of those who had been deported sued.

The judge of the Upper Tribunal, Mr. Justice McCloskey, said that neither of the two people who gave evidence on behalf of the Home Office had "any qualifications or expertise, vocational or otherwise, in the scientific subject matter of these appeals"(Dunt 2016a). At no time, in fact, had the Home Office had advice or input from a suitable expert. The criticisms of their witness statements "were not addressed, much less answered, in their evidence."

The Home Office's case that these students had committed fraud was "entirely dependent" on ETS. The tribunal found the Home Office accepted uncritically everything reported by the firm. Ironically, ETS provided no evidence in the case, either written or oral, nor was the voice recording on which the allegations of fraud by the two students who sued made available. The Home Office appealed this decision; that appeal was dismissed in October 2016 (Dunt 2016b). The Home Office appeal "originally claimed that the case was unfair, that the deputy judge was biased, that witnesses had not been given an opportunity to explain evidence properly, and that the tribunal had misunderstood expert evidence" (ibid.).

Later, the Home Office wrote to the lawyers representing the students, admitting there were "no compelling reasons to pursue the appeal." It also offered to pay costs if the appeal was withdrawn, but the Court chose nevertheless to decide the case, even though the Home Office wanted to withdraw their appeal.

Voice recording fraud provides another example of the misuse of technology by the Home Office and their agents whose unsupported claims were uncritically accepted by the government, possibly motivated by the desire to identify fraudulent practices among migrants. The issue is now being dealt with in various legal cases, including those by other students who were among those whose tests were declared invalid because they had allegedly cheated. There is likely to be a public inquiry about this scandal, and the cases continue to come to the courts.

FINGERPRINTING

The use of fingerprints has become an important element in Europe in what are known as "Dublin" cases, basically the rule that a person must claim asylum in the first safe place she reaches. Despite many problems with the Dublin rules, the system is currently still in force. The fingerprinting system, called Eurodac, is considered an accurate indication of where a person has been, another example of heavy reliance on technology. Despite its widespread use in many areas of the law, there is some dispute about how accurate fingerprints are (Zabell 2005; but see Biometrics in Large Scale IT 2015). In a number of cases, asylum seekers claim either that they were not in the country or that they were there but not at the time the Eurodac database claims. This is not necessarily an issue of the accuracy of the fingerprinting itself, but of the Eurodac system. As there is no independent evidence, determining the accuracy of the system is difficult. It is unlikely the EU will devote much attention to this question because fingerprinting is so central to the way the EU tries to manage asylum. Also troubling is that, in some cases, asylum seekers claim that they were fingerprinted by force. Human Rights organizations have been very concerned about the recent efforts to expand the access to the Eurodac files. A spokesman from the German Institute of Human Rights is reported to have argued that, because the automatically transmitted data are not reviewed by an actual person in all EU member states involved, it has been mixed up before. "We are dealing with a truth machine." But that is fatal, Töpfer explained, because "the fingerprint has become the decisive evidence" (Dernbach 2015).

LIE DETECTORS

The use of lie detectors in criminal prosecution is not unusual. In some cases, police used polygraphs to test women who have claimed to have been raped, and the results are used to assess the "veracity" of the claim as a prerequisite for further investigation. The use of polygraphs was banned in the USA by the Violence Against Women Act of 2005. Explaining the ethical problem of using lie detectors on vulnerable people such as asylum seekers, one asylum lawyer said, "Imagine the horror of strapping torture survivors into the lie detector equipment and what that would do to them" (Jacobsen 2016).

One of the reasons for the skepticism about the use of lie detectors is their inadequate validity (see, e.g. Iacono and Lykken 1997; APA 2004). Despite their known unreliability, there have been recent calls for their use in the USA as a tool for determining the veracity of the claims of Syrian refugees. One House lawmaker introduced legislation that requires Syrian and Iraqi refugees to take a polygraph test, while the head of the Department of Public Safety, Steve McCraw, told a Texas House committee that such a test should be introduced before refugees could come to Texas. "I don't know if would be sufficient, but it would certainly be a technique that would provide a greater level of confidence," he said (Carney 2015; WOAI News Radio 2015). This is a very interesting example of the ways in which people can be made to feel secure despite the fact that lie detector tests are sufficiently unreliable that they cannot provide true security. Many courts have rejected lie detectors as unreliable means of proving the veracity of claims such as asylum. Their unreliability does not, however, prevent the subject coming up now and again, sometimes as a way for asylum seekers themselves to prove their claims. Commercial firms offer polygraph tests in such contexts, and one company even provides instruction for polygraph tests for asylum seekers, among others, as part of their "theory of polygraph science" (Centre for Forensic Neuroscience, n.d.). As further evidence of the continued attraction of lie detectors in this area, despite their ethical and scientific problems, an asylum lawyer we interviewed reported that at a recent meeting a judge suggested the use of lie detectors (Jacobsen 2016).

According to media reports, in 2010, the Czech Republic used what was described as an "erotic lie detector" to determine the validity of the claims of gay asylum seekers (Puhl 2010). The phallometric device is used in research and in cases of pedophiles and others as a way of determining arousal. When the EU Agency for Fundamental Rights got wind of this, there was a public outcry (ibid.).

MEDICAL EVIDENCE

Medical evidence, unlike the other technologies of surveillance and corroboration, is primarily used in asylum cases to buttress, rather than discredit, the claim. When used to discredit a case, the authorities may reject the validity of the medical evidence and its role in explaining causation. Medical evidence is used often in asylum cases, mostly to support claims of torture or post-traumatic stress disorder (PTSD). As with other issues, some argue that the authorities ignore concerns about torture, as, for example, the belief that the Home Office disregarded torture claims of asylum applicants and detained them (Townsend 2010).

One of the most fraught issues is the extent to which medico-legal reports can determine whether injuries and bodily scars are caused by torture. Doctors who write such reports use the Istanbul Protocol, outlined in a UN Handbook (OHCHR 2004). The Protocol describes a process for clinicians to match up scars with the account of the survivor to assess whether the scar in question was caused by torture, as claimed. There are five possible levels: (1) not consistent: the lesion could not have been caused by the trauma described; (2) consistent: the lesion could have been caused by the trauma described, but there are many other possibilities; (3)

highly consistent: the lesion could have been caused by the trauma described, and there are few other possible causes; (4) typical of: this is an appearance that is usually found with this type, but there are other possible causes; and (5) diagnostic of: this appearance could not have been caused in anyway other than that described (34–5). While this typology is undoubtedly very helpful for clinicians asked to provide expert medical reports, when used in asylum hearings, the lack of a definitive determination that a scar was caused by torture often fuels skepticism and is used to support hearing officers' denials of asylum claims. Some clinicians have advocated the use of various techniques to make the determination of cause more convincing, such as the use of photographs and bone scans, but the problem of medical judgment remains (Park and Oomen 2010; Kezwer 1998). In addition, classification systems in which experts profess to determine causation are not well-received by the law because judges believe that a decision about the cause is their job alone. Judges are not, however, averse to using experts when they think it will help them. One lawyer told us that judges have asked psychologists who examine asylum seekers to tell them whether the applicants are "telling the truth" (Jacobsen 2016).

Some forms of torture do not leave physical scars. In fact, there is evidence that some torturers purposefully choose methods of torture that do not leave scars (Park and Oomen 2010)). They target a person's feet or genitals, where scars are not likely to be visible, or use methods such as waterboarding, which do not leave marks on the body. In such cases, the Istanbul Protocol furnishes no assistance to an examining medical expert.

The claim of PTSD is a widespread medical diagnosis in asylum cases. Estimates of its prevalence vary; one meta-analysis found the incidence of PTSD to be about ten times that of the normal population (Fazel et al. 2005). The analysis indicated that about 9% of resettled refugees suffered from PTSD, though some studies had a much higher rate (ibid.). There is some consensus that PTSD can affect a claimant's ability to provide credible evidence of her claim. As, Rogers, Fox, and Herlihy put it, "There is evidence that mental health problems, including PTSD, could have a negative impact on asylum seekers' credibility through affecting the consistency of their verbal accounts of their experiences" (2014: 2). In addition, although some individuals with PTSD are able to narrate the central elements of their stories accurately, they might, nonetheless, narrate discrepancies in the surrounding details (Herlihy and Turner 2006).

The lawyers and NGOs who represent asylum seekers and the immigration authorities have very different perceptions of the significance of

PTSD. Those who work with asylum seekers argue that the authorities do not take psychiatric diagnoses sufficiently into account, and the authorities in response argue that a person presents inconsistent evidence because their story is untrue and then is used as evidence of a deliberate deception. As with cases of proving torture, the medical profession is involved in preparing reports to explain the effect of PTSD on the ability, or lack thereof, to remember traumatic events. As we have discussed in Chapter 2, being able to narrate such events in convincing detail is often crucial to a successful asylum claim.

The authorities, especially in the UK, sometimes regard medical experts as insufficiently objective and instead as partisan representatives of the interests of the asylum claimants (Bohmer and Shuman 2007: 130–2). Judges often justify their disbelief in the medical report by deciding that the doctors' assessments are opinions based on an applicant's untrue statements (Kelly 2012). Further, Conlan reports that in some Irish cases, officials identified what they saw as discrepancies between what an applicant told the official and what was reported to the doctor, resulting in an assessment that the applicant's case was not credible (Conlan et al. 2012: 35). The fact that one expert was found to have provided a report on an asylum seeker he had not seen further raises questions about the reliance on medical testimony (Ahluwalia 2005).

The importance of medical evidence is another issue that differs between the USA and the UK. In the USA, it appears that medical evidence is more likely to be believed and accepted by judges. One lawyer told us, "I have had times where it is clear in the process where the judge was leaning towards the belief that the person was not credible, I have engaged a psychiatrist to conduct a forensic exam and testify why he believed the client was credible. He used research on credibility; it was very compelling. I think it changed the outcome" (Feal 2016). And, "Survivors of Torture Organization provides assessments, about physical scars, to say they are consistent with the story…. The judges here, they really like it when someone whose status he might respect tells him something, he is not going out on a limb" (ibid.). One lawyer went so far as to say, "The judges are expecting it nowadays. If you don't present it, the government lawyer points it out to the judge. The first question the government attorney asks is 'Have you got a medical report?' They'll take that as significant, they are expecting it now" (Marszalkowski 2016). The respect for a medical professional's status seems a lot less significant in the UK, and the reliance on medical testimony much lower.

OTHER EXPERT TESTIMONY

The Home Office especially downgrades expert evidence as of a lesser order than their idea of "hard science." Several anthropologists familiar with the cultural practices of particular groups and with language dialects have been called upon as experts. These experts are able to provide extensive information about the structure and history of a community. However, when asked to predict the future and assess whether claimants would be in danger if they were to return to their home country, they cannot always answer with any certainty, resulting in a possible loss of credibility in the court (McDougall 2015).[2]

The anthology *Asylum at a Crossroads* provides a thorough discussion of the reliance on expertise in the asylum process. Written by anthropologists, the book provides a much needed historical context for understanding other legal domains and for reconsidering how plausibility and credibility were evaluated in the establishment of rights more generally (2015: 4). As they point out, experts do not exist independently of the systems in which they serve; their information is managed as part of legal and cultural systems. In particular, they point to three elements of expert knowledge, "the exigencies of juridical proof, the substantiation of the claimant's credibility, and the humanitarian trope of the deserving refugee" (Berger et al. 2015: 6) .

DIGITAL TECHNOLOGIES

Digital technologies, including cellular phones and social media, have become a central dimension of the migration experience, important at all levels of the process, from connecting migrants to each other and to smugglers to the asylum hearing itself, where immediate access to information has changed the kinds of evidence that are available and that can be challenged. The availability of immediate translation on a cell phone, for example, makes it possible for people to attempt to communicate without knowing each other's language. New technologies have altered the landscape so that migrants can no longer be regarded as persons with a singular identity from a particular place. Instead, displaced peoples often have vast networks beyond their local origins, and their movement across borders includes both virtual and literal migration. At the same time, the new technologies are available to individuals attempting to deceive asylum officials.

The authorities frequently engage with digital technologies to provide evidence of credibility. Marco Jacquemet writes, "Digitalization has allowed asylum courts to become 'smart courtrooms,' fully wired with access to the digital information infrastructure 24/7. In particular, digitalization has enabled the staff of asylum courts to conduct immediate online searches to verify proper names cited by applicants, even while the applicants are in process of giving their testimonies" (2016b: np). The officials use Google maps to corroborate an applicant's testimony about locations, and inconsistencies are considered as evidence of deception. Several lawyers in the USA described this use of digital technologies in asylum hearings (Nesbit 2016).

In a close examination of the use of digital technologies in "smart courtrooms," Jacquemet has identified significant errors. He writes, "Proper names are (erroneously) believed to survive the translation from one language to another in a fairly constant, recognizable form" (2016b: np). However, he provides several examples in which proper names are variable, especially among non-native speakers. In several cases Jacquemet documented, proper names were mistranslated or resulted in confusion (2016b).

The primary digital technology is the smart phone, and the phone itself has become a central piece of documentary evidence. The German government has proposed a plan whereby border police would pilot a scheme under which refugees resettled in Germany under the recent deal made between Turkey and the EU would have to hand over their smartphones for security checks if they did not have passports. The German minister proposing this plan said, "We frequently encounter cases where refugees often don't carry identity documents, but do nearly all carry their smartphones" (Oltermann and Henley 2016). The smartphone is the most important asset for any asylum seeker, especially during their flight to safety, because it is the only way they can stay in touch with family and friends and also learn crucial information. The German authorities are also planning that refugees hand over access to their Facebook contacts. These proposals come on the heels of attacks by asylum seekers in Europe, which has increased the fear that people calling themselves asylum seekers are in fact terrorists.

Since 2013, UK immigration officials have had permission to hack the phones of refugees under an amendment to the 1997 Police Act. According to the *Observer*, the Home Office has "been granted the power to use 'property interference, including interference with equipment', which can include planting a listening device in a home, car or detention centre, as well as hacking into phones or computers" (Townsend 2016) . The government claims that such techniques have been made possible for the purpose of preventing serious crime, including disrupting the supply of counterfeit travel documents. They did not address whether the powers had been used to ascertain the veracity of asylum claims, so we cannot determine one way or the other whether this use of technology is a method to determine credibility; it is certainly possible.

After the terrorist attack in San Bernardino, California, in 2015, where the couple involved had allegedly become radicalized through the Internet, Congress requested that the Department of Homeland Security (DHS) investigate the social media accounts of immigrant applicants (Dzubow 2017). As a result, the DHS is conducting a task force and several pilot projects to expand social media screening of asylum applicants as well as other immigration applications, despite the fact that at the time the project was initiated, the ability to investigate social media accounts was limited by technology (ibid.: 3).

DOCUMENTING THE BODY AS A SOURCE OF EVIDENCE

The asylum applicant's body is itself a source of evidence of the trauma he or she claims to have experienced. Asylum courts have sometimes relied on their own medical examiners to ascertain the validity of torture claims, and unlike the applicant's narrative, the examination of the body has been regarded as less open to deception. In recent years, new technologies have been employed in courtrooms, provided by both the courts and the applicants. For example, to prove that they are victims of China's one-child policy, applicants have provided X-rays and ultrasounds showing the presence of an intrauterine contraceptive device (Nesbit 2016). To prove that they are gay, men in the UK have provided video records of sexual intercourse with other men, which is discussed in Chapter 5, and, as we shall see, is a form of documentation that is no longer accepted (Lewis 2014).

As Fassin and Halluin observe, the availability of new technologies as evidence of bodily harm or intrusion has resulted in the expectation that applicants will produce medical certificates or other documentation (2005: 598). They argue, "the body has become the place of production of truth on the asylum seeker" (2005: 599). Further, they cite statements by doctors who are justifiably worried that their testimonies about the medical credibility of an applicant's claim place them in the ethically problematic role of determining whether a claim is valid (2005: 601). The medical testimonies often carry more weight than those of the applicant, a situation that is especially problematic when an applicant claims to have been tortured but has no bodily markings, as discussed earlier. Medical examinations can be inconclusive, for example, when an applicant describes ongoing pain resulting from torture, and the medical practitioner is able to identify a medical condition but not certify its source.

As Dove points out: "Identity documents-the written and visual texts, and the spoken word of the applicant-lose their power of truth in the face of science. There are various reasons for this reliance on genetic truth, but one of the most apparent is the post-9/11 climate that has induced a culture of risk and its apparent control" (2013: 472). This reliance on using the body to produce "scientific" results, which is seen as "objective," comes with the implication that this evidence is somehow more "true" than the narrative evidence otherwise relied on by the asylum authorities. In reality, however, as Kelly (2012) points out, despite the search for the body as the "authentic ground of suffering," it does not provide a solution to the credibility problem in asylum policy. Rather, "the corporeal is treated as just as problematic a source of evidence as the linguistic" (Kelly 2012: 762) .

Fassin and Halluin describe the use of medical certificates as evidence of torture in France as the result of a "profound delegitimization of asylum in the last two decades all over Europe" (2005: 598). As a result, authorities look to the body as evidence, but the applicant faces the aforementioned barrier, that the effects torture are increasingly hard to see, because torturers pick their methods for this very reason. Fassin and Halluin write, "When war is over or when the oppressor is defeated, the torture may be brought in front of an international or a national court of justice. The war criminal's elementary rule is, thus, to leave no physical mark. It is in this context of concealment favorable to all types of subsequent denial that the medical certificate assumes increasing importance in societies in which the victims of political violence are supposed to be accepted and protected" (2005: 598).

As political asylum hearings increasingly rely upon documentary evidence to support narrative claims related to the body (including torture, sexual identification, rape, forced contraception, or F.G.M.), applicants without documentation are under suspicion. Medical examinations, including DNA testing, are not necessarily reliable indicators, and as with other technologies, are open to fraudulent use and manipulation.

Conclusion

The efforts to use science and technology as a way of providing "objective" measures of credibility are understandable in an area where it is so difficult to obtain a satisfactory narrative and to be confident that it is true. Further, the increased availability of new forms of global surveillance combined with the fact that some asylum seekers have various kinds of records on their phones has changed both the kinds of evidence and attitudes toward evidence. At the same time, the new technologies are also part of the culture of suspicion, in which many immigration officials view asylum seekers as guilty until proven innocent. This phenomenon is not new, but it is intensified by the use of technologies deemed more scientific. As we have seen, new technologies are sometimes employed without regard for privacy rights; instead, in many cases, asylum seekers are perceived as criminals, whose rights are denied. In some cases, asylum seekers are used as test subjects for untested and unreliable methods, with very little attention to the research that shows them to be not only less than useful but in some cases faulty.

Migrants and asylum seekers are increasingly aware of new methods of surveillance, evidenced by applicants who discard their cell phones before arriving at the border of a country of refuge. To some extent, the wide availability of cell phones has democratized systems of surveillance and corroboration, providing migrants and asylum seekers with technological proof that once remained only in the hands of the powerful.

Although intended to provide better means for identifying fraudulent asylum seekers, the technologies we have discussed in this chapter often not only fail but also serve to delegitimize the process as a whole.

Notes

1. Medical genetics has been the subject of extensive inquiry. For example, a team of researchers wrote, "Human genetics is about relationships—biological and social relationships—and it can be argued that any rigorous ethical justification of informed consent to genetic testing needs to take this into account" (Hallowell et al. 2003: 78).
2. Lawrance, et al. provide an extensive discussion of the roles of expert witnesses in asylum cases, (2015, pp. 1–37).

CHAPTER 5

New Forms of Evidence: Membership in a Particular Social Group

Of all of the political asylum categories, membership in a particular social group (PSG) has seen the most change as new groups have been recognized as victims of persecution. At the same time, PSG is the most nebulous of the categories that qualify an individual for asylum, and thus the most open to interpretation (Helton 1983). People claiming membership in relatively newly recognized persecuted groups have been the subject of suspicion not only because the group itself is not fully recognized but also because policy makers and some members of the general public in the receiving countries suspect both that economic migrants are taking advantage of these newly recognized forms of persecution and that criminals, the persecutors of those very groups, might portray themselves as victims. We will return to the particular problem of differentiating between perpetrators and victims in Chapter 8.

Some of the issues that emerge in any political asylum claim, including the importance of credibility, demeanor, producing a coherent narrative, and the plausibility of the case, are intensified in claims to membership in a persecuted social group. In addition, applicants for social group asylum are required to meet additional criteria. First, membership in a social group is expected to be immutable, that is unchanging. Second, and this criterion is rarely articulated as such, members of a social group are expected to have awareness of the circumstances of their persecution. Finally, people claiming membership in a social group must be able to prove their affiliation with the group. These three dimensions invoke additional suspicions—first, that an applicant might be able to change their association with the group to avoid

© The Author(s) 2018
C. Bohmer, A. Shuman, *Political Asylum Deceptions*,
https://doi.org/10.1007/978-3-319-67404-9_5

persecution; second, that applicants' lack of knowledge might be an indication of pretense, a sign that the applicants are using the newly identified category as a means of entry into the receiving country.

Fauziya Kassindja was a young woman who fled Togo because she was about to be forced to undergo female genital mutilation (FGM; also known as female cutting or female circumcision) before entering a forced marriage with a man more than twice her age (Kassindja 1998). She was of mixed tribal origin; her father was Koussountu and Tchamba and her mother was Fulani and Dendi. Her father was very liberal and believed in educating his daughters. He did not want Fauziya to undergo FGM, but when he died, her mother was sent back to her village and Fauziya'a upbringing was taken over by her aunt and uncle. They decided she should undergo FGM and arranged her marriage. Days before the circumcision was to be performed and the marriage to take place, Fuaziya fled to Ghana with the help of her older sister. She flew from Ghana to Germany and eventually arrived in the USA. She was detained and spent many months going through the asylum system. The eventual decision in her case was a landmark one, in which the Board of Immigration Appeal accepted her claim of persecution based on the fear of FGM. The particular social group to which she was found to be a member, for purposes of asylum law, was "women of the Tchamba-Kuntsuntu Tribe of Northern Togo who oppose the practice of FGM.[1]" By describing her membership so narrowly, as a member of a particular cultural group that opposed FGM, rather than as a member of the larger group of women threatened by FGM, the officials strategically narrowed the social group.

Minta del Carmen Rivera-Barrientos is a young woman from El Salvador who was asked to join a gang. She refused, because she did not want to participate in gang coercion and violence. The gang threatened to harm her family if she didn't join. The gang members continued to harass her and pressure her to join the gang over the next few months. Later, she was kidnapped by gang members, hit in the face, and gang-raped. She did not report the attack to the police because she didn't think they could help her. The gang came to her house several times after the attack asking if she had changed her mind. She fled to Mexico and was then caught trying to enter the USA. She claimed asylum as a member of a particular social group, that of young women who refused gang membership. The court denied her claim because it believed that the social group she claimed as a basis for her claim was not "defined with particularity" or "socially visible" (Rivera-Barrientos v. Holder 2012).

In recognition that people are persecuted for a broader range of reasons than were anticipated in the original Convention in 1951, the category of membership in a particular social group has been expanded recently and, for example, now includes claims on the basis of gender and the persecution of sexual minorities.[2] It is the only category that is expanding to take into account recent ideas of people who should be protected. The category of a particular social group often raises questions about the conditions in which people deserve protection, and in this sense, it's connected to changes in human rights discourses, for example, pointing to the ways that the original 1951 construction of the policy did not attend equally to well-founded fears of persecution.

As the cases at the beginning of this chapter illustrate, recent claims show how difficult it is to adapt the catchall category of PSG to current conditions that were not anticipated in the discussions that set up the Convention. The expanded category of social group also has fostered new forms of suspicion. In all five of the asylum categories, an applicant can be accused of not being credible, or the persecution can be deemed insufficient to warrant asylum, but the category of social group opens up the question of whether the social group is itself legitimate.

THE ORIGIN OF MEMBERSHIP IN A PSG

Little documentation exists to explain the intentions of the drafters of the Convention when they added membership in a particular social group to the list of grounds as a basis for a well-founded fear of persecution. Apparently, the Swedish delegate added the category, saying that such cases exist, and they should be mentioned explicitly. The category of PSG was adopted unanimously without discussion by the delegates a few meetings after it was proposed by the Swedish delegate (Conference on Plenipotentiaries 1951). Political asylum scholars have offered possible explanations. For example, Helton argues:

> The intent of the framers of the Refugee Convention was not to redress prior persecution of social groups, but rather to save individuals from future injustice. The "social group" category was meant to be a catch-all which could include all the bases for and types of persecution which an imaginative despot might conjure up. Thus, the framers' general intent is illustrated by the subsequent recognition of the many types of invidious persecution prevalent in the world today. (Helton 1983: 45)

The opinion in the landmark case known as *Shah* elaborated on the understanding of the impetus behind the category:

> In choosing to use the general term "particular social group" rather than an enumeration of specific social groups, the framers of the Convention were in my opinion intending to include whatever groups might be regarded as coming within the anti-discriminatory objectives of the Convention. (Shah and Islam 1999)

The Meaning and Use of the Category of PSG

Because the term was specifically not defined in the Convention itself, scholars and judges have been struggling to determine exactly what is involved in a PSG. One consequence of the lack of clarity is that the law is thereby unclear. At the same time, the openness of the category of PSG provides an opportunity to expand the kinds of persecution that can be considered for asylum. This expansion is evident in the fact that in the USA, PSG is the second most used basis for asylum claims (Gallagher and Dizon 2010).

One of the landmark cases on the category of social group in the USA clarified the definition as requiring immutable characteristics of the members. Julio César Acosta, an El Salvadoran, claimed persecution as a member of a social group, COTAXI, where about 150 taxi drivers had refused to participate in a work stoppage called by anti-State El Salvadoran guerrillas. He claimed that he and others received death threats from the guerrillas. His application for asylum was denied because if he were to return to El Salvador and not return to driving a taxi, he would no longer be a target of persecution (Matter of Acosta 1985). His claim was denied because he did not meet the requirement of an immutable characteristic. The decision stated:

> Applying the doctrine of ejusdem generis, we interpret the phrase "persecution on account of membership in a particular social group" to mean persecution that is directed toward an individual who is a member of a group of persons all of whom share a common, immutable characteristic. The shared characteristic might be an innate one such as sex, color, or kinship ties, or in some circumstances it might be a shared past experience such as former military leadership or land ownership... whatever the common characteristic that defines the group, it must be one that the members of the group either cannot change, or should not be required to change because it is fundamental to their individual identities or consciences.[3] (233)

Although Acosta was able to meet the requirement of fear of persecution, he was not able to meet the requirements for the category "member in a social group." The issue of "immutable characteristics" established by this case continues to be debated, and the decision also has consequences for people targeted by gang violence in Central America such as Minta del Carmen Rivera-Barrientos (Rivera-Barrientos v. Holder 2012). For the most part, their claims to be part of a social group have been denied on the same grounds as the Acosta case. In Chapter 8, we return to another dimension of applications based on fleeing gang violence in Mexico and Central America. Not only do these asylum seekers fail to meet the criterion of PSG, but in some cases, the officials also suspect them of being connected to the corruption and criminality of the drug trade.

Thus, people fleeing drug-related gang violence in Central America face the difficulty of proving that they are members of a social group; in addition, they are suspected of being drug traffickers.[4] With the increased reporting of drug-related gang violence in Central America, and increased asylum applications from people claiming to escape that violence, discourses about fraudulent claims have also increased. Reporting for the *Los Angeles Times*, Chang and Linthicum write:

> With the jump in asylum applications has come concerns about possible fraud and abuse. On Thursday, the House Judiciary Committee held a hearing to address reports that the asylum system is being exploited, including by Mexican drug traffickers. If indeed we allow that process to be abused … then those that we disserve the most are those who are genuinely persecuted, said Rep. Trent Franks (R-Ariz.). (2013. Np)

Sometimes evidence is available to identify an applicant within a narrower, more distinctive group, as in the Kassindja case discussed earlier. In one case, a Salvadoran woman was granted asylum on the basis of her membership in a PSG, which was defined as, "Salvadoran women who are viewed as gang 'property' by virtue of the fact that they were successfully victimized by gang members once before" (In the matter of *** 2011: 15). The woman witnessed members of the M-18 gang murder two young men. She spoke to the police about it, and later, four members of M-18 raped her. The next day, the rapists told her that she was "their woman" (ibid.: 6). She became pregnant; she and the four rapists believed that one of the rapists was the father and that "they had rights over her daughter" (ibid.: 7). Then, the rapists demanded "rent" of USD 200 per month, which was her monthly salary. At that point, she fled to the USA.

Scholars have offered a variety of reasons why refusing to join a gang fails to meet the criteria of membership in a PSG. Paul Kan documents the surge of Mexicans requesting political asylum, including not only poor villagers but also business owners, journalists, and other professionals fleeing drug-related violence. As Kan points out, what he calls "narco-refugees" are caught in the intersection of the war against drugs and efforts to curb Mexican migration. Writing during the Obama administration, he observed that in 2011, very few Mexicans had been successful in their asylum claims (Kan 2011: 10). More recently, discussing the same situation, retired immigration judge Bruce Einhorn says that such individuals might be able to credibly argue that they cannot "obtain protection from...the government of their country" (Becker and McDonnell 2017). Where corruption and forced migration visibly intersect, as in the case of the Mexicans, asylum seekers are often seen as a threat, a "surge" of people crossing the border (Kan 2011: 18). Mark Krikorian, executive director of the Center for Immigration Studies in Washington, says, "Clearly, if we start granting asylum to Mexicans, it could start a real flood of applications, even from people with no plausible cause" (Becker and McDonnell 2017).

Claims to gang membership are constituted differently and raise different questions than other PSG categories, especially the categories from past decades. For example, Grahl-Madsen, the first major treaty writer on refugee law, wrote in 1966, "[n]obility, capitalists, landowners, civil servants, businessmen, professional people, farmers, workers, members of a linguistic or other minority, even members of certain associations, clubs, or societies, all constitute social groups of various kinds" (Grahl-Madsen 1966: 219–220). Nowadays, the groups most frequently used as grounds for asylum are more likely to be connected to issues of sexual orientation, gender persecution (e.g. domestic violence, FGM, forced marriage, honor killings, forced abortion), clan membership, or gang membership.

According to the classic textbooks on refugee law, membership in a PSG is the ground with the least clarity, subject to the most rigorous examination by the courts (Hathaway and Foster 2014: 424). Even though Hathaway and Foster argue that the group should not be artificially limited, and its size is irrelevant, it is possible that part of the intense legal focus stems from a fear that it will be used to open the floodgates of asylum to vast numbers of claimants (the situation faced by people fleeing gang violence). Johnson claims, with regard to immigration generally, that at least in the USA, "the deep-seated fear persists that, absent strict migration controls, the United States risks being overwhelmed by hordes of immigrants of different races, cultures, and creeds who will 'take over' the country" (Johnson 2007: 27).

Some groups are indeed, potentially very large (e.g. women), though many courts have made efforts to limit the claims in other ways. Most descriptions of PSGs are narrower than merely "women." Rather, the group defines particular women from a particular country. Although the case of *Shah* represented the two Pakistani women as members of a general category of people who were denied protection because of their gender, more recent cases have narrowed the description to something more specific. For example, the US Board of Immigration Appeals recently decided that "married women in Guatemala who are unable to leave their relationship" constituted a PSG (Matter of A-R-C-G 2014). The Canadian Court considered a "Westernized Tajik woman in a society moving towards Islamic orthodoxy, with no male protection," to be a member of a PSG (Re J, C.R.D.D. 1993).

One of the difficulties in constructing a PSG is that it can't be defined solely by reference to a well-founded fear of persecution. Reasoning that a group is defined by the fact that everyone who belongs to it is persecuted is clearly tautological. But there is a Catch 22 problem here, as Baroness Hale points out in *Fornah*, "If not all the group is at risk, then the persecution cannot be caused by their membership of the group; if the group is reduced to those who are at risk, it is then defined by the persecution" (Fornah (FC) (Appellant) v. Secretary of State for the Home Department (2006): 466). This membership requirement means that many descriptions of groups are convoluted and not cohesive, for example, the description of the group ("women of the Tchamba-Kuntsuntu Tribe of Northern Togo who oppose the practice of FGM") at the beginning of this chapter.

Although different countries have similar laws because they are all based on the 1951 Convention, there is considerable variation in emphasis and treatment. In the UK, most of the attention is on LGBTI claims. In the USA, there is some attention given to these claims, but the current focus is directed more to the issues of persecution in Latin America by drug-related gangs, as the case of Minta del Carmen Rivera-Barrientos, discussed earlier, illustrates (Rivera-Barrientos v. Holder 2012).

In France, in contrast to the US ruling permitting Fauziya Kassindja to receive asylum according to a very narrowly defined social group, Didier Fassin reports that more recently, Malian women fleeing FGM became the largest group of successful asylum applicants in 2010 (2013). At a time when Chechens had a 14% rate of acceptance, and applicants from the Congo were accepted at a rate of 12%, Malians fleeing FGM had a 75% acceptance rate.

PROBLEMS OF EVIDENCE

As is always the case in asylum, proof is central to the claim. The difficulties faced by people who claim persecution on the basis of membership in a particular social group can be greater for a number of reasons. First, the very nature of the claim requires that an applicant prove the existence of the group in addition to the usual need to prove the other elements of the claim. Second, an applicant needs to prove their membership in that group, especially that they are not "faking" membership. Some of the claims are based on private activities and are by definition harder to prove. Third, as more asylum seekers make PSG claims, suspicion about its use has increased.

Proving the Existence of the Group

The case of Fauziya Kassindja is a good example of the struggle to formulate a group, which is not so big that it includes vast numbers of people, and clear enough that it includes those who fit the requirements of social group discussed earlier. If the court had made the group "those in fear of FGM," for example, they would have faced the claim that they had opened the floodgates to all of the millions of women in this category.

In the case of gang violence, as we saw earlier in the case of Minta del Carmen Rivera-Barrientos, the problem is proving that a social group exists. If the group the claimant claims to belong to is not considered a PSG under the law, then their membership in it is irrelevant. As we have discussed elsewhere, the category of "disability" is also problematic, though no one doubts that a claimant is disabled (Shuman and Bohmer 2012, 2016). Generally, the courts have not accepted it as a PSG, and usually the cases address persecution on other grounds.

Proving Membership in the PSG

The current typical case of membership of a PSG is that of a group based on sexual orientation. The existence of such a group as "gay men from Country X" is clear in current asylum law. Thus, courts recognize that being a sexual minority[5] in many countries risks criminal prosecution that may result in long prison sentences. As part of that focus, many sexual minorities in such countries suffer serious persecution in addition to being at risk of imprisonment. Not surprisingly, sexual minorities are very reluctant to express their sexuality openly in their countries of origin. For many, that reluctance doesn't change after they arrive in the host country. People who have been persecuted for being a member of a sexual minority may continue to be closeted even though they are no longer at risk. Therefore, finding evidence to support the claim of membership in PSG can be difficult.

Joshua was a Ugandan who was rejected by his family because he was gay (Robinson 2016). He arrived in the UK and was initially detained and treated under the fast track system, which assumes that someone is unlikely to have a valid asylum claim. His lawyers stopped representing him when he was in detention, so he represented himself on appeal and produced no evidence to support the claim that he was persecuted because he was gay. When he was finally represented by competent lawyers, they built a case by getting a number of the people who knew him to give evidence. Jill Parr, who ran the UKLGIG (UK Lesbian and Gay Immigration Group), agreed to give evidence, which she was able to do because she had extensive experience and she knew Joshua. Also, an administrator of Say It Loud, an organization of Ugandans in the UK committed to supporting Ugandan sexual minorities and to decriminalizing homosexuality in Uganda, gave evidence about Joshua's sexual orientation. This administrator said that he was aware that people sometimes used his organization (to fake a claim) and said that he had his own checks (which supported the veracity of Joshua's claim). One of Joshua's tutors from school testified, even though he had never given evidence before. Also, a woman from a youth group he attended called Project Indigo, which provides support to LBGTQ youth in Hackney, London, provided effective testimony. She said that he hadn't had any relationships, but, "We have seen him interact in this setting over 18 months, he has become more and more comfortable, able to share." Joshua's lawyers also acquired a report from the Beobab Centre, which provides support to young survivors of torture and political violence. In addition, a young woman flew in from Norway to testify on Joshua's behalf. She had known him when she was a student at SOAS studying for a Master's degree. She was able to say that she worked for IOM (International Organization of Migration, the leading intergovernmental migration organization). This gave her and Joshua's case credibility, because the Home Office characterized the others who gave evidence as, "all well-meaning NGO people, they are not lying but...." The Norwegian woman was treated differently because of her governmental connection. They also obtained a psychiatric report, and the psychiatrist who wrote it also testified. All these people talked about how long they had known him and the kind of situations they had seen him in. Joshua himself didn't give evidence; he was not well enough, but he provided a witness statement.

Despite not giving evidence himself, Joshua was granted asylum, perhaps because of the extensive collection of evidence produced by the various people who testified in support of his claim. All of the evidence proved his status as a sexual minority, even without providing any actual evidence of gay sexual practice. Joshua had an unusual amount of evidence in support of his claim. Often, applicants do not have much available evidence to prove that they are sexual minorities, especially if they have not come out in public in their host countries. One informant told us that of the 69 people she had seen at her organization, Reachout, in Leeds, an estimated 85% are not out except in the support situation (MacIntyre 2016a).

Immigration authorities face the difficulty of assessing the legitimacy of sexual minority persecution claims based primarily on claimants' accounts. The UK Home Office guidelines state that officers are not supposed to ask questions about behavior, nor intrude into someone's privacy to do so (Home Office Asylum Policy Instruction 2015). This instruction is in response to a leaked Home Office document about over-intrusive questions that were being asked by asylum officers. One example, quoted by *The Daily Telegraph,* asked, "When x was penetrating you, did you have an erection?" And, "What is it about men's backsides that attracts you?" (2014). One study of lesbian asylum seekers in the UK found that intrusive questions were asked including questions about sexual positions (Bennett and Thomas 2013). The report of that study in the *Independent* added to the negative publicity of the behavior of asylum officers (Taylor 2016). As a result of all this publicity, the Secretary of State ordered an independent review by the Independent Chief Inspector of Borders and Immigration (Home Office Asylum Policy Instructions 2015).

However, anecdotal evidence reveals that some officers still do not adhere to these guidelines and do in fact ask intrusive and inappropriate questions about private behavior. We were told by one person who runs an LGBTI NGO, "There is a serious lack of information about what the HO does or doesn't currently do in interviews, irrespective of best practice documents or advisory guidance notes state. The only thing we have to go on is anecdotal evidence. Whilst it is no longer allowed to ask sexually-focused questions or accept explicit videos or photographs in interviews or at court, I have been told by ReachOUT members that this is still happening" (McIntyre 2016a). A recent report also described problems with the conduct of asylum interviews (Right to Remain 2017).

Rachel Lewis reports that claimants in Canada are asked, "What day the gay Pride parade was on; where the gay bars in Toronto are located" (2013: 179). As she argues, these questions represent stereotypical assumptions about LGBTI practices. "The privileging of these skewed credibility assessments in women's and LGBTI asylum claims means that lesbian asylum cases are repeatedly evaluated on the basis of heteronormative assumptions about lesbian sexuality" (ibid.).

In the USA, the use of intrusive questions seems less frequent, though it is difficult to be sure. Several lawyers we spoke to had no experience of coming across such questions. One lawyer was confident of his ability to prevent such questioning: "I had a case where the AO tried to ask intrusive questions and I said, 'Enough. I want to speak to the supervisor'" (Kolken 2016). Presumably, if this applicant faced intrusive questions, they likely were asked when the lawyer was absent.

In Australia, the courts are apparently more willing to ask intrusive questions about sexual behavior, despite the views of other jurisdictions that this is a violation of privacy and human rights (Dawson 2016a, b). Dawson attributes the use of intrusive questions to the lack of training of hearing officers and insufficient guidance from the Australian Administrative Appeals Tribunal.

The Home Office sometimes considers an applicant's membership in gay groups to be required for proof of LGBT status. The case of Maiba, an asylum seeker from Zimbabwe, illustrates the contradiction here, "When I went to court the barrister said to me, 'You say you're a lesbian but you've never been involved in any groups or so on and so forth', I said 'Well, I am a lesbian I don't need to be involved in a group to show that I'm a lesbian. Since I've been in this country I don't feel the need for protection of a group'" (Bachmann 2016: 24). The fact that someone is not a member of a gay group can mean that they are still afraid to come out, that such groups do not exist in their home country, or that they no longer feel the need to be part of such a group, rather than that they are not gay, as the HO might assume. In any case, they may, nevertheless, have a legitimate fear of persecution in their home country on the basis of their LGBTI status.

Sometimes the questions asked by the officials are not useful to determine what they are intended to prove. For example, we have heard that hearing officers ask claimants whether they went to gay bars. Such a question is both irrelevant (going to gay bars is only one way gays perform their gay identity), and it also neglects the cultural chasm between the experience of the hearing officers and asylum seekers. Asylum seekers in the USA receive no benefits and are not allowed to work until six months after their application is received; in the UK, they receive a pittance to cover food, transport, clothing, and so forth. Neither the USA nor the UK asylum seekers have the financial resources to go to gay bars, even assuming they know about them and feel comfortable with this public display of their LGBTI status.

At other times, the questions are pointless. In one case, the "Home Office quizzed a bisexual asylum seeker from Pakistan about LGBT terminology. The Home Office interviewer went on to say 'Okay, so considering that you claim to have been at the London Pride event, and you are going to the Big Weekend event also for the LGBT community, how is it that you incorrectly refer to the T in LGBT as trans, when it in fact means transgender?'" (Right to Remain 2017: 4).

The problem such questioning raises is that it is based on stereotypical notions of what it means to be gay, something that has been prohibited by the Court of Justice of the EU (CJEU) in a recent case, though not specifically in the UK (Chelvan 2014). Basing decisions on how the applicant comes across is also prohibited by the CJEU decision, though doubtless still practiced in individual cases. A "butch" woman or an effeminate man will have less trouble convincing the authorities of their LGBT status than someone who does not "look gay." Similarly, one transgender applicant said, "The interviewing officer was surprised to see a person like me talking about these things. He doesn't believe I am transgender. 'You don't look transgender!'" (Bachmann 2016).

For many, identity as a sexual minority is a private matter. Vani, a lesbian asylum seeker from India, puts it bluntly: "Before I ended up in detention I didn't feel the need to go outside and shout yes I'm a lesbian. Now everything I do I have to prove something. If I don't put pictures of myself or my new haircut up on my Facebook, they will be saying I'm not open enough. That's how it is: 'how much of a lesbian are you? Do you go to gay clubs? Do you hang around with other lesbians? How many lesbians can write a letter for you to say yes I know her she's a lesbian? And of those lesbians how many of those lesbians have been accepted by the Home Office or are British?'" (Bachmann 2016: 24).

Extra Suspicion About LGBTI Claims

The perception, at least in the UK, that LGBTI cases are less credible than other bases for asylum claims is based in part on the high rates of denial. The NGO UKGLIG argued in a 2010 report that 98–99% of LGBT applicants brought to their attention were denied their claims, which is much higher than typical denial rate of 73% for asylum based on other grounds (Failing the Grade 2010). While this estimate includes those brought to the attention of the organization, which may be biased in favor of those applications that are denied, and only addresses refusal at the hearing stage, it is certain that a high percentage of LGBT claims are indeed refused. The Home Office has been under pressure about LGBT claims recently, but still does not provide statistics about the current rates of application and refusal in different types of claims (McVeigh 2011). It is hard to know how many people fake an LGBT status in order to obtain asylum fraudulently, but there is anecdotal evidence that this does happen, though it is unlikely to be as high as this denial rate would lead one to believe.

The fear that someone would fake an LGBT claim seems to be much less widespread in the USA. One lawyer we interviewed said, "Most men would not lie about being gay. Culturally speaking, it is very shameful. A man who is not homosexual would not 'humiliate' himself. There is still a sense that this taboo is so powerful, he would not lie, the repercussions would be so serious" (Feal 2016). Another lawyer admitted the possibility, but believed he had not had a client who faked the claim, "You can make up cases, I'm gay, I've converted. I've never knowingly had anyone who made it up" (Siman 2016).

The authorities' suspicion about the credibility of LGBT claimants has resulted in desperate measures on the part of those trying to prove they are gay. One expert on LGBT asylum seekers, S. Chelvan, said in 2013, "I know of at least two cases in the last six weeks where I have had asylum seekers filming themselves [having sex] to demonstrate that they are gay. … There's such a huge culture of disbelief that they feel forced to be in this position and submit such evidence. … They go to desperate measures. It shows the asylum system has broken down to push gay asylum seekers to have to go to such extremes" (BBC Today 2013).

The UK authorities are not supposed to accept such material, and we are told that requests for such material "seemed to have waned" since all this publicity (McIntyre 2016b). In their Asylum Policy Instructions (2016), the Home Office clearly states, "A claimant is never be (sic) asked to supply video or photographic evidence of sexually intimate acts, any such evidence of a person engaging in sexual activity is not in and of itself evidence of sexual orientation and has no evidential value" (at 31). This ban seems to be in response to the Home Office select committee report in 2013, which found that "Claimants have resorted to desperate measures to stay in the UK, including handing over photographic and video evidence of 'highly personal sexual activity' to caseworkers" (ITV News 2013). This kind of evidence has been prohibited by the Court of Justice in the EU in a decision in a case from the Netherlands (Chelvan 2014). The basis for the decision was both the practical understanding that such evidence could easily be fabricated, and the recognition that it was a violation of human rights.

The suspicion that LGBT claims are not credible, while strong in the UK, does not seem to be unique. As we mentioned in Chapter 3, in 2010, authorities in the Czech and Slovak Republic began using an "erotic lie detector" as a way of determining whether an applicant was "truly" gay. Such devices, called phallometers, measure responses to pornography and are used in research to assess arousal rates, and in some criminal cases involving pedophiles. Use of phallometers for asylum seekers caused international outrage and was stopped in 2011 (Chelvan 2014). In 2014, the CJEU in the decision mentioned earlier decided that such evidence was prohibited under the EU Charter of Fundamental Rights, because it was of little value and would infringe human dignity (ibid.).

Conclusion

Although membership in a particular social group was one of the original Convention grounds, it has been expanded significantly in recent years. The expansion has made possible many claims that would previously have been rejected. It has not come without difficulty, not only because very little is known of the intentions of the framers of the Convention, but also because, as we have seen, it is difficult to determine what a group is and who belongs to it. The expansion of this category is a response to the recognition that people are persecuted for a broader range of reasons than was anticipated in the original policy.

The category of membership in a particular social group raises special problems for claims based on gender and LGBTI persecution, which are vulnerable to even more suspicion than other bases for asylum on the part of the asylum authorities. These problems are exacerbated by the fact that many applicants whose claims are based on their LGBTI status kept their sexual orientation hidden in various ways before fleeing, out of fear of the consequences of publicity. Many gay men and women married and had children in their home countries, either because doing so was customary, or as a way of protecting themselves and their identity; others were celibate for the same reason. In addition, LGBTI status is about private behavior, which makes it much more difficult to prove than claims based on other grounds where public activity can provide supporting evidence. Those cases that do succeed are more likely to involve extensive evidence of various kinds, as was the case of Joshua, the Ugandan described earlier in the chapter. The US lawyers we interviewed also described a careful process of building a credible case through the use of testimony from family and friends.

Given these difficulties of proof, it is not surprising that the authorities are tempted to ask intrusive questions about the private behavior of applicants in the hope of satisfying themselves that the claimants are telling the truth. It is also not surprising that it is easier than in claims based on other grounds to say that a claimant is lying.

NOTES

1. The name of the tribe is spelled both Kuntsuntu and Koussountu.
2. We have attempted to use the most appropriate terms in our discussion of sexual minorities. Charlotte Walker-Said uses the term sexual minorities to refer to individuals "who face an exceptional level of violence as a result of their nonnormative sexual or conjugal status and also to those who, because of their sexual and conjugal roles, are vulnerable to cultural, social, and religious criticism" (in Berger et al. 2015: 203). When possible, we use the terms used by the people we interviewed. LGBT (lesbian, gay, bisexual, transsexual) is the most common term, but some people also refer to intersexed individuals (I).
3. *"Persecution on account of membership in a particular social group" mean[s] persecution that is directed toward an individual who is a member of a group of persons all of whom share a common, immutable characteristic. The shared characteristic might be an innate one such as sex, color, or kinship ties, or in some circumstances it might be a shared past experience such as former military leadership or land ownership. The particular kind of group characteristic that will qualify under this construction remains to be determined on a case-by-case basis. However, whatever the common characteristic that defines the group, it must be one that the members of the group either cannot change, or should not be required to change because it is fundamental to their individual identities or consciences.*

4. See also Cabot (2014)

5. The Western categories LGBTQI (lesbian, gay, bisexual, transgender, queer, intersex) do not map onto the categories used in all cultures, so we use the all-encompassing term sexual minorities unless a particular claimant uses a different term.

CHAPTER 6

Your Bribery Is My Networking: Understanding the Meaning of the Exchange of Favors

It's not what you know, it's who you know.

In the USA, we often consider favors exchanged for money to be a sign of corruption. We call that bribery.[1] We are not surprised or disdainful when we learn of favors exchanged for less tangible benefits. That is called networking. The former is not acceptable, while the latter is an important part of doing business, the "who you know" part of life. As Johns and Bagaric point out, bribery "is seen as a third world phenomenon" (2002: 159).[2] Other societies have a more nuanced view of the importance of the exchange of favors rather than our dichotomized view of bribery as possibly illegal and networking as possibly beneficial. They recognize the importance of contacts in all social relations, and they are less shocked to learn of corrupt officials. As business has become more global, there has been an increase of interest in the use of connections in business and a modest literature on the subject, resulting, for example, in the OECD *Convention on Combating Bribery of Foreign Officials in International Business Transactions.*[3] None of that interest or literature has extended, however, to the use of connections by those fleeing persecution. This chapter will fill that gap by examining the role of bribery/networking in the narratives of those fleeing persecution, its meaning, and the reaction of asylum authorities to asylum narratives that describe potentially illegal acts

© The Author(s) 2018
C. Bohmer, A. Shuman, *Political Asylum Deceptions,*
https://doi.org/10.1007/978-3-319-67404-9_6

used in the process of escape and in the journey to the host country. We are particularly interested in how reports of accepting or paying bribes lead to the determination of a fraudulent asylum case. We begin this examination with a case study that illustrates the significance of bribery/networking for those fleeing persecution.

The question of an applicant's affiliations has always been one of the primary considerations in determining whether someone receives asylum, and with current concerns about immigrant terrorists, these affiliations are receiving even more scrutiny. Engagements and arrangements that cross enemy lines, whether in the form of bribery or other forms of influence, raise suspicions in asylum cases. We argue that a more precise and careful understanding of how bribery, influence, and networking operate in the applicant's home country is called for, especially regarding what counts as governmental corruption and what counts as mere influence, or slippery categories that both change in time and are difficult to apply universally (Rothstein and Torsello 2013).

In their consideration of what might appear to be contradictory evidence, the asylum officials are interested not only in assessing applicants' credibility but also in determining whether or not applicants pose a threat, and associations across enemy lines can easily trigger suspicion. However, safe and dangerous affiliations are rarely simple. People fleeing persecution often are victims of corrupt governmental practices, and in many cases, they rely on their knowledge of insiders who might be willing to cross loyalty lines to help them. They often report that an enemy helped them cross a border or accepted a bribe that made escape possible. Thus, immigration officials are often faced with evidence of illegal, if not corrupt, affiliations, requiring a complex understanding of the relationships among various forms of corruption, strategic use of influence, and bribery, all of which can be reported by legitimate as well as fraudulent asylum seekers.

A Cameroonian woman, whom we will call Margaret, was arrested, tortured, and raped in response to demonstrating peacefully as part of a student protest. Her brother was killed because of his relationship with her. However, the asylum officials denied her application twice because of inconsistencies that raised suspicions about her claim to membership in a persecuted political group. Margaret did not initially choose to be part of a political resistance movement, but instead found herself forced into a situation of political conflict because of her experience of social injustice. She is from the southern part of Cameroon. When Cameroon received its independence, the southern, Anglophone, part was given the choice of joining English-speaking Nigeria, joining the northern, French-speaking part of Cameroon, or standing on its own. The British eliminated the third option, which would have required substantial British support, and in an election, southern Cameroonians decided to join northern Cameroon. There was to be a vote after a year to review the decision, but that never happened, and southern Cameroonians have continued to face discrimination, if not persecution, from the dominant francophone government.[4]

Margaret studied to be a nurse at the only English-speaking university in Cameroon, the University of Buea. In her narrative, she recounts many inequities in the system, including the requirement to do clinical practice in French-speaking hospitals—the closest English-speaking hospitals are outside of Cameroon. At a point, the Cameroonian government decided not to grant credentials to the students at the University of Buea. The students decided to go on strike. As Margaret reports in her affidavit for political asylum:

> In December 2001 the newly appointed Minister of Higher Education, in collaboration with the Minister of Public Health, decided to limit the Nursing and Medical Laboratory Science Bachelor's programs at the University of Buea to two-year Diploma programs. This decision was based on the fact that there were no French speaking equivalent programs. I believed that this decision was part of the plan by the government of Cameroon to further marginalise Anglophone Cameroonians and prevent them from having access to educational and professional opportunities.

In response to the Minister's decision, Margaret and other student leaders attempted to meet with the administration, and when they received no response, they decided to go on a strike. Some of the student leaders were killed; many were imprisoned and tortured. With the help of a police officer, whom she bribed, Margaret escaped from prison after having been arrested three times, and because she had already been awarded a Fulbright Fellowship, she was able to get entry into to the USA on a student visa; she then applied for political asylum.

Margaret's account offers a good example of the difficulties of translating a human rights story into a successful political asylum case. Our analysis of her narrative focuses on how she accounts for social networks including her family, her co-activists, the people who aided her escape, and the people, including Carol, who were involved in her asylum application process. It is these social networks (sometimes including bribery), or kinship affiliations, that are one of the central areas of dispute in asylum decisions. Both denials of Margaret's asylum application rested on the asylum officials' suspicions of her social networks. Asylum officials' suspicions often focus on the legitimacy of the applicant's claim to belong to a political group, and connections across lines of dispute, especially aid provided in an escape, appear (to the officials) to suggest contradictions. Complex, seemingly contradictory connections, especially the use of bribery, offend the officials' unarticulated belief in the idea that lines of conflict ought to be clear-cut and that government officials ought not be corrupt. Further, officials are especially suspicious when people are helped by people who should be their enemies.

Part of her narrative involves her escape from prison because of the contact she made with a prison guard, with whom she had several connections.

In her affidavit, Margaret describes how she escaped:

> I overheard the Commissioner telling a police officer to prepare for my departure to Kondengui prison.
>
> I recognized the police officer that was assigned to supervise me. We knew each other because he had brought his father to the National Center for Diabetes and Hypertension at the Yaounde Central Hospital, where I worked from July 2002 to May 2003. He was also from Babessi, my hometown.
>
> I struck a deal with the police officer—he would help me escape, and I would pay him 500,000 CFA francs. We arranged that I would bring the money to his wife's house after I escaped.

Margaret gave a similar version of the story a couple of years later when she was a guest speaker in Carol's class:

> I was taken to the French speaking prison, jailed there. The letter I had signed was distributed everywhere. I knew I would be locked up in the prison where I had been a nurse. I had to do something where I was or I would go to jail. They gave you assignments. They tortured you in the morning and you worked in the afternoon. Someone I knew happened to be one of the law enforcement officers. "What are you doing here?" "I got arrested. You need to help me." I struck a deal with him. I was assigned to clean floors…I just walked away. That's' how I left. I was in hiding. I went to a friend's house, a friend from the University of Buea.

In this version, Margaret includes the actual conversation with the police-man rather than the details of how she knew him. In a version she told to Amy, she explained that she was given a cleaning job at the prison and that she had to go outside to get water. She was returning with the water when she saw the policeman:

> So when he saw me he was shocked
> He said "what are you doing, what happened?"
> I explained to him
> I told him I said, "please you really need to help me
> If you don't help me, this is the end of it
> I really need you to help me"
> So, he wouldn't do it without a price
> So we had to strike a deal
> And that's how I walked away.

Margaret elaborated on her connection with the policeman; not only was he from her town, but she also lived in a building with his wife's relative:

> His wife was related to someone I knew in the university
> She lived in the same building
> We lived in university apartments for students
> I lived with her in the same building.

Country Reports describe Cameroon as a country with a rich history of bribery and corruption. This perception translated into a deep suspicion by the US State Department, which was very concerned about Cameroonians who were considered to have lied about the basis for their asylum claims. Meredith Terretta describes various cables and reports from the US Consulate in Yaounde, Cameroon, beginning in 2003, and for several years thereafter, that specifically point to corruption in Cameroon. The 2003 cable reads, "Post believes that most of these original asylum claims [from Cameroon] are frivolous or fraudulent. Post advises DHS to view such Cameroonian asylum requests with skepticism and use all tools available to adjudicate follow-to-join derivative applications" (2015: 61). The Consulate also argued that the political situation in Cameroon had not deteriorated over the last few years, contrary to the State Department's own reports. The Consulate used the fact that Cameroon had a high rate of corruption in support of the assessment that most asylum claims were fraudulent (See Transparency International Corruption Index 2012). In that index, Cameroon was the most corrupt country in 1999, and since then has been in the bottom quartile.[5] We believe that, ironically, it is in part because of the frequency of corruption that Margaret was able to make the arrangement she did to escape from prison. We also suggest, though we cannot be certain, that part of the problem for the asylum officers is the Cameroonians' complex social networks, especially their reports of being aided in their escape by people who look like their enemies.

Asylum applicants are rarely aware of the suspicion created by an account of a bribe during the hearing itself. Instead, the refusal letter describes bribery as a rationale for denying asylum. The following explanation was provided in a manual designed to help asylum seekers and their representatives to better understand conditions of refusal:

> The refusal letter will say that the Secretary of State considers that someone would have acted differently in the scenario your client describes and, solely on that basis, conclude that your client's account is a lie. The Secretary of State may consider that the local police would not have released your client if they were still suspicious of her; that officials would not have accepted bribes to release her or allow her through immigration control; that she would not have been arrested just because her family were active; that guerillas would not have anything against her just because she refused to help them; or that drug barons would not pursue her to a particular town. (Henderson and Pickup 2012: 1.34)

As the authors of the manual point out, the officials question the plausibility of an event that includes bribery. They ask why someone would act in the manner described by the applicant. Having determined that the events aren't plausible, the officials do not pursue further explanation, to consider, for example, an account of the complex relations and networks at work. Margaret was not questioned about using bribery to escape during her hearing. In a version of her story, told after she received asylum, she describes a more complex relationship with the policeman and her vulnerability in the prison.

The reciprocity of their relationship is too complex to chart completely, and in any case, for Margaret, as for many other victims who receive aid from enemies, it is possibly ongoing. Some asylum officials in the West are completely unfamiliar with this sort of relationship and obligation, especially when people maintain their enemy status but still step across it to aid each other. One could say that the policeman was interested only in the monetary reward, but this is probably an over-simplification. One could interpret his request for money as compensation for the great risk he was taking. In other cases we observed, the opposite is true; people aided "enemies," and it was not a particularly risky action, though it was interpreted as risky by the asylum officials. Interestingly, in all three versions of the story, Margaret describes her arrangement with the policeman as "striking a deal," as a mutually beneficial proposal rather than as an illegal act. The obligations of reciprocity go beyond the two individuals involved and usually implicate whole families. In Margaret's case, as she explains, it involves a relative who lives in her building as well as the father and wife of the policeman. This same larger kinship connection is at work when relatives of a targeted individual are killed.

Many survivors of genocide describe relying on these networks. For example, Tutsi survivors of the Rwandan genocide recount finding Hutu neighbors who were willing to shelter them. In addition to telling his own story of relying on Hutu friends, Tutsi Eduard Kayihura describes the greater complexity of these relations of reciprocity, trust, and betrayal in a detailed account of his experiences in the Hotel des Mille Collines, the same hotel in which the Hutu manager is depicted (incorrectly according to Kayihura) as a hero, a protector. Kayihura describes him as an opportunist and provides an excellent example of the complexity of influence and favors exchanged across enemy lines in a time of extreme violence (Kayihura and Zukus 2014).

Violations of human rights fundamentally alter connections, loyalties, and obligations humans have to one another. Margaret was able to prevail on the prison guard's loyalties to her and persuade him that she would keep her word in offering him a bribe. Her escape depended on bribery, which in itself is a kind of reconfiguration of loyalties.

Most of the literature about bribery focuses on the business context, and, not surprisingly, presents it in a negative light. The occasional article does highlight the role of the exchange of favors within the business context, as in Hutchings and Weirs' comparison of the Chinese and Arab versions of networking, guanxi and wasta. Their focus is on getting foreign entrepreneurs to understand these processes. They stress the religious origins of both these concepts and argue that social relationships are key to business connections (Hutchings and Weir 2006) . While this is clearly a very different situation than that which we address in this chapter, it does recognize the fact that bribery and networking are not completely different things.

Johns and Bagaric differentiate between bribery and networking as business practices to understand how they differ on moral and legal grounds. They understand bribery as a form of networking, differentiated by the exchange of money (2002: 160). They further differentiate between the more casual sort of networking to create associations for some future connection and what they call "expenditure networking" in which services or goods are provided to clients (2002: 162). As they point out, business requires social networks, and it is difficult to draw an absolute line between acceptable and corrupt forms of influence.

The everyday life of a community depends upon, and can even be defined as, social networking. Social networks include both the kinship relations that assign responsibilities of care and the institutional networks for allocating and distributing goods and services, from education to forms of transportation. Social networks are situational, and, at the same time, members of the community can count on some stability to know how their society works. Influence is a small part of those networks, but it can become hugely significant in times of crisis. In periods of upheaval, some social networks remain reliable, for example, kinship connections, and others are completely overturned, making neighbors into enemies and replacing trust with betrayal.

Social networks are, by definition, culturally specific, and what look like gestures of loyalty in one culture will look like corruption in another. "Corruption is a complex phenomenon which, in everyday practices, is inextricably tied with numerous other forms of social interaction, such as, for instance: gift, reciprocity, friendship, kin ties, patronage, identity, affection, and even love" (Rothstein and Torsello 2013: 9). In a cross-cultural comparison based on the Human Relations Area Files, Rothstein and Torsello) found a general agreement that corruption is wrong (2013: 4) but also that even though people might condemn it, if they believe everyone is accepting bribes and kick-backs, they would not refrain from using these means of influence (2013: 5). The greatest differences among cultural practices depend on (1) what is defined as a public resource, and (2) how gift-giving is categorized. "The gift is to be seen as a fee for a service, not a bribe. It would only be a bribe, and would also by the local people be seen as a bribe, if it was given in a way to influence adjudication by favoring one party over another. In this case, the public good is converted into a private one, and this is perceived as corruption" (2013: 8). In his classic study of the gift, Marcel Mauss (1954) distinguished between gift exchanges in archaic societies and modern states, but the countries the asylum seekers are fleeing from often belong to a third category, of failed states, which, Polese argues, can be considered similar to archaic states (2008: 53). He writes, "Once the state fails to respect its obligations, there is a spectrum of 'acceptable' reactions by the public worker" (2008: 51), thus shifting the legitimacy of public versus private "gift" exchanges. One of the Ukranian subjects of Polese's research said, "If I receive it, then it is a gift; if I demand it, then it is a bribe" (ibid.).

In times of war and genocide, social networks are often reconfigured. Defining a social network as "persons (network nodes) linked by different kinds of relationships (edges)" (2008: 540), Elizabeth Wood writes, "Wartime polarization may reshape friendship networks in a village, fracturing the network into two distinct networks with no edge between them" (2008: 540). Wood's work focuses on the networks used to mobilize combatants rather than the networks used by those who flee violence, but she does point out how, in some cases, new networks of victims replace former relationships (2008: 544). However, isolation, rather than new networks, is just as possible. She writes, "The pattern of dissolution may be one of increased social isolation rather than new network ties, particularly where armed groups coerce support" (2008: 544). Also, in times of conflict, "What appears at the national level to be the key issue—for example, class relations, constitutions, or ethnic secession—may not be salient at the local level, which may be dominated by conflicts between families or clans or other social groups concerning particular local grievances" (2008: 547–8), and newly configured gender roles can "break traditional social norms" (2008: 552).

Bribery and other strategies of influence exist at many levels in the narratives of flight told by asylum seekers. They range from a public official who takes money for providing a service, to a private person doing another a favor for no apparent gain. In fact, the latter activity is not considered bribery in the general meaning of the word. Many forms of exchange of gifts and reciprocity, although used to influence behavior, are not considered corrupt. Bribery in the context of war is not unconnected to the cultural practices conducted by politicians and businesses in times of peace, where bribery is a key element of corruption, thus inviting suspicion. Although asylum seekers often describe their use of influence, bribes, and other favors as corresponding to customary practices, they differentiate between the desperate efforts of a victim of violence and the corrupt practices of businesses and governments.

The kind of connection described by Margaret in her narrative is often the crucial element in someone's escape. We hear of it so often from asylum seekers that it seems to be a "normal" way in which people get themselves out of prison so they are able to flee. A chronicle of another Cameroonian asylum seeker also describes bribing a guard to escape.[6] However, bribery often requires something other than money, and several of the asylum seekers we have worked with have described a situation in which an "enemy" helped in an escape. As we report in *Rejecting Refugees* (Bohmer and Shuman, 2007: 166):

> Henri was questioned at his asylum hearing at great length about why someone would let him escape from the Central African Republic to Cameroon. He described how an "enemy" (someone from the current leader's party, Patasse) helped him cross the border. It was clear that the officer couldn't understand why an "enemy" would help someone. In fact, as Henri told him over and over, he was also a childhood friend. In that society, long-standing friendships trump party affiliation. Similarly, the AsylumAid report describes the case of: "J.L., for instance, was allowed to get away by Zairian soldiers who had captured him on orders, because he spoke in Tshiluba, their language. But shared loyalties are not a motive the Home Office recognises". (AsylumAid Report 1999: 41). (2007: 166)

One reason that the asylum officials, like the one in Henri's hearing, don't recognize shared loyalties across enemy lines is that doing so contradicts basic understandings of justice and injustice. Political asylum is designed to protect innocent people against unjust aggression, and if the aggressors are sometimes sympathetic, identifying legitimate asylum cases is more complicated, if not compromised. Of course, receiving preferential treatment from someone one knows is as common in modern democracies as it is in situations of persecution. In a sense, it's nothing more than being well-connected. In politically fraught situations, especially those involving violence, being well-connected is crucial, and those connections often, if not always, cross enemy boundaries. Avoiding or escaping persecution often relies on these connections.

It is ironic that decision makers may have trouble accepting the power of allegiances and the ways in which people help those whom they know even when they are on opposite sides of a political divide. Because our system has different ways of differentiating among legitimate and corrupt exchange of gifts and favors, asylum officials are perhaps less likely to see that networking and the help Margaret received to get out of prison are part of the same social system. In this case, ironically, we have an example of the importance of "contacts" in our society. After the second denial, Margaret's lawyer called someone he knew in the Department of Homeland Security to ask them to re-evaluate her case, and as a result, she was finally granted asylum. But we do not call this corruption or bribery or even favoritism, which is how we negatively label the actions of those who help asylum seekers.

Political asylum officials are particularly suspicious of what looks to them like contradictory affiliations. As we saw earlier, the person who helped Henri was an "enemy" in that he was a member of the party against whom Henri and his colleagues were fighting, but he was also a childhood friend. However, these contradictions are endemic to the political asylum process at all levels, from the irresolvable goals of human rights protection and border control to the local entanglements that make people rely on their enemies for assistance in escaping. The problem is not only finding sufficient documentation to overcome the officials' identifications of inconsistencies in the applicants' accounts. In many cases, no amount of documentation could overcome the larger contradictions in both the political asylum process and in the applicants' complex experiences of violence and loss. Political asylum cases are rarely simple, and hearings, understandably, expose this complexity. The question facing the asylum officials is whether the applicant's affiliations across enemy lines warrant suspicion that someone pretending to be a victim might actually be a perpetrator.

Asylum officials also may have more difficulty with those cases that are not clear cases of what we consider bribery, that is, in which money is exchanged in return for the favor, for example, looking the other way so the person can escape. The idea that a person will do another a favor without expecting some benefit, either symbolic or monetary, flies in the face of the Western transactional view of the way the world works.[7] Yet we have heard of many cases of such favors, like the one accorded to Henri described earlier. Eric, a Burundian fleeing during the Rwandan genocide, was captured by the rebels who accused him of being a Hutu sympathizer (largely because Eric's father was a known Hutu militant). Eric tried to persuade the rebels that he was a pacifist, a difficult position in a time of war. Eventually, he was freed by a rebel officer who recognized Eric as a former classmate. The officer let him go because he remembered Eric as a scholar who should not be forced to fight.

As we have already mentioned, narratives involving bribery are so common that they would be hardly worth mentioning except for the disbelief on the part of the authorities. There are few empirical studies that include analysis of the frequency of bribery, but those that do support our personal experiences with asylum seekers. For example, the following is a transcript of part of a case heard of an Iranian man in the Asylum and Immigration Tribunal in London:

J[8]: I'm not sure I understand. Was the confession on the 3rd or 4th day?
AP: In the 3rd day, it was a confession, and on the 4/5th I was still detained.
HO: After the confession you were still detained 2 days? The authorities didn't arrest your colleagues during these days?
AP: I was in a cell, no information was coming in or going out. I had no information what was happening.
HO: I'll move on. You were released on a bribe by your father. When were you notified of a date by the court?
AP: Before I was released or after?
HO: You tell me.
AP: Well, the date of the hearing was not clear yet when I was released. After my father paid the bribe, after 10 days we'll send you the hearing date, but I didn't receive anything, and I started my normal routine. It was several months after I received a letter that I had a hearing date and I should appear in court. (AIT, May 3, 2006).

Support for the frequency of the use of bribery to obtain release from prison can be found in an article about asylum seekers from what was then Zaire:

Of the 81 imprisoned, only two were recorded as having been charged and sentenced, and both escaped before the completion of their full term. Twenty three were released, two after appeals from Amnesty International, but 19 were subsequently rearrested. *The others all escaped, either through bribery by family or friends, or because a guard was from the same tribe or part of the country.* (italics ours) (Peel 1996)

In another study, in this case of Ethiopian asylum seekers in the UK, the authors report:

Most claimants in this study had been detained and over one third reported escaping from detention, most with the aid of bribery (table 1). However, despite a Home Office Country of Origin Information report of widespread corruption in Ethiopia, not one account of escape was accepted and the incredibility of escape procured by bribery was used to deny asylum in at least 42 cases. (Trueman 2008: 11)

They cite this example of asylum authorities' approach to such cases: Magarssa, 21, RFRL, May 2005.

> *You state that ... the police officers helped you to escape from prison because your brother paid them a bribe ... if you had been a person of any importance to the Ethiopian authorities, your brother would not have been able to do this as the police officers concerned would have feared possible serious punishment or dismissal by their superiors more than their wish to take a bribe. In light of the above your claim is therefore not accepted.* (Trueman 2008)

As in other cases, the officials in this case assume that police officers who take bribes fear punishment or dismissal. In some places, it is just as likely that the police officer would be required to hand over or share the bribe, but in any case, bribery in many places is tolerated.

In some of the asylum seekers' home countries, bribery is rampant in everyday life, so it is hardly surprising to find evidence of it in narratives of flight and forced return. In Cameroon, which we saw in Margaret's case, is a country with high rates of corruption, it is a criminal offence to leave the country without permission. When a failed asylum seeker is deported from the receiving country, she risks imprisonment for this offence. A report on the return of Cameroonian deportees describes how deportees avoid prison by paying "fees" that could be construed as a form of bribery:

> Although imprisonment is no longer systematic, deportees may nonetheless face detention, monetary extractions and threats of imprisonment. In principle, deporting states first contact the consulate of the country to which they want to deport a person. By issuing a laissez-passer, deportee-receiving states confirm the nationality of and guarantee safe passage for persons to be deported. As repressive practices by the Cameroonian state are still alive in public memory, many Cameroonian deportees prefer to call family members before being deported. These family members are then charged with locating contacts at the airport (preferably in the police) who, in return for some financial recompense, will guarantee safe passage and avoid preventive detention and the threat of imprisonment. Even if deportees have a laissez-passer, police officers may still ask them to "regularise their situation" by paying CFA Franc 150,000, plus a further 50,000 for the costs of detention (approximately EUR 300 in total). When faced with the threat of New Bell prison, many deportees understandably prefer to pay. (Alpes 2015: 750)

In addition to the common narrative of using bribery or networking to get out of prison, many asylum seekers use social networks and favors to obtain passports so they can leave without attracting the attention of their persecutors. As Dieudionne said in his application for asylum:

> Mr. Jacques [a person who was helping him to escape] explained that he had a friend named Gordon Baccard who is a Canadian citizen who might be willing to loan me his passport. Mr. Jacques put me in contact with Mr. Baccard and I agreed to pay him for the use of his passport and that I would mail him the passport upon coming to the United States. (Affidavit of Dieudionne 2004)

In another familiar form of payment for a less than legal exchange, asylum seekers buy documents from corrupt public officials. For Chan, getting someone else to buy her a Burmese passport was the only way she could leave:

> Because the Thai government monitored my activities and began to support the Burmese government, I believed I had to travel to the United States. I did not have a passport and I was convinced that the Burmese government would not issue me one. Therefore, I contacted my friends in Burma and they paid Burmese Immigration officials to issue me a Burmese passport. (Affidavit Chan Aye 2005)

CONCLUSION

The exchange of favors often implicates victims as affiliated in some way with their perpetrators, raising the suspicion of immigration hearing officials. We have suggested several explanations for these affiliations, including (1) how wars reconfigure social networks, but victims often attempt to rely on the former peacetime affiliations when they seek help, (2) how the exchange of favors is a culturally based system, and what counts as corruption in one society might be interpreted as acceptable in another, and (3) how relying on people affiliated with the enemy is not necessarily a discrediting practice.

Although we have evidence of the peacetime strategies of exchanging favors in different cultures, those practices do not necessarily apply to wartime. At the very least, as Wood (2008) observed, traditional class and gender roles are often reconfigured, affording new social networks and obliterating familiar ones.

The assessment of affiliations, evidenced through social networking, as well as the applicant's narratives, is likely to receive even more attention in the coming years, and these affiliations can be important in differentiating between victims and perpetrators, and legitimate asylum seekers and people affiliated with terrorist organizations. However, as these modes of scrutiny intensify, it will become even more important to attend to cultural practices of social networking to understand the differences between corrupt and accepted uses of the exchange of favors.

NOTES

1. See Walton Douglas' discussion of the difficulty of assessing the ethical implications and situational justifications of bribery. 2005: 167.
2. According to Transparency International, one in four people reported paying a bribe in the last year. They found a world average of 27% and listed the countries in which people reported most frequently paying bribes as follows:

   Top countries:

   1. Sierra Leone 84%
   2. Liberia 75%
   3. Yemen 74%
   4. Kenya 70%
   5. Cameroon 62%
   6. Libya 62%
   7. Mozambique 62%
   8. Zimbabwe 62%
   9. Uganda 61%

   http://www.bbc.com/news/business-23231318. Accessed 12-2-2015.

3. The convention states:

   Each Party shall take such measures as may be necessary to establish that it is a criminal offence under its law for any person intentionally to offer, promise or give any undue pecuniary or other advantage, whether directly or through intermediaries, to a foreign public official, for that official or for a third party, in order that the official act or refrain from acting in relation to the performance of official duties, in order to obtain or retain business or other improper advantage in the conduct of international business. (cited in Johns and Bagaric 2002: 159)

4. *Cameroon: Information on the Relationship between the Anglophone and Francophone Communities* (2002), available at: http://www.unhcr.org/refworld/publisher, USCIS,CMR,3f51eaad4,0.html.

5. Meredith Terretta reports that "Cameroon was ranked the most corrupt country in the world on Transparency International's Corruption Perceptions Index" (2015: 60).

6. See http://www.jonesday.com/experience/experience_detail.aspx?exID=S20985

7. However, scholars of corruption observe multiple ways of assessing legitimate and corrupt transactions (Pardo 2004; Taormina and Gao 2010; Steidlmeier 1999).

8. J is the judge, AP is the applicant, R is his representative, HO is the Home Office representative.

CHAPTER 7

False Pretenses

Introduction

As we discussed in the introduction to this book, the legitimacy of the asylum seeker has faced increasing scrutiny. Determining the legitimacy of an asylum seeker is no longer (if it ever was) simply a matter of identifying whether or not people who have fled adverse circumstances meet the criteria for eligibility. Today, the categories of the asylum seeker, the refugee, and the migrant can overlap, and migrants increasingly are suspected of being potential or actual terrorists. In addition, asylum policy is also changing and incorporating new categories, for example, to include persecution based on gender. As part of the evolving concept of refugee and asylum seeker, the category of what counts as fraud has also changed.

We have thus far looked at a number of different means for assessing credibility, which remains the central issue in the asylum process. In this chapter, we address the problem from a different angle. We examine cases that have been identified as fraudulent, either because a court has made such a decision or because of other reasons, such as a confession by the claimant that s/he lied. We discuss the specific pieces of information given by the applicant that were later shown to be lies in order to better understand the varieties of deception and fraud used in the asylum process.

© The Author(s) 2018
C. Bohmer, A. Shuman, *Political Asylum Deceptions*,
https://doi.org/10.1007/978-3-319-67404-9_7

113

CREDIBILITY AND DECEPTION

In the cases we describe in this chapter, the asylum applicants were deemed to be credible, and they received asylum status. Only later, in some cases as part of an application for citizen status, and in other cases as part of other inquiries, were they determined to have lied on their applications. In many cases, they were not asked to provide evidence for their claims, perhaps because they presented a credible narrative. If they used forged passports, the fraud was not identified. These cases raise larger questions about the evaluation of credibility.[1]

Many asylum policy scholars discuss credibility and how it is (mis)used in the asylum hearing process (Einhorn 2009; Tinti and Reitano 2016). Sweeney argues that the evaluation of credibility is a legitimate legal activity but claims that the term "'credibility' is employed with a range of descriptive intentions and legal consequences" and also argues that some of the directives on how to assess credibility confuse it with proof (Sweeney 2009). Some scholars, journalists, and policy makers point to an underlying assumption that the authorities are in the business of disbelieving truthful applicants (Ramji-Nogales et al. 2009). Rarely do policy scholars discuss how asylum seekers use deceptive practices or acknowledge that people may not be credible. Instead, many scholars, including our own earlier work, refer to the "culture of disbelief" as a pervasive attitude. One exception is Melanie Griffiths, a scholar, who describes individuals who admit that they have distorted the evidence for strategic reasons (to work in the UK or better their immigration chances) (2012).

For most part, the credibility scholarship has identified flaws in the asylum process, for example, the misused scrutiny of inconsistencies and failures of logic we discussed in Chapter 2. In our discussion of the role of narrative in the political asylum process, we observed that the immigration officials sometimes fail to look for explanations (or even argue that it is not their job to do so) that would account for the inconsistencies. We argued that this process is not an effective means for identifying fraudulent applicants. As we discuss in the examples later in the chapter, cases that have been proven fraudulent rest on a variety of credibility issues, especially the misleading use of information, the embellishment of information, and rehearsed performances of potentially credible accounts by individuals who did not experience the events they describe, often with the help of guides who create the stories and coach the applicants.

In this chapter, we examine several categories of deception. Some of these categories overlap; some cases are clearly lies; others may better be categorized as strategic deceptions. First, we consider cases in which an individual strategically embellishes a case because s/he thinks it is more likely to result in asylum. Exaggerations might contain lies about details, or they may alter something more fundamental to the claim. Second, we consider fabrications based on a borrowed script. Like the first category, the applicant may have a legitimate truthful claim to asylum, but in some of the cases we identified, the applicant was convinced by a third party to memorize and reproduce a fabricated, scripted case that seemed more likely to be successful. Third, we discuss cases in which individuals lied about the basic facts of who they are, where they come from, and what happened to them. Fourth, we consider cases of persecutors who claimed to be victims. Fifth, we review some of the ways that people "launder" or reframe their cases using what they consider will be a more successful framework. For example, they claim religious persecution, or they do something to gain media attention. Finally, we discuss some of the larger issues that arise in these cases of identified asylum deception. Deceptions are regarded differently in the courts, in the media, and in the personal narratives told by the applicants. In some cases of people found years later to have been deceptive on their asylum applications, applicants are able to explain their actions as necessary and strategic. In other cases, especially when a persecutor has masqueraded as a victim, the fraud is considered to be a misuse of the system. As we discussed in Chapter 2, applicants also use cultural conventions for relating events in their asylum narratives.

Embellishments

Some applicants have a genuine asylum case but nonetheless feel the need (accurately or not) to embellish it to make it "worse" to enhance their chances of receiving asylum. Some have suffered discrimination or bad treatment that in itself would not be enough for an asylum claim. The strategic use of deception to enhance a case represents the applicant's (often incorrect) assessment of the immigration official's expectations. Describing the situation, one lawyer said, "Sometimes they feel they need to exaggerate, they want to do everything they possibly can. You say you got arrested, severely hurt but you need to get hospital records. The guy may have been beaten, but not necessarily required treatment. I had a kid from Bangladesh, he was Hindu (99% of population is Muslim). He says

'I fell down, cut my hand, the doctor said I had to have bed rest for 30 days.' How come if they just slapped you, you needed 30 days bed rest? They are not inherently lying, they need to exaggerate" (Siman 2016). Several lawyers similarly reported that applicants stretched the truth to convey their sense of fear of returning to their homeland.

Sometimes people embellish their story even though it does not benefit them (Bianchini 2016). In fact, they may make their situation worse. We can't assume that asylum applicants know which lies will be beneficial. They can just as easily misjudge the situation. We have spoken to a number of lawyers who have had to pick up the pieces after an embellished story, when the real story would have sufficed (Bohmer and Shuman 2007: 39).

Lawyers argue that even clients who have a good asylum claim lie. They report that in some cases, clients have received legal advice to exaggerate or alter their accounts, and a subsequent lawyer is left to explain why applicants lied, even though they had a legitimate (and true) claim (Bohmer and Shuman 2007: 168). In an article in the *Daily Beast*, Emily Arnold-Fernandez of Asylum Access says,

> 'We have had clients whose real circumstances are more compelling than the stories they have been advised by others to use. But there's such a lack of adequate legal advice…. And in the absence of accurate information and legal assistance, refugee communities may end up filling in the gaps with inaccurate information.' The temptation is so great, she says, that some asylum seekers have been exploited by people charging $100 a pop for stories that 'work'. (Ellison 2011)

Some cases are a combination of lies and embellishments. Nafissatou Diallo's exaggerated claim was discovered when, as a housekeeper in a New York hotel, she accused Dominique Strauss-Kahn of sexual assault. In a letter from the District Attorney of New York to the defense lawyers in the Strauss-Kahn case, a number of the claims made by the housekeeper who accused Strauss-Kahn of rape were later admitted by her to be lies (McConnell 2011). Strauss-Kahn himself clearly did as much as he could to discredit her claims.

Diallo, a refugee from Guinea, had received political asylum, but as part of the Strauss-Kahn inquiry was discovered to have memorized a story of gang rape rather than to have told about her actual experience. Her true story was that she was forced to undergo female circumcision as a child and was raped by soldiers for violating curfew as a teenager. Her husband had died of AIDS, but in her application, she claimed that she and her husband were persecuted political dissidents. In the inquiry following her accusations of Strauss-Kahn, it was discovered that Diallo also lied about her income and taxes. The charges against Strauss-Kahn were dropped, though Diallo later received an undisclosed settlement in a lawsuit.

Celeste Montoya argues that the "DSK Affair…follows a 'rape script,' a gendered grammar of violence with rules and a structure that assign people to positions within the script" (2016: 147). Diallo's narrative became entwined with that of Strauss-Kahn, and others, including the media and lawyers. According to *The New York Times*, it was a "signature case" for her lawyer, Kenneth P. Thompson, who used the case to launch his political career. Thompson said, "Ms. Diallo was being vilified to the world, being called a liar…I was not going to stand on the sidelines while Ms. Diallo was being portrayed that way. But I was able to get her some justice" (Yee 2013). As we discuss in Chap. 2, the prosecutor in Beatrice Munyenyezi's case also invested his reputation on an asylum case. After it became clear that Nafissatou Diallo had embellished the narrative for her asylum claim, many articles in the press described cases of immigrants with no possible claim for asylum who were taught how to present suitable stories in order to convince the authorities that they had been persecuted in their country of origin.

In one of the most circulated articles in the *New Yorker*, Suketu Metha exposed corruption in asylum claims (2011). She recounted the story of a woman who came to the USA from Central Africa on a tourist visa for a wedding, who was using three different identities. In one of them, she was claiming asylum based on a (false) claim that she had been raped by soldiers. She apparently chose this lie because she believed, based on informal information networks, that it would be the most likely route. "A clerk in Caroline's lawyer's office had suggested, 'Why don't you say you were circumcised?' Caroline told her that female circumcision wasn't practiced in her country. So she learned how to play a rape victim" (ibid.). "Caroline" (one of her three identities) did have some basis for fear when she left her country. Her "parents are supporters of a controversial opposition leader. Government soldiers ransacked their house in the city twice. Caroline remembered the soldiers as being very stupid, and from the countryside. Although they didn't rape her or her sisters, once they broke a dish over one sister's head, and they beat her brother. They were looking for her father" (ibid.). Whether this would have been enough for a successful asylum claim or not, she was not taking the risk of denial. Instead, she devoted a great deal of time and attention to building a case, including attending group and individual therapy sessions for survivors of torture, gynecological exams, and the writing of an extended description of the (nonexistent) rape. "Caroline" seems to have been a gifted liar, who was developing her own case, though she did take advice from various sources about the best way to present her claim.

When an applicant lies, it is not always clear whether there is *any* truth to the claim, or to what extent the applicant is consciously lying. As we have seen earlier, sometimes the applicant has followed the advice (misplaced or not) of the "agent" or whoever has advised them and has presented a false story, even though the real story was strong enough for a successful asylum claim.

Borrowing a Script

Other cases are complete fabrications, rather than embellishment of a story of persecution. Asylum applicants who fabricate their claims sometimes memorize a script of lies and hope they won't be caught. Scripted narratives can correspond to the hearing officer's preconceptions, but as we discussed in Chapter 2, scripts can become overly familiar and can be a source of suspicion.

Fake applicants often learn stories that the authorities are expecting to hear, from other successful applicants, or from "agents" (smugglers), or lawyers. In 2012, as a result of an investigation in New York, 26 people, including 6 lawyers, were charged with helping Chinese immigrants submit false asylum claims (Goldstein and Semple 2012). Women were encouraged to watch soap operas so they could learn about forced abortions and then claim they had undergone such treatment resulting from the one-child policy (ibid.). Others were set up to claim religious persecution as members of Falun Gong. Some applicants were tutored in religion so they could claim they were persecuted as practicing Christians. The preparation included visiting a particular church and obtaining a certificate of participation. In the article reporting the arrests, Peter Kwong, an academic, was quoted as saying that in his opinion, most Chinese cases in New York City were fabricated, "This is an industry. Everybody knows about it, and these violations go on all the time" (ibid.).

In Canada, fake stories from Russians came to light when counsel gave a manual to the IRB "which went through a sample of five or six different scenarios, claims for gender persecution, claims for Jewish persecution, whatever the standard ones [were] that were likely to succeed. 'Here are the questions you will be asked and her is the answer you will give'" (Rousseau and Foxen 2005: 19).

Lying About the Basic Facts

The well-known public figure, previously a politician in the Netherlands, Ayaan Hirsi Ali, provides an example of lying about details as well as more central issues. Hirsi Ali made a name for herself both in Europe and the USA as an outspoken critic of Islam. She is a feminist who speaks out against FGM and also in favor of the rights of Muslim women. She received asylum in the Netherlands in 1992, and in 2003 she became a member of the Dutch parliament.

Hirsi Ali provides us with a very clear case in which a relatively straightforward piece of information central to her asylum claim turned out to be a lie. She claimed that she fled the prospect of an arranged marriage in her native Somalia. On a Dutch talk show, when asked if "she had lied—'as everybody else did'—when she sought asylum in 1992...[she said] she had because she feared for her life if her family found her" (Scroggins 2012: 200). A 2006 television program about her featured interviews with her relatives who denied that she fled from a forced marriage. Later, in her autobiography, she claimed that her father wanted her to have an arranged marriage, but there was no evidence she was being forced into one. From the point of view of an asylum claim, this difference is fundamental. Her actual marital status is murky; she may in fact have been married twice, though it remains unclear if either of these marriages was legal (Scroggins 2012: 52–3).

Ali also lied about several other important facts that could have led to a denial of asylum. She lied about her full name, her date of birth, and the circumstances that brought her to the Netherlands. She used her grandfather's name (though that seems to be legal under Dutch law). Later she said she used that name to escape retaliation by her clan. She also neglected to tell the authorities that, rather than fleeing from Somalia, she and her family had lived for many years outside Somalia in relative comfort. She had a UNHCR-issued refugee document from Kenya and was therefore eligible for asylum in the Netherlands. She admitted to lying on her asylum application, explaining that she thought it would enhance her chances of gaining asylum. We have seen this motivation in many of those who seek asylum. Scroggins claims, "Many Somalis who arrived (in Europe)...were in fact refugees...but their passage to the West was often greased with fraud" (2012: 51).

What is remarkable about this case is that, unlike other cases we have seen, Ali suffered few consequences as a result of the revelations of her lies. She has admitted to lying on many occasions, including when she was being considered as a candidate for the Liberal Party (Scroggins 2012: 214). In 2006, Rita Verdonk, the immigration minister at the time, ordered that Ali surrender her Dutch passport. Rita Verdonk was at this time involved in a Liberal Party leadership contest with Mark Rutte. She couldn't afford to look lenient toward a fellow party member and political friend because it would undermine the credibility of her leadership challenge. Also, in 2006, a TV documentary highlighted the asylum lies of Hirsi Ali, which were already known in Liberal Party circles. Later, however, in the face of public opposition, and the concern about where she could go, she got her citizenship back (Scroggins 2012: 351). This was despite the fact a new naturalization law, which the Liberal Party had helped draft, required that asylum seekers who were found to have lied on their applications were to be stripped of their citizenship (ibid.: 350).

Ali has been a polarizing figure who had, and continues to have, a large following, perhaps because of her willingness to speak out against Islam. She has since relocated to the USA and holds American citizenship. She is now a successful commentator, author, and a research fellow at the Hoover Institute at Stanford University.

Several cases in the UK have been found to have been fabricated. For example, the *Daily Mail* reported the criminal conviction of an asylum seeker who apparently engaged in a breathtaking number of deceptions in order to receive an array of benefits (Seamark and Cohen 2011). At her trial, it turned out that she had obtained asylum in Sweden as a Somali under the bogus name of Ayan Abdulle and received £50,000 in benefits from the Swedish government, which she is said to have spent on "luxury living" (ibid.). Then under the name of Amina Muse she claimed asylum in the UK, but it later turned out that she was living in Sweden at the time, having just given birth to a child. On the basis of a harrowing account of being brutally gang-raped by armed militiamen in Somalia, she obtained asylum in Britain, and became a British citizen in 2009. Investigators now believe that she is actually Kenyan.

Perpetrator as Victim

In some cases, perpetrators have claimed to be victims, as we discuss in detail in Chapter 8. Who knows better the details of the persecution than the person who perpetrated it? In Chapter 2, we described the case of Beatrice Munyenyezi, purported to be a perpetrator of the Rwandan genocide. She came to the USA in 1998 as a refugee from Rwanda after the 1994 genocide. As the Manchester Union Leader reported, she

> spoke often of the pain and suffering that genocide caused in her homeland. She even peddled a memoir, 'Life In The Middle of Nowhere,' based on her life and hard times. (Tuohy 2010)

Munyenyezi was an exemplary refugee, working as an advocate for other refugees and taking advantage of educational opportunities. She applied for citizenship in 2003. This application became the basis for her subsequent two federal trials (the first one ended in a mistrial). She was accused and convicted of lying on a question on her citizenship application that asked whether she was a member of a political organization. The decision described her as "entering the United States and securing citizenship by lying about her role as a commander of one of the notorious roadblocks where Tutsis were singled out for slaughter. She also denied affiliation with any political party, despite her husband's leadership role in the extremist Hutu militia party. 'She was not a mere spectator,' McAuliffe (the judge) said. 'I find this defendant was actively involved, actively participated, in the mass killing of men, women and children simply because they were Tutsis'"(Tuohy 2013).

As we discussed in Chapter 2, individuals who have lied on their applications are positioned very differently; in some cases, such as that of Munyenyezi, living an exemplary life in the USA does not resolve the accusations of deception. In others, such as that of Hirsi Ali, the deception is reframed within another narrative of suffering and necessary escape, and the good work done on behalf of others further removes the refugee from accusations of fraud. These and other cases are part of complex ideologies that weigh lies and deceptions differently and often reference ongoing assessments of blame, corruption, and persecution, among other political circumstances, in the individual's homeland.

Laundering the Case and Media Attention

In another category of deception, a person develops a claim for asylum after having arrived in the host country by deliberately undertaking activities that would make it dangerous for them to return to the home country. It is not necessarily a "lie" as it is commonly understood. It is called a *sur place* claim and can be legitimate, for example, when political conditions in the homeland change after an applicant arrives, or can be used when an applicant genuinely continues to be involved with the activism that forced them to flee in the first place. However, such cases are fraudulent when the basis for the claim is set up after the person has arrived, for example, when someone starts practicing a religion that would get them in trouble in the home country, for the purpose of making an asylum claim. In effect, they are laundering their case from that of economic migrant to asylum claimant. In the case of *Re HB*, a New Zealand court heard that the Iranian applicant, who had arrived on a false French passport, initially told authorities that he was not in fear of persecution in Iran (*Re HB* 1994). Later, he told them that he had bought a copy of *The Satanic Verses* in Japan (which he later confessed was untrue), and that he had told some friends that he was interested in finding out about Christianity. He also alerted the news media to his case, and an interview was aired on television. He claimed that an article in the Wellington newspaper, where the Iranian Embassy was located, would draw the attention of the authorities to his activity and provoke future persecution in Iran. All of this activity in New Zealand seems to have been consciously designed by the applicant to set up a claim for asylum. After very careful consideration of the case, the court decided that he was not in fact a refugee, because he did not have a well-founded fear of persecution. They devoted a lot of attention to the very real tension in the law between the need to provide safe haven for individuals whose activities in the host country might subject them to persecution and the possibility that applicants can manipulate the system to gain asylum status. Such situations are at the heart of the culture of suspicion in asylum hearings; on one hand, the court makes every effort to avoid being manipulated by applicants playing the system, and on the other, they are also aware that publicity surrounding the claim may itself actually generate the possibility of persecution on return. This is clearly what HB was hoping for when he took his claim to the media. Courts in various countries have come to different conclusions on the need for good faith in the claim, sometimes punishing applicants who engage in activities in the host country solely for the purpose of setting up a claim (see Driver 2011). Gaining media attention may be manipulative, but it isn't necessarily deceptive.

Adverse publicity post-flight (including lies) can, in fact, trigger the possibility of persecution on return. A professor of asylum law at the University of Denver and a former counsel to the UNHCR describes a 1997 case "in which a man calling himself Edwin Matara Bulus applied for political asylum based on the fact that his older brother was the leader of an attempted coup in his home country, Nigeria. His claim was denied, and Bulus made his case public, telling his story to newspapers across New York. When it turned out that he was not, in fact, a relative of the man behind the coup, representatives of the Nigerian government visited him in his detention center, and accused him of portraying Nigeria in a negative light. 'They threatened him, which actually gave him a legitimate claim'" (Ellison 2011).

Asylum seekers can falsify claims to religious conversion to improve their asylum chances, and genuine conversions can be difficult to prove. *The Guardian* describes the increasing number of Muslim asylum seekers in Europe who are converting to Christianity. "Complex factors behind the trend include heartfelt faith in a new religion, gratitude to Christian groups offering support during perilous and frightening journeys, and an expectation that conversion may aid asylum applications" (Sherwood and Oltermann 2016). Differentiating between the fraudulent and genuine is a difficult exercise both for the asylum authorities and the churches themselves, who are concerned that they only accept genuine converts into their ranks.

All these cases can be distinguished from legitimate post-flight activity by asylum seekers. Phyu Phyu, a client from Burma, worked in Washington, DC, for an NGO developing a case against the then-Burmese government in the International Criminal Court. Such activity was for her a genuine extension of her pre-flight activism, rather than a strategic effort to set up (false) grounds for asylum. It added to the evidence of her risk on return, which, in turn, resulted in a grant of asylum.

THE MORAL ECONOMY OF LYING

Roberto Beneduce describes the arrangement of biographical facts in a political asylum narrative as "the moral economy of lying." Beneduce is particularly interested in threats attributed to what he calls "specific imaginaries (threats of witchcraft, occult forces) or to ritual violence"

(2015: 552). He recounts the story told by a Nigerian asylum applicant in Italy who initially described herself as a victim of violent conflict between the Muslim Hausa and the Christian minority. The woman showed Beneduce and others at the Frantz Fanon Centre a scar on her abdomen as proof of the violence she had suffered, but it was obviously the scar from a Cesarean section. She was caught in her lie but then told a different story, also about suffering and violence. Beneduce writes,

> Her story was full of every kind of lie, but it also contained important truths: that there was another, equally violent, tale (the social and family violence in her country) and a need to cope with the authorities' changing attitudes, now less inclined to grant benefits to the victims of the international sex trade. (2015: 555)

Beneduce also tells the story of a man from Congo who said that he was a member of the BDK movement; he had been arrested but had bribed a guard and escaped. He had received asylum and a year later told Beneduce that the whole story was false and that he had left the Congo because he had a lymphoma and had been abandoned by his Catholic religious society. The passport, name, and age he gave to the officials in Italy were all false. Beneduce writes:

> The use of violence, and the arbitrariness and illegality of the systems of government in certain areas of the world, are sometimes taken as given, and thereby the commission participates in the expansion of a gray area where the credible and the incredible, truth and untruth, escape any possibility of being distinguished without ambiguity. (2015: 556)

Not only individuals but also groups have been identified as fraudulent. Didier Fassin describes the case of 900 men, women, and children who claimed to be Kurds fleeing Iraq and seeking asylum in Germany when they were shipwrecked in France. It turned out they were actually Yazidis from Syria. Fassin describes this as "the moral geography of tyranny, as it is constructed in the contemporary world and translated into local imaginaries" (2013: 12).

THE DISCOVERY OF DECEPTION

Deception can be discovered in several ways. First, the applicants themselves may later reveal that they were lying. Several lawyers report cases in which the client later admits that, for example, he was from Rwanda, and not Burundi, as he initially claimed.

The Hirsi Ali case provides an interesting example of the complexity of determining what exactly is a lie. On the one hand, she sometimes admitted her lies: "(s)he wrote in *Infidel* that she had concocted a tale based on the experiences of the real Somali refugees she had met in Kenya, plus her own experience leaving Mogadishu in 1991 (Scroggins 2012: 63)." And in an interview she said, "I was lucky and felt guilty for getting refugee status so quickly, on false pretenses, when so many people were being turned down" (ibid.: 80). Hirsi Ali's stories varied significantly both in accounts told to various people in the media and in her autobiographical writing.

In other cases, the person may not admit to lying, but the story may be so inconsistent that not all of it could be true. In the case of HB, the Iranian in New Zealand described earlier, the applicant kept changing his story in the hope of making it more suitable for a valid claim (RE HB 1994), and the court that heard his case realized that his story was a fabrication.

In a second possible way of identifying fraud, those who know the facts come forward to reveal that the story was a lie. Such cases depend on being able to verify the facts. For example, witnesses came forward to dispute the case of Adelaide Abankwah, a woman from Ghana who claimed asylum on the basis that she was fleeing FGM. She alleged that she was the eldest daughter of the Queen of the Nkumssa people and that her mother had just died. She claimed that because she was next in line to assume the throne, and because she was not a virgin, she had to be circumcised to avoid detection of her lack of purity. She attracted considerable public support from people including Hillary Clinton, Julia Roberts, and Vanessa Redgrave. Her path to asylum was a rocky one, including time spent in detention and several appeals before she was ultimately granted asylum.

When Abankwah/Danson's application was originally denied in 1998, the BIA denial stated, "We find that the applicant has failed to meet her burden of proof" (Martin 2005). In the appeal, the lawyers argued that the request for proof of FGM practices among the Nkumssa was unreasonable. They said that such proof "may not – and probably does not – exist.... Ms. Abankwah is from a small tribe in a rural area of Ghana. Furthermore, the practice of FGM in Ghana is particularly secretive" (Martin 2005). The court agreed with the lawyers and wrote:

[h]aving established that Abankwah is credible, we accept as fact her assertion that Nkumssa custom includes FGM as a punishment for premarital sex. Abankwah's position is particularly compelling in light of the general conditions present in Ghana.

The court noted that 15–30% of the women had been subjected to FGM. The Ghanaian government's efforts to criminalize the practice were labeled "insignificant." Abankwah/Danson received asylum. Seventeen months later, *The Washington Post* reported that her case was fraudulent. According to David Martin, the initial review considered Abankwah to have a "weak case." The support of celebrities and politicians seems to have made a difference for her subsequent approval (Martin 2005).

An in-depth INS investigation confirmed that she had fabricated details of her background (Murray 2000). Her real name was in fact Regina Norman Danson, and she was not a member of the royal family: she was a former hotel worker, and she had stolen the identity of Adelaide Abankwah. Moreover, her mother was still alive, and it was unclear whether she and her mother were members of the Nkumssa tribe. Leaders from the community she claimed to belong to in Ghana reported that they did not have a practice circumcising adult women about to become queen, nor did they circumcise women as a form of punishment. At her subsequent trial for lying, the tribal chief, Nan Kwa Bonko, testified that Danson was not part of the tribe's royal family and that female genital mutilation was not practiced in his region of Ghana (Ossa 2003). She was convicted on nine counts in the Federal District Court in 2003 and sentenced to time served and a fine. It is not clear whether she was subsequently deported (Martin 2005).

Many of the well-known cases of fraud were identified retrospectively, after the individual received asylum. In these cases, such as Danson's, the applicant is later discovered to have lied. In the process of investigating the case, or in Beatrice Munzenyezi's citizenship application, immigration officials, reporters, and representatives of human rights organizations unravel the lies. In Munzenyezi's case, the political situation remains so muddy that it is difficult to finally prove whether or not she was a perpetrator. It can be argued that in the legal system a lie is something declared as such by a court, although as we discuss in Chapter 2, the witnesses in a court hearing can have their own agendas. Munzenyezi continues to claim that she is innocent, as do others involved in her case, including her lawyer (Ruoff 2014).

Perhaps the most notorious of such claims is that of John Demjanjuk, also known as "Ivan the Terrible." Demjanjuk, a Ukrainian, came to the USA in 1952 as a refugee, from a Displaced Person's Camp in Europe. He lived for many years in Ohio, where he worked for Ford as a diesel mechanic. He became a naturalized American in 1958. His problems with the US government started in 1975, when his name was on a list provided by an editor of "Ukrainian News" to INS of Ukrainians accused of collaborating with the Germans in World War II. Efforts then began to strip Demjanjuk of his US citizenship on the ground that he allegedly concealed his involvement with Nazi death camps on his immigration application in 1951. The problems continued throughout his life, involving "a tortuous odyssey of denunciations by Nazi hunters and Holocaust survivors, of questions over his identity, citizenship revocations, deportation orders and eventually trials in Israel and Germany for war crimes" (McFadden 2012). He lost his citizenship, then had it restored in 1998 when a federal appeals court ruled that prosecutors had suppressed exculpatory evidence concerning his identity. Then later, with new evidence, he was charged again and once again lost his US citizenship, which rendered him stateless in 2002. He remained stateless for the rest of his life, and died in a nursing home in Germany where he had been tried for war crimes. The case against him in Germany was under appeal at the time of his death.

The USA is currently involved in an ongoing effort to deport a number of Bosnians who were granted asylum, but have now been found to be perpetrators of war crimes (Lichtblau 2015). The war crimes section of the Immigration and Enforcement, set up in 2008, has been investigating up to 300 Bosnians in the USA, many of them alleged to have been involved in the Srebrenica massacre in 1995. The identification of Bosnian war crimes suspects arose almost by happenstance. It began with an arrest in Boston more than a decade ago. A series of tips, along with a book by a Boston Globe reporter, led federal agents in Massachusetts in 2004 to a construction worker named Marko Boskic, a Bosnian Serb accused of carrying out executions in the Srebrenica region. He was convicted of concealing his army service, then sent back to Bosnia, and was sentenced to 10 years in prison for crimes against humanity.

As is typical in the aftermath of refugee-generating conflicts, the authorities rely on the honesty of the evidence supplied by the refugees themselves, with little effort to investigate their stories. Such was also the case in the aftermath of the Rwandan genocide (O'Neill et al. 2000). The issue of proof is also a difficult one here, with the war crimes unit hampered by lack of funding and delays caused by backlogs in immigration courts, not to mention the problems of building cases based on the chaos of a civil war (Lichtblau 2015). As in the Munzenyezi case and Boskic who was convicted of concealing his army service, the authorities often use the fact that some lies are easier to prove than others. Despite these difficulties, however, a total of 64 people have already left the USA, after having been expelled or fleeing during the legal proceedings (ibid.).

Not surprisingly, the same issue came up in the UK where a number of applicants were originally given leave as Kosovan refugees and then Indefinite Leave to Remain (ILR). Later, the Home Office learned, sometimes in the course of a citizenship application, sometimes after they had been recognized as British, that they were Albanian, rather than Kosovan as they had claimed (Seamark and Cohen 2011). The UK authorities then cancelled their grant of leave or citizenship. There were so many of these cases that the Home Office instigated a five-year review, the result of which was to say that these citizenship applications were a nullity. They were returned to a status of ILR, leading to a re-examination of their status and a decision about whether or not they could stay. For a while, if they were in the UK long enough, they were allowed to stay, though it is unlikely that they would ever satisfy the good character requirement for citizenship (Naik 2016). In some of these Albanian cases, the matter came up when they applied to bring women to the UK from Albania to marry, and it became clear that since the women were Albanian, it was likely that the men were as well (Free Movement 2009).

One of the lawyers we interviewed said, "Some of my clients in their witness statements say the situation in Albania was so terrible at the time, so lawless, that they said they were Kosovan, but now we are here, all hard working. Lots of them don't think they did anything wrong. Or it was so long ago it shouldn't matter" (Naik 2016). This is another illustration of the complexity of such deceptions, and also their long reaching effect. Often a lie can build and become impossible to undo.

In one case, the applicant decided he had to disclose the deception himself, even though it was years later. The lawyer said, "A young Kosovan guy, had been refused, came when he was very young, spoke amazing English, well integrated, lots of friends. The HO sent him a letter, at time of legacy, wanted to confirm all his details. So I was checking with him, and he said, 'I've got something to tell you, I'm Albanian, not Kosovan.' He took the view, he'd done security guard training, he said 'I've got to disclose this now rather than later.' He got lucky because the Home Office gave him ILR anyway, though it may have been because no one realized what had happened" (Robinson 2016).

Sometimes lies come out because subsequent legal procedures bring out the inherent inconsistencies, as was the case when the "Kosovans" applied to bring over Albanian wives. Or the lies make future legal benefits impossible to obtain. For example, "Somalis send a woman first from the refugee camp on the theory that they are more likely to get asylum. One woman said she was a widow, with the idea that this would get her asylum more readily. Later, after she thought her second husband was dead, she remarried for a third time in the UK, and had another kid. The problem is that she wants to bring her children from the second husband, who are in a refugee camp, to the UK but she can't because she said she was a widow and has remarried" (Naik 2016).

Another way for lies to be revealed is as a result of a criminal investigation of one of a number of possibly fraudulent cases. In the Chinese case in New York described earlier, the authorities found a system in which asylum seekers were being coached in lying. For example, in a wiretap in New York, a man was heard urging his client to "fabricate a tragic past if he wanted asylum in the United States. To say that he was a victim of political repression in Albania. Or police brutality. Or even a blood feud. 'Maybe you had to leave because someone threatened to kill you,' the man suggested. 'Because of something that your father did to somebody else or something to do with the land. You understand? That can be a way to get asylum'" (Dolnick 2011).

Fraud in immigration applications is not limited to asylum claims; the authorities work constantly to expose the fraud that extends from sham marriages for immigration purposes to business visas. The EB5 program, which offers foreign investors a fast track to a green card, was recently the subject of an investigation by federal agents, the DHS, as well as the Securities and Exchange Commission. They uncovered a 50 million dollar visa fraud operation that enabled Chinese citizens, including fugitives from the law, to obtain these visas illegitimately (Jordan 2017). In some cases, the fraud is actually undertaken by a government itself. The British authorities have recently accused three members of Ghana's Parliament and a former lawmaker of visa fraud, saying the men abused their diplomatic privileges to help people travel to Britain (Boakaye-Yiadom and Searcey 2017). They were accused of falsifying visa documents and helping secure travel documents for family members who overstayed their visas, a practice that mirrors the widespread visa fraud in some parts of Africa (ibid.).

People who work with asylum applicants, whether lawyers or refugee services providers, hear similar stories about the reasons applicants give for fabricating their stories (Bohmer and Shuman 2007: 166–9). The rationales change over time, paralleling the current need for asylum. The difficulty is in distinguishing the stories that are similar, because similar things happen to people in times of war or upheaval, from those that are invented for the purpose of getting asylum and parroted by applicants.

One lawyer makes the distinction between stories that are identical and those that are similar. He says, "In certain countries—China—it's basically family planning, sexual orientation, Falun Gong-the cases are identical. For other countries, the stories are similar. From Afghanistan, the stories are similar but not identical to what you've heard before, like the Chinese ones. The story gets around, everyone copies…In the case of Afghanistan there are problems with the Taliban, in Yemen, problems with the rebels, in Sudan problems with the government. In the Chinese cases, it seems they use the same exact thing. 'I was arrested three times in March,' exactly the same categories, same over and over again. I've had 2 or 3 cases of Chinese (applicants). Two people file the same application, they are not even related, the hospital is the same, the events the same" (Siman 2016).

Another lawyer also makes the distinction between real and fabricated stories. He reports, "There are lots of blood feuds, Albanians…If you're going to pick a claim, don't pick blood feuds—they are more problematic because there is a really small number of people in Albania affected. The Afghan one is fear of the Taliban, which is a bit less obvious. My sympathies are with the young Afghans not the Albanians" (Robinson 2016).

SLIPPERY TRUTH

The cases we have discussed show that sometimes it is possible to lie and get away with it, and sometimes old fabrications catch up with the liars. In some of those cases, serendipity caused the matter to come to light. The implication is that there must be many other cases in which the authorities do not find out that the asylum claim is based on lies. It is hardly surprising that this possibility contributes to the culture of suspicion among asylum hearing officers and judges, even though, as we discussed in our introduction, identified deceptions are rare. However, suspicion of fraud is at the root of the wide-ranging efforts by the courts to prevent such claims from getting through.

The question of how central the lie must be before someone is denied asylum or granted citizenship is an important one, particularly give the propensity of the authorities to latch onto small inconsistencies to deny the claim. The US Supreme Court recently decided to hear a case to determine whether naturalized US citizens may be stripped of their citizenship in criminal proceedings even though the false statements were immaterial to their claim (Maslenjak v. U.S. 2017). In the case before the court, Divna Maslenjak, a Bosnian refugee, told a US immigration official that she feared persecution because her husband had not served in the Bosnian Serb army during the civil war, but in fact he had served, according to government evidence. She also claimed she and her husband had lived apart from 1992 to 1997 so he could avoid military service, though in fact they had lived together. Citizenship applications require that the applicant swear that they did not lie to obtain asylum (which was the basis for the case against Beatrice Munyenyezi discussed earlier and in Chapter 2). Identified lies resulted in Maslenjak being convicted of the criminal charge against her, even though she argues in her appeal that they are immaterial to her asylum claim (the question considered in the Supreme Court case).

Many of the aforementioned cases describe lying that is recognizably different from telling the truth. In such cases, a person makes claims that are verifiably false, as in the Danson case of the Ghanaian Queen, or a person's country of origin. The case of the NBC news anchor, Brian Williams, who lied about his presence in a helicopter that came under fire in Iraq shows that this kind of lying happens elsewhere; checking the veracity of statements made by public figures like Williams is relatively easy (Mahler et al. 2015).

Embellishment, however, is not always recognizably different from telling the truth.[2] Someone who is raped once may say they were gang-raped; someone who was assaulted makes it sound worse, and calls it "torture." Such diversions from the "truth," whether they be embellishments of omissions, may be the result of cultural conventions of truth-telling. "Rather than conceived as lying by the claimant, these might follow culturally-ascribed dictums of honor, shame, politeness, respect, etc, regarding what is appropriate to express in a public domain (Rousseau and Foxen 2005: 59)."

The case of Somaly Mam, although not about asylum, is helpful for understanding the kinds of lies some applicants construct. Mam, a prominent social activist, whose charitable organization is named after her, claimed that she was an orphan who had been trafficked as a sex worker. She and her organization received acclaim from celebrities and politicians until she was exposed by a *Newsweek* reporter who discovered that she had embellished her tale (Marks 2014).

The cover article of *Newsweek* featured a photo of Mam with the title, "Sex, Slavery, & Slippery Truth." Disputing her claim to be either an orphan or the victim of sex trafficking, the article also identified possible corruption in Mam's organization, which offered sanctuary to sex traffickers. Mam stepped down from her position, but the story continued, with some of her defenders mounting a defense. A sympathetic journalist, Abigail Pesta, asked Mam, "Why her personal history seems jumbled and contradictory—there have been discrepancies in her own telling of the details," and reported, "Mam acknowledges scrambling the facts. Her explanation: 'I was enslaved since I was a child' When a person is raped and abused for years, Mam says, dates and memories blur" (Pesta 2014).

This explanation, the blurring of memories due to trauma, is not uncommon and not far from other justifications by people who embellish or alter the facts. A great controversy followed Nobel Prize winner, Rigoberta Menchú's declaration that she had altered some of the facts in her memoir (1984). Menchú's memoir included two falsehoods: that she had attended her brother's funeral and that she had worked in the field as a laborer. She explained the latter by noting that, in fact, she had been sheltered in a convent at that time, and had she told the truth about it, she would have exposed the nuns who gave her refuge, to violence and possibly death.

Trauma does create extraordinary circumstances that are sometimes untellable, whether because to do so would put someone else in danger or because the memories are jumbled. In the case of Somali Mam, some human rights workers have argued that embellishment additionally causes harm. In a *Salon* article reviewing the Mam case, Anne Elizabeth Moore writes that the fact that the facts don't add up "doesn't account for the damage Mam's Enterprise of Cards has wrought. Her downtrodden-girl-overcomes-it-all-to jail-abusers narrative is extremely compelling, both to Cambodians, who need more women heroes, and to young women in the U.S. On top of the credibility problem she has created for real victims of rape and abuse. Mam has made freeing women from oppression look easy, in her boldest and most damaging lie. It's not" (Moore 2014).

Moore describes the embellishment of Mam's personal story in order to attract the attention of celebrities and politicians as part of what she calls the "expression of colonialism" in celebrity visits to sites of rescued women who have been trafficked. She writes,

In the world of NGOs, visits by a raft of different characters are viewed as an unfortunate but necessary part of survival. Whole days are dedicated to showing outsiders tidbits of projects in the hope that flattering reports will reach donors' eyes. Those receiving visits carefully orchestrate them to be entertaining and rewarding for visitors, including by arranging photo opportunities. It is totally conventional for the same objects of pity to be wheeled out every time; they have learned their lines and how to behave appropriately, they know how to hug visitors and smile for the camera. It would be too time-consuming to set up a new scenario for every visit. (Moore 2014)

Moore continues, "The repetition of stories by the same inmates is well known, as is the phenomenon by which victims learn to embellish their stories to provoke more sympathy in listeners (including researchers and program evaluators). That these narrations are often exaggerated in performance or fabricated out of whole cloth is so well known in NGO circles as to be banal. *Everyone does it*, one old hand wrote me" (Moore 2014).

The problem may be also the difference between big lies and small lies and what is in between. The big lie is the person masquerading as an asylum seeker who is in fact not a victim of persecution or worse, a persecutor. A small lie can be seen as a strategic use of the system. A big lie is an abuse of the system. Too many small lies, as in the case of the frequent claim of Chinese persecution based on the one-child policy, can add up to a big lie. Small lies can be attributed to inadvertent contradictions. Big lies are viewed as intention to defraud. Deception falls somewhere in between, and the difference is often the measure of moral outrage. Public rhetorics generally support the idea that a child soldier can be redeemed but not Demjanjuk.

CONCLUSION

The research on how to tell if someone is lying shows we aren't very good at it, despite a fundamental belief to the contrary. Much of the legal belief in the ability of judges and juries to determine if someone is lying depends on demeanor evidence—that one can tell by the way a person presents herself and her facial expressions whether she is telling the truth (Ekman and Friesen 2003). However, the research shows that accuracy is often no better than chance (Minzer 2007–2008, at 2561; Gray 2011). The psychological literature shows that there are better ways of determining that someone is lying, but that they generally require the kind of training and practice that the asylum authorities do not have (Gray 2011). Much of the research on lying is directed at the criminal justice system rather than at the asylum system. It thus neglects to take into account potential complicating factors of cultural differences, discussed extensively in the asylum literature (Daniel and Knudsen 1995; Neumayer 2005; Fassin and d'Halluin 2005; Coutin 2001).[3] In addition, it seems to be based on a related assumption that the person in question believes their statements to be lies. In some of the situations discussed earlier, the applicant may not have believed that their statements are "lies" in the legal sense.

Didier Fassin proposes a distinction between "'truth' as substance and 'true' as evidence in political asylum cases" (2013: 40). With the changing policies and sentiments toward asylum, refugees can, in substance, be afraid to return to their countries of origin, but they may lack the evidence for those claims. Further, Fassin observes that the response to fraudulence also can attend to or refuse those differences, resulting in repression or compassion, criminalization or humanitarianization, which "do not simply function as alternative policies" (2013: 52). Often the two modes of response coexist; humanitarian aid workers and police occupy the same spaces.

Adding to the murky and changing categories of what constitutes asylum and the effort to differentiate between the migrant and the asylum seeker, both groups are suspected of being possible terrorists. Proving that someone lied when making an asylum claim has become a high-stakes matter. The possibility that a claimant might be a terrorist is the reason that both the US State Department and the Department of Homeland Security are involved in vetting refugees and asylum seekers. Rooting out potential terrorists is a very difficult proposition, given that they are a very small minority among the thousands of people each year who obtain refugee status either from abroad or through application in the USA. Not surprisingly, both the departments that address this issue operate in secrecy, which makes it virtually impossible to know anything about their methods. It would seem that they have sophisticated protocols for determining whether an applicant is lying. We have no way of knowing how successful these protocols are.

Sympathy for tragedy can produce a willingness to believe, and further, learning that one has been conned, deceived, in such cases can produce outrage. It is one thing to be lied to, but another to be drawn in to sympathy. In a Canadian study, the authors describe differences in hearing officers' willingness to be sympathetic to the narratives they are presented with (Rousseau and Foxen 2005). In her study of volunteer human rights workers aiding asylum seekers in Israel, Ilil Benjamin reports that the possibly fraudulent applicants were called, "imposters" and that the human rights workers had little sympathy for them (2015). In the Danson case, described earlier, by contrast, there was initially a lot of public sympathy and celebrity support for her. When it turned out that she was lying, that support turned to outrage. Some people believed that the case would have a negative effect on other (reliable) claims, both on the part of the public and also those deciding such cases (Kurylo 2013).

The possibility that a fraudulent claim may have a negative effect on other claims is borne out by the research done by Schoenholtz and his colleagues of asylum officers around the USA. "It is clear, however, that suspicions of fraud related to a particular country's nationals can affect asylum officers in challenging and sometimes troubling ways where enough fraud is encountered. For some officers, these suspicions change their approach to the interview.... When there are multiple applications from the same country with the same story, same evidence, same preparer/attorney, the credibility of the applicant is in question" (Schoenholtz et al. 2014: 157).

Each culture has its own understandings of what counts as the truth, its own expectations about when truth-telling is required, and its own consequences, including emotional responses. In their study of Canadian Refugee Board members mentioned earlier, Rousseau and Foxen found a huge gap between those board members who saw their role as being lie detectors and those who believed they had to deal with the complexity of the narratives they heard (2005). This was connected to whether the board members believed that lying was a moral issue or a response to a difficult situation. The latter group was much more understanding of the many reasons why applicants feel the need to lie, while the former was intent on finding some objective "truth." More sympathetic board members echoed the widespread belief that the system is in fact structured to encourage lying, especially given the high stakes of asylum hearings (ibid.). It may also be argued that the system pushes people into deception; if the authorities need material, as they do increasingly, the asylum seeker feels compelled to provide it (Naik 2016).

Where does this leave the asylum system (or indeed the legal system), which is dependent on truth-telling for a variety of purposes? The suspicion surrounding asylum applicants can serve as a rationale for not accepting many applicants (Zetter 2007). Rousseau and Foxen point out that the myth of the lying refugee makes it possible for people to combine the contradictory beliefs in Canada as a haven for refugees while turning many applicants away.

The asylum application process produces suspicion in part by creating untenable and unresolvable relationships between being in a state of knowing and being in a state of doubt. The legal process does not accommodate understanding the ways in which knowledge is constructed and situational, and the traumas the applicants have experienced do not often lend themselves to coherent narratives. Instead, the asylum process exists at the untenable meeting ground of tragic choices (Calabresi and Bobbit 1978) and legal procedures.

NOTES

1. We note that in a unanimous decision, the US Supreme Court recently ruled that citizenship cannot be revoked when an applicant has made minor errors in their naturalization proceedings. Maslenjak v. United States, No. 16-309.
2. See Fassin's distinction among objective coherence, subjective coherence, and sincerity (2013).
3. For a discussion of the meaning of "truth" in asylum cases, see Fassin (2013).

CHAPTER 8

Victim or Perpetrator?

MT was a police officer in the Zimbabwe Republic Police (ZRP), from 2000 until she went AWOL in 2007, traveling to Sudan in mid-July of that year (MT v. Secretary of State for the Home Department 2012). She returned to Zimbabwe for a brief period in the second half of September 2007, in an effort to obtain (unsuccessfully) a passport for her daughter. She then traveled, via South Africa, to the UK, where she claimed asylum in 2009, after having been arrested as an overstayer while working for Asda, the supermarket chain. She admitted in her asylum hearing that she had lied when she told her employer that her passport was with the Home Office.

In her asylum claim, MT argued that in Zimbabwe she had been a police officer stationed at Bulawayo between 2000 and 2007. She herself had never been politically active. She had never supported ZANU-PF; she did not think that to be a police officer that it was necessary to support ZANU-PF, but she had heard that a police commissioner had said all police should be ZANU-PF.

At her asylum hearing, she said she was a uniformed duty officer; however, she had said in her screening interview that she was a police detective and had submitted a January 2007 pay slip describing her position as part of criminal investigations. Her explanation for this discrepancy was that she was only a detective for three months for training purposes, though later she said she had also been to court to present cases. Until 2007, MT said that she did not know that the police force had a record of brutality against political opponents and others. She said she had not seen anything herself to suggest that this was the case before then, except when it came to the Riot Squad.

In 2007, MT came under pressure from her superiors to participate in various acts against political opponents of ZANU-PF (the political party of Robert Mugabe, the president of Zimbabwe). This included attendance at the rallies of MDC, the opposition party, where police beat MDC supporters with batons. MT argued that as a way of dealing with these requirements of her role, she took several days of sick leave before she deserted the police force.

In her asylum claim, she described three incidents in which torture was used, and although she claimed not to have been responsible, she was nonetheless implicated. The first was the "Stephen Mhlanga incident" in February 2007. She was with five other police who raided his house, arrested him, and, en route back to the police station, took him to a bushy area by a river, where he was questioned for about two hours about his MDC connections. She was the most junior officer there, and her role was just taking notes. Some of the officers there were verbally aggressive and poked him and threatened to throw him in the river. He was very scared. He gave them the information they wanted. After they had taken him to the police station, he was put in the cells. She did not inquire if they had ill-treated him there, although she knew he was released the next day. She did not protest to her superiors about his ill-treatment as they would, she said, have labeled her as an MDC sympathizer.

Second, MT described the "Gibson Sibanda incident," which occurred in April 2007. She was one of the seven police officers present on a raid of Sibanda's house. Others had hit him with batons, but she had only slapped him. She did not think he had been offered or received any medical treatment for his injuries. After the interrogation, conduct of his case was left to the detectives. She saw him the next day. She did not notice any new injuries.

Third, in March 2007, she had also been ordered to go to a village near Plumtree, where ZANU-PF supporters had set fire to houses of MDC supporters. About 30 were killed, including children. When she arrived the next morning, the village was deserted. No one knew where the perpetrators had gone. The CID officers present told her and others to bury the bodies in shallow graves. She testified that she was shocked and traumatized, but did not leave the force then because she was scared to do so.

MT also said that in 2007, she had been involved in policing 11 MDC rallies/demonstrations. She and her colleagues had been deployed as a second line behind the Riot Squad, helping chase and disperse the demonstrators. She said that excessive force had only been used on some of these occasions; the Riot Squad used tear gas and batons; they claimed that they needed to use force against the MDC mob. She did not participate in any beatings; she used her baton just as a form of prodding to encourage people to disperse.

MT's asylum claim was refused, and the Home Office decided in January 2010 to remove her from the UK. They also certified her claim under s.55 of the Immigration, Asylum and Nationality Act 2006. They determined that Article 1F(a) and (c) of the Refugee Convention excluded her from the protection of the Refugee Convention because there were serious reasons for considering she had committed crimes against humanity.

MT claimed asylum on the basis that she was a victim of persecution. She argued that she was afraid that she would be persecuted should she return, having deserted the police in Zimbabwe. The government, on the other hand, argued that she was a perpetrator and was not, therefore, eligible for asylum under the 1951 Convention. MT also claimed that the actions which were the subject of the exclusion clause on Article 1F were undertaken under duress.

The original 1951 Convention on the Status of Refugees included a section (1F), which stated that it "shall not apply to any person with respect to whom there are serious reasons for considering" [that]:

(a) he [or she] has committed a crime against peace, a war crime, or a crime against humanity, as defined in the international instruments drawn up to make provision in respect of such crimes;

(b) he [or she] has committed a serious non-political crime outside the country of refuge prior to his [or her] admission to that country as a refugee; or.

(c) he [or she] has been guilty of acts contrary to the purposes and principles of the United Nations.

Further, UNHCR policy states:

Certain acts are so grave as to render their perpetrators undeserving of international protection as refugees. Their primary purpose is to deprive those guilty of heinous acts, and serious common crimes, of international refugee protection and to ensure that such persons do not abuse the institution of asylum in order to avoid being held legally accountable for their acts. (UNHCR 1997)

This policy statement is at issue in the case of MT. The court decided that MT was excludable under Art.1F (a) because she had aided and abetted in the commission of a crime against humanity. They considered her defense of duress and decided that it did not apply in this case.

First of all, we find that at no point was she faced with a threat of imminent death or of continuing or imminent serious bodily harm. The background evidence does not show that police officers who resigned or deserted – and there were very significant numbers of them – ordinarily met with threats of ill-treatment. (MT v. Secretary of State for the Home Department 2012: para. 107)

According to the court, MT's participation in the several incidents described earlier:

Shows she must have been trusted to be loyal. She voluntarily joined a brutal police force, she had personal involvement in the "cover-up" of a mass murder and in two incidents of torture. The test of duress is a high one requiring a person to show that not to follow an order put them in grave and imminent peril. Yet even after these incidents she did not leave immediately. (ibid.: para. 64)

The court argued that the fact that she did take some modest action, by feigning illness without anything negative happening to her, is further proof that she was not under duress.

The question facing the court was whether MT was a perpetrator or a victim. The court decided she was a perpetrator because she participated in crimes against humanity under 1F (a) as an aider and abettor even though she was not an instigator of the events described in the case. MT frames herself as a victim who was caught up in something about which she claims to be ignorant and over which she had no control. Her flight to Sudan was, apparently, in her mind, a way of removing herself from a situation that was traumatic to her, and she describes her travel to London as part of her flight from persecution. The court, however, framed her flight differently because they did not believe she was in fear of persecution should she return to Zimbabwe. The fact that she was able to return to try to get a passport for her daughter showed the authorities her lack of fear, as did her visit to the Zimbabwe Embassy in London after her arrival in 2007 to renew her passport.

She played down her role as a member of the police, saying that she was merely a member of the force, rather than a part of criminal investigations as she was, although only for a short period. She also played down her political sophistication, her knowledge of the role played by the police in brutality directed against the opposition as well as her knowledge of the connection between the police and ZANU-PF. These can all be called strategic deceptions rather than verifiable lies.

The decision about whether MT was a perpetrator or a victim combined an evaluation of available facts and legal analysis. There is a large body of legal analysis of the exclusion clause, or perpetrator bar, as it is known in the USA, which is not the focus of this chapter (e.g. see Hathaway and Foster 2014; Goodwin-Gill and McAdam 2007; Gilbert 2003). Rather, our interest lies in the ways in which such decisions are framed and the issues they raise about how to decide whether someone is a victim or a perpetrator. In individual cases from countries that are not in the throes of a civil war, this is a matter of gathering sufficient evidence and evaluating it, which is difficult enough. These were the cases imagined by those who drafted the 1951 Convention and its Article 1F.

Nowadays the situation is often very different. Cases of civil war are even more difficult because the nature of the violence itself makes it difficult to sharply divide perpetrators and victims. The importance of this issue has exploded with the awareness that the violence is being exported, because it feeds into our current fears about terrorism perpetrated in the host countries of asylum seekers. The issue is not only whether people committed human rights violations in their home countries but also whether they would commit violence in the receiving country. We are making two observations here: first, that in current civil wars, it may be difficult to differentiate between perpetrators and victims, and second, that even victims are under suspicion. In this climate of suspicion, the category of the innocent victim of civil wars has been under attack, creating a shift in perception of asylum applicants as potential terrorists. Some scholars argue that current ideas about Article 1F risk undermining "the Refugee Convention under which fugitives from political conflicts, from around the world, could traditionally always seek sanctuary in a safe country" (Juss 2012: 467).

In contemporary asylum hearings, examiners often apply similar measures of human rights violations to a variety of political situations. Efforts to sharply differentiate between perpetrator and victim are fraught with difficulty, but continue nonetheless, perhaps only as a moral exercise of seeking justice. In a remarkably frank assessment post Rwanda, O'Neill, Rutinwa, and Verdirame make clear how extremely challenging it can be to try to discover with any certainty who was responsible for the killing and therefore who was barred from refugee status by the exclusion clause (2000). These authors conducted a study in Kenya, Tanzania, and the Central African Republic to try to understand whether and how these states applied the exclusion clause. They pointed out that the genocide in Rwanda was a planned operation in which significant numbers of people were involved in the killing. "(T)he Rwanda genocide was accomplished by what has been called 'artisanal' means. The weapon of choice was a machete or a nail-studded club. Sometimes firearms and grenades were used, but most of the killing was done by individuals and by hand. To kill at a minimum one-half million people in three months with such low-level weapons means that thousands had to have participated. Adding to the figure are those who did not kill but were somehow complicit. Neighbours informed the death squads where Tutsis were hiding, or identified the children of mixed marriages as Tutsis. Others ordered people to kill, especially the town mayors (bourgmestres) and officials in the prefectures" (2000: 136).

Determining who is a perpetrator and who is a victim is made even more difficult by powerful individuals and politicians who obscure and control access to information (Des Forges 1999: 628). In many cases, O'Neill, Rutinwa, and Verdirame report that people were given refugee status because it was easier for various reasons, even though they may well have been excludable based on Article 1F. They argue that this "undermined support for genuine refugees but also weakened the humanitarian aid effort and destabilized the security of the entire region" (2000: 170). From our point of view, the instabilities both during and following genocide illustrate how unlikely it is for the authorities to get these determinations right, to separate out those who participated in mass killings. People can be complicit in many ways, further complicating the possibility of discovering accurate details of their participation. In so many cases, a person is not either a victim or a perpetrator, but a bit of both. This is especially true in cases of mass civil disturbances like Rwanda and Bosnia in which so many of the citizens were involved.

As we discussed in Chapter 2, the portrayals of participants in civil wars encompass many categories, not only persecutor and victim, but also those who unwillingly participate in violence, such as child soldiers, those who were in the wrong place at the wrong time, and those whose status in the conflict is assumed but not provable. For example, we discussed the case of Beatrice Muyenyezi, who was convicted not of being a perpetrator of the Rwandan genocide but of lying on her citizenship application about her position in the MRND government responsible for the killings. Within the conflict itself, innocent bystanders are easily misread as conspirators.

The difficulty of determining responsibility does not make it less important. The use of the exclusion clause has become more frequent in the aftermath of civil wars in the 1990s. Although the exclusion clause was written into the 1951 Convention, it was not used very often until the late twentieth century. Individual cases were considered earlier but became salient again following the wars in Yugoslavia and Rwanda. Reijven and van Wijk write, the "idea that perpetrators of severe human rights violations should not find a sanctuary abroad nor gain impunity resurfaced when the atrocities of the war in former Yugoslavia and the genocide in Rwanda became apparent" (Reijven and van Wijk 2014: 2).

Even though the use of Article 1F is more frequent than it was, it is still only used in a fraction of the asylum applications. It is very difficult to obtain figures about its use, but in the UK, Singer has conducted extensive research on the subject (2015). She was able to discover that Article 1F refusals represented a tiny fraction of a percentage of all initial asylum decisions. The highest number was in 2011, with 31 cases out of 17,380 decisions, which represented 0.18% (ibid.: 173). Singer also argues that its use is limited by the fact that it is very hard to prove such cases, so the Home Office is more likely to use two other ways of denying asylum to possible cases: they either say that the person is lying and the claim is not credible, or they argue that the person is not really in fear of persecution on return (ibid.: 202–3). She also believes that it is lack of resources that prevent the Home Office developing the necessary proof to invoke Article 1F (Singer 2016).

There is a difficult line to walk, on the one hand forbidding persecutors access to asylum, while on the other not barring everyone involved in civil wars. As the court in the case of Miranda Alvarado versus Gonzales pointed out, "Injury inflicted by opposing political or other groups on each other during a civil conflict will not necessarily equate to persecution" (2006: 41–2), and "It is untenable to impose a blanket exclusion on asylum-seekers who come from places beset by civil war and are affiliated in some respect with one side or the other in the conflict" (ibid.: 43). However, they also stated that courts have "not hesitated to impute motivation on account of political opinion in factually-compelling circumstances where someone fighting on one side of a politically-based civil war persecutes someone affiliated with the group fighting on the other side" (ibid.).

In the case of Miranda Alvarado, the asylum applicant was a Quechua-speaking member of the Peruvian Civil Guard in Lima who was assigned to serve as a community leader in a Quecha-speaking neighborhood (Miranda Alvarado v. Gonzales 2006). One of his tasks was preventing infiltration by the guerrilla organization Sendero Luminoso (Shining Path), the guerilla organization that opposed the Peruvian government. Later he became an interpreter for other officers who interrogated suspected Shining Path members. During these interrogations, suspects were often subjected to electric shock, torture, and beatings on the legs and feet with rubber batons. The applicant did not conduct the torture personally, but did witness it. He acted as a translator over a seven-year period, at which point he tried to resign, because, he told the authorities in the USA, he didn't like the way the people conducted the interrogations, though he put "family reasons" on his resignation form. Later, he requested and received "anti-terrorist and survival training." In the course of his training, he was involved in the capture of three Shining Path members who had attacked the training group. These guerrillas threatened Miranda and his companions with death. When he returned home, he found that his wife and children had been visited by masked men who had stolen his police uniforms and put Shining Path slogans on the walls. The following year, Shining Path members vandalized his property once again, killed his dog, and left a note on the corpse saying that he would die in the same way. At that point, he fled to the USA. Miranda Alvarado did not lie about his involvement as a translator during the interrogations of suspected members of Shining Path, but rather claimed that he was not actually involved in the torture himself.

The court decided that Miranda was barred from asylum because he was personally involved in the persecution. He was undisputedly a regular part of interrogation teams who questioned Shining Path members. He clearly was a necessary part of the interrogation. Without his services as a Quechua interpreter, the interrogations could not proceed, so he materially aided the persecution process, rather than merely being peripheral to the persecution. Thus, the court was able to make an individual judgment about a situation of major civil unrest in which the applicant was considered to have played a part in the persecution of the government's political opponents.

In some cases, although the immigration authorities can't tell who is a victim and who is a perpetrator, people on the ground can, though not in ways that are generalizable. The Tutsi refugees who have settled in Columbus, Ohio, claim that some of the Hutu Rwandans, who received asylum and live in nearby Dayton, Ohio, were perpetrators in the Rwandan genocide. The Hutu claim to have been persecuted by vigilantes who would have killed anyone sympathetic with the Tutsis.

MATERIAL SUPPORT

In addition to applying the exclusion clause of the 1951 Convention, since 1990, US legislation has also prohibited the granting of asylum to people who have provided material support to designated foreign terrorist organizations.[1] This prohibition was subsequently incorporated in the Anti-Terrorism and Effective Death Penalty Act of 1996, and was intended to combat terrorist financing and support in the USA. After 9/11, the definition of "terrorist activity" and "terrorist organization" was expanded in the USA PATRIOT Act of 2001 and the REAL ID Act of 2005. The USA PATRIOT Act divides the list of terrorist organization into three tiers, which have different implications. Aiding a Tier I organization is a criminal offense, which is not the case for Tier II, though someone who aids anyone on either list is barred from the USA. Both these lists contain specific organizations and are public. The same cannot be said about Tier III, which includes a "group of two or more individuals, whether organized or not, which engaged in, or has a subgroup which engages in terrorist activities." There is no public list of organizations and no review process. Even members of an umbrella, nonviolent group, or movement will be classified as engaging in terrorist activities if a subgroup allied with the umbrella group engages in any form of terrorist activity, or is a spouse or child of someone who fits in this category (Kidane 2009–10: 319–320).

The current material support provision states that someone is ineligible for entry into the USA if they have committed:

"an act that the actor knows, or reasonably should know, affords material support (1) for the commission of a terrorist act; (2) to any individual who the actor knows, or reasonably should know, has committed or plans to commit a terrorist activity; or (3) to a designated or non-designated terrorist organization. Material support involves providing even once 'a safe house, transportation, communications, funds, transfer of funds or other material financial benefit, false documentation or identification, weapons, explosives or training.'"

The definition of terrorism has been at the heart of much scholarly and policy debate. The results of this debate have been inconclusive and confusing. Efforts to define terrorism have dated back to the 1930s, and although various international instruments have been used to define the term, there is no internationally accepted definition. If no one is able to decide who is a terrorist and how asylum-receiving states can protect themselves from them, how can we design appropriate immigration policy to respond to the threat presented by terrorism? Part of the difficulty is that the activities defined by some as terrorism are often defined by others as political activism. As the saying goes, "your terrorist is my freedom fighter." One scholar points out that Nelson Mandela, former president of South Africa and Nobel Peace Prize winner, was considered by many to be a terrorist for his anti-apartheid activities with the African National Congress (Kidane 2009–10: 304–5). He was not removed from the US terrorist watch list until his 90th birthday in 2008.

As mentioned above, one of the ways the USA has responded to this definitional conundrum is by forbidding entry to anyone who has provided support to one of a list of terrorist organizations. Making such lists can be a fraught activity requiring extensive knowledge of the activities and focus of the organization, as well as constant adaptation to changing conditions. Because terrorism generates so much fear and concern, the authorities err on the side of caution in compiling these lists. As we complete this book, the courts are still evaluating President Trump's ban on immigrants from Islamic countries, a particularly drastic example of a response to terrorism.

The War on Terror that followed 9/11 increased the connections between asylum law and national security. As a result, the process of claiming asylum and the refugee resettlement program have become more complex and drawn out. Refugees who are potential candidates for resettlement in the USA are now subject to an enhanced and drawn out evaluation process, based on the concern that the resettlement process was being misused as a way into the USA by terrorists. Now many refugees are stuck for months and years in camps while their applications are being processed.

The New York Times interview with a Syrian refugee family (now reset-tled in Illinois) describes their problems and some of the general problems Syrian families face in their attempts to get asylum in the USA (Griswold 2016). They are having a difficult time financially, in part because they were relying on having the help of their son, Waseem, who, at the last minute, with everything completed except the medical exam, didn't get a visa with the rest of the family. He was told that something had come up in the security clearance. Many months later, he and his wife and children remain in limbo in Jordan, without any explanation of why his visa did not come through. *The New York Times* asked the authorities to explain why the visa was on hold; they were not able to get an answer for this case, but were told that it "could be as simple as an applicant's security clearance having expired while a family member waited to be vetted. Or maybe Waseem's name sounds like a name on a terrorist watch-list. Or maybe, at the very last minute, 'recurrent vetting' raised a red flag." The family worry that the problem is Waseem's uncle, who was a former military member of Assad's regime before he defected. Family members were asked various questions about him. They were asked, for example, "Did they serve him coffee or tea when he was in their homes? This was most likely a question to determine whether the family had provided material support — which could include a cup of coffee, a glass of water, a ride — to someone designated to be an enemy of the United States"(ibid.).

The US bar on giving asylum to someone who has provided material sup-port to a terrorist organization has had the ironic effect of turning some genuine victims into "perpetrators" or at least those barred from receiving asylum. Here the classification of the organization as terrorist is not in doubt; what is in doubt is the role of the person providing the support. A person can fit into this category even if they have been forced to help the terrorists.

One of the most egregious and publicized cases involves a nurse from Colombia who was kidnapped and assaulted by the Revolutionary Armed Forces of Colombia (FARC). She was forced to give medical treatment to their members. She fled to the USA and sought asylum. Her application was denied on the ground that she had provided material support to a ter-rorist organization (Human Rights First Report 2006).

Much has been written over the last decade chronicling the stories of those who have fallen into this material support abyss and have been mostly unable to extract themselves. Unlike in other common law coun-tries (Canada, UK, New Zealand, Australia, as well as the EU and

Germany), there is no duress provision in the law that would exempt those who, like the Colombian nurse, were *forced* to provide the "support" to a terrorist organization. So even though the forced assistance was in fact part of the persecution, which resulted in flight, those who were unlucky enough to be persecuted by members of the groups classified as terrorist organizations cannot obtain asylum. There are many examples of such cases in the Human Rights First report and elsewhere. Two will provide illustration of the bizarre results of this policy: in one case, a journalist from Nepal who was beaten, threatened, and forced to hand over money to Maoists was denied asylum because the Maoists are a terrorist organization; in another case, a fisherman from Sri Lanka who was abducted by the Tamil Tigers, another terrorist organization, and forced to pay his own ransom, was also barred under the material support rule.

However, despite the publicity about the inequity of the absence of a duress exception, the law has not yet changed. It still does not include a *de minimus* exception so that even nominal support is sufficient to trigger the bar. But in 2007, perhaps as a result of the pressure, Congress granted the Secretary of Homeland Security, in consultation with the Attorney General, the authority to issue waivers to the material support bar in certain limited circumstances including that the support has been provided under duress (Consolidated Appropriations Act 2008). As a result, DHS has recently been more willing to grant waivers in individual cases, though according to Human Rights First, that has always been legally possible (Human Rights First Report 2006). The question of material support continues to trouble the court system. The Board of Immigration Appeals is currently working on it, having called for amicus briefs on the meaning of material support and on the application of the "de minimus" to contributions of money (Amicus Invitation 2016).

Individuals can also be included in the category of giving material support to a terrorist organization if they were "legitimate, if irregular, combatants in struggles supported at one time by U.S. policies" (Wenski 2007). The definition is so expansive that people can be caught whether they were involved with an organization that the USA opposes or supports. The DHS have said that someone who provided support to Afghanistan's Northern Alliance in the 1990s would be prohibited from obtaining asylum, even though the Northern Alliance was fighting the Taliban government that the USA considered illegitimate (Swarns 2006). The DHS has apparently also put on hold some ethnic minorities fighting alongside the USA in Vietnam (ibid.). Others may be caught up in changes in US policy in which they may have been granted refugee status but are stuck in limbo when it comes time for them to obtain permanent residence, or for the resettlement of family members. Such is the case of Cubans who fought against Castro in the 1960s whose family members are barred from joining them in the USA (ibid.).

Although the law has not changed so that genuine refugees are not caught up in this problems generated by the material support bar, the situation in most cases seems to be resolved eventually (a situation that is changing as we complete this book). As one lawyer points out, "In practice, these cases are often referred to court by the asylum office and the IJ resolves the material support issue. Sometimes there are designated DHS trial attorneys that handle all material support cases in an office. So it can work in the end unless there the client has really done some awful things himself, but it can be slow" (Berger 2015).

The problem is that often people have no idea what is going on because they are not told why their claim has been delayed. In the USA, cases in a number of categories, including those that have a Terrorism Related Inadmissibility Grounds (TRIG) bar, or persecutor-related issues, have to be sent to Headquarters for special consideration. Often these cases languish there for months, even years, and the applicant is not told what is happening, or even that their case falls into these categories, though it is often possible for the applicant's lawyer to find out (Dzubow 2015).

FROM VICTIM TO PERPETRATOR

Some cases come to the attention of the authorities well after asylum (or another immigration status) is granted. In this situation, a person is granted asylum initially, and the basis for the asylum claim is questioned only when they apply for permanent status (usually citizenship or permanent settlement). There are several reasons that the interest of the authorities is triggered at this stage: the definition of terrorism may have changed, or new information may have come to light, or it could be that when attention is drawn to the case, as happens in further proceedings, the authorities decide they were not in fact eligible in the first place. The results of this change are various and may range from criminal charges that result in prosecution to deportation to long, unexplained delays.

Sometimes the change in label of an asylum applicant can be the result of more than one of the aforementioned reasons. As we saw in Chapter 2, Ibrahim Parlak, a café owner in a small town in Michigan, obtained political asylum in the USA in 1992 after he fled Turkey, where he said he had been imprisoned, charged with separatism, and tortured for his activities with the Kurdistan Workers' Party, or P.K.K., a Kurdish insurgent group (Lewin 2015). After he applied for citizenship a decade or so later, his asylum was revoked, because by that time the P.K.K. had been designated a terrorist organization by Washington. The Department of Homeland Security accused Mr. Parlak of lying on his green card application by checking a box saying he had never been arrested or supported a terrorist organization. The agency said he did not mention that he had been arrested after being involved in a 1987 border gunfight in which the P.K.K. killed two Turkish soldiers. Mr. Parlak claims that he had disclosed the arrest and his P.K.K. affiliation on a previous asylum application. The USA deemed Mr. Parlak a terrorist, and incarcerated him in the Calhoun County Jail in July 2004. Five months later, a federal immigration judge issued a deportation order. This case has gained a lot of public attention, as a result of which he was allowed to stay in the USA because of a personal bill introduced in the Senate that year by Carl Lewin. Representative Fred Upton reintroduced the bill in January 2017. In December 2015, he obtained a 90-day stay of the deportation proceedings, though the DHS apparently had obtained the necessary documents so he could return to Turkey, despite having previously lost his Turkish passport. This case illustrates the potential effects of changes in US definitions of terrorism. Mr. Parlak's lawyers have also argued that the situation in Turkey has deteriorated for Kurds, which would make his return to Turkey problematic (Osnos 2015).

The case of Beatrice Munyenyezi, discussed in detail in Chapter 2, provides another example of a person who claimed to be a victim but was found later to be a perpetrator, as a result of new information coming to light. It is not clear how the authorities acquired this new information, but it resulted in a charge and subsequent conviction of lying on her citizenship application. She came to the USA in 1998 as a refugee from Rwanda after the 1994 genocide, and applied for citizenship in 2003. The decision described her as "entering the United States and securing citizenship by lying about her role as a commander of one of the notorious roadblocks where Tutsis were singled out for slaughter. 'She was not a mere spectator,' McAuliffe (the judge) said. 'I find this defendant was actively involved, actively participated, in the mass killing of men, women and children simply because they were Tutsis'" (Tuohy 2013).

The case of Edin Sakoč provides an illustration of how the authorities respond to changed information after an applicant has been granted asylum. In 2001, Sakoč, a Bosnia Muslim, was granted refugee status in the

USA. In 2004, he obtained a green card. In February 2007, he applied for US citizenship. On the application form and in a subsequent interview with a US immigration officer, which was part of the application process, Sakoč reportedly denied having committed any crimes or acts of persecution. In September 2007, he was granted citizenship (United States of America v. Edin SAKOC 2015).

In 2010, the government became aware of allegations that Sakoč had engaged in criminal acts prior to coming to the USA. In July 1992, while serving in the Bosnian army, Sakoč allegedly raped a Serbian woman before taking her to a prison camp, aided another Bosnian soldier named "Boban" in shooting and killing the woman's family members and burning the bodies, and, finally, aided Boban in burning down the family's home. In 2013, he was charged with knowingly procuring naturalization on the basis of false statements in which he denied committing any acts of persecution while in the military.

The case was complicated by the passage of time since the acts Sakoč was alleged to have committed in 1992. Evidence was collected in Sarajevo by deposition to support the government's claim in 2013. Sakoč argued that the delay had meant that the key witness, Boban, had disappeared and therefore could not testify, and that he would have told the court that Sakoč did not rape the Serbian woman, nor did he know or help Boban kill her family members. The court did not dismiss the charges on this basis, but later granted Sakoč a new trial on the grounds that they had changed the terms of the charges against him midstream, putting him at risk of being charged with what was basically the same offenses twice. Sakoč decided instead to leave the country and return to Bosnia (Ring 2015).

Sakoč's case explains the difficulty faced by the authorities attempting to show that someone lied on their claim for asylum, or in this case, on their citizenship application when the events at issue are already old. It is hardly surprising that neither the government nor Sakoč was able to trace Boban after so much time had elapsed, though, as the government pointed out, it would anyway be unlikely that he would implicate himself in the process of exonerating Sakoč. In addition, the evidence collected in Sarajevo was disputed; Sakoč argued, without success, that the unwillingness of one of the witnesses to answer questions about a possible bribery claim, in which he was asked to change his testimony, meant that his evidence about the case in general was inadmissible.

Cases such as Sakoč's appear to be part of a widespread investigation by the Department of Homeland Security's war crimes division, which was set up in 2008. In February 2015, *The New York Times*, in an extensive article on the subject, wrote that a number of Bosnians had already been deported or had fled the country (Lichtblau 2015). Inquiry into the history of the many Bosnians who sought asylum in the USA in the 1990s revealed, "When more than 120,000 Bosnian refugees began applying for American visas in the mid-1990s, they were required to disclose military service or other allegiances that might have suggested involvement in war crimes. But the system relied largely on the honesty of the applicants, and there was little effort to verify their statements" (Lichtblau 2015). The problems of checking every applicant at a time when there were a large number is similar to the problems described earlier in the aftermath of the Rwandan genocide (O'Neill et al. 2000). Recent evidence show that verification remains a problem in situations where the authorities must process many asylum claims at once. *The New York Times* reported a recent case in which a "German Army lieutenant appears to have taken advantage of his country's chaotic system of processing migrants in 2015 to pose as a Syrian asylum seeker with the intention of carrying out an attack" (Eddy 2017). Further evidence of the absence of true screening can be seen in the fact that he appeared to speak no Arabic (ibid.).

The investigations into Bosnian refugees in the USA began by chance in 2004, when federal agents in Massachusetts arrested Marko Boskic, a Bosnian Serb who was accused of carrying out executions in the Srebrenica region. They had been alerted to his case by a book written by a journalist from *The Boston Globe* (Neuffer 2001). Like Sakoč, Boskic was convicted of concealing his army service, then sent back to Bosnia and sentenced to 10 years in prison for crimes against humanity. Until these investigations, Bosnians who had committed war crimes were able to live openly in the USA, something that caused great anguish to those who were genuine refugees from that war.

Most of the Bosnian investigations by the war crimes division were of Bosnian Serbs, but Bosnian Muslims, like Sakoč, and Croats also were found to have committed war crimes (Lichtblau 2015). The US courts decided that Azra Basic could be extradited to face charges in Bosnia for her actions as a guard at a military detention center. Basic, a Croatian woman, was charged with inflicting torture on some Serb prisoners, which included, among other things, making them drink gasoline and human blood, and kneel on broken glass (Chicago Tribune 2015). Basic had been living in the USA for nearly two decades under the name of Issabell Basic when the extradition case was implemented in the USA, though the formal request from the Bosnian government dates from 2007 (Gay 2011). Such cases do not require the legal proceedings usually undertaken to deport potential war criminals in the USA.

Lichtblau describes the effort to identify suspects, including "an appeal broadcast to Bosnians around the world in February, urging witnesses to come forward with any information about war crimes" (ibid.). In addition, the war crimes division has a "trove of Bosnian war crimes files and military rosters" (ibid.). What they don't have is enough money to follow all leads; the budget of the unit has been cut to $65,000. In addition, the backlog in the entire immigration legal system is such that these cases can be delayed for years. Many of these cases involve multiple legal hearings and appeals, as was the case for Sakoč.

With the exception of celebrated cases, individuals who commit human rights violations are rarely prosecuted in their home countries or by international tribunals. Asylum hearings and the prosecution of fraudulent asylum cases increasingly have played a role in the adjudication of human rights violations.

In some cases, someone who didn't personally commit acts of violence is nonetheless prosecuted for condoning, not preventing, or affording them. For example, the film *The Uncondemned* documents the first UN tribunal prosecution of rape as an international war crime (Mitchell and Louvel 2015). With the help of women who were willing to testify, the mayor of a small town was convicted of permitting the rape of Tutsi women in his office during the Rwandan genocide.

CHILD SOLDIERS: VICTIMS OR PERPETRATORS OR BOTH?

Child soldiers present the classic case in which the determination of whether one is a perpetrator or a victim is impossible. The law that we discussed earlier about the perpetrator bar/exclusion clause and the material support bar would lead to a fairly clear conclusion that child soldiers are barred from asylum by virtue of their participation in persecution. And yet, it seems morally questionable that the same rules should apply to children as to adults.

Millions of children have been recruited as child soldiers, despite universal recognition that such recruitment is a violation of human rights. Some of these children have been forced to become soldiers, while others are recruited "voluntarily," though it is clear that these children are under various pressures (economic, social, or psychological), which may mean that becoming a child soldier is a tool for survival. Some are brainwashed and/or drugged during their time as soldiers.

Researchers have demonstrated that children cannot make the same decision as adults because their brains are not yet as well developed in their decision-making capacity (Sebastian 2007). Children are more easily coerced and are less able to judge the consequences of their actions (Modecki 2008). As a result, they cannot always be said to participate voluntarily when they become child soldiers and participate in atrocities, even when they are not forced to do so.

In fact, it is their very vulnerability and malleability that makes children such good candidates for soldiers. This is especially true now that it is no longer necessary to have physical strength to wield weapons. A report by Quillam, a counter-extremist think tank, has described how the Islamic State trains children:

> The organisation ... focuses a large number of its efforts on indoctrinating children through an extremism-based education curriculum, and fostering them to become future terrorists. The current generation of fighters sees these children as better and more lethal fighters than themselves, because rather than being converted into radical ideologies they have been indoctrinated into these extreme values from birth, or a very young age. (Benotman and Malik 2016: 27–8)

Many scholars advocate a change in the rules about duress in the USA to make it possible that some child soldiers could be recognized as victims rather than perpetrators (e.g. Note 2010: 220–1; Thomas 2013). In such situations, it would be possible that child soldiers would be considered to be victims by virtue of their having been coerced rather than perpetrators who committed war crimes, not unlike the situation we discussed earlier with respect to material support. Support for this approach comes from some scholars who believe that children under 18 years of age cannot be prosecuted for war crimes. Prosecution also seems not to happen in practice (s. 8, Rome Statute of the International Criminal Court n.d.; Gilbert 2017).

One possible way to reconsider the status of child soldiers would be to use the UNHCR guidelines. The UNHCR, in its nonbinding guidelines on child asylum claims, describes a three-pronged test for deciding whether a child should be excluded from asylum for persecuting others. The first is whether the child had the requisite intent to commit the act, which requires determining the child's mental development and maturity. The second prong asks whether the child was acting under duress or in self-defense. The third prong asks whether the acts committed were proportional to the consequences of asylum denial (UNHCR 2009).

CONCLUSION

The line between perpetrator and victim is not always clear, both making assessment difficult and affording perpetrators the possibility of passing as victims. Further, the categories of victim and perpetrator are not rigid, as we observed in the cases of refugees belonging to groups later defined as terrorist organizations. In many of the contemporary civil wars, relatively peaceful associations across groups have turned violent, requiring everyone to choose sides. Individuals who refuse or who have multiple affiliations are vulnerable to suspicion not only during the violence but also in the asylum process.

The pursuit of perpetrators who fraudulently present themselves as victims is motivated both by social justice and by the fear of terrorism. Given limited funding, and perhaps also the current climate in which the fear of terrorism outweighs concerns about social justice, some cases are not pursued or are left to the work of NGOs such as Elie Wiesel's organization, Foundation for Humanity, or Human Rights Watch.

The relationships between perpetrator and victim can shift when a violent situation has been, for the most part anyway, resolved, especially in situations with active reconciliation efforts. People who illegally helped refugees to flee can become heroes rather than criminals. People who were coerced into violence can be seen as victims. Persecutors who are remorseful can sometimes participate in reconciliation efforts. The political asylum process operates in a complex, often retrospective position that assesses events that occurred both in the recent and not so recent past; some people are caught in the middle, as unwilling participants in violence. Others, more clearly persecutors, can take advantage of the gray area that emerges from such conflicts. Given the complexity of these categories, it is not surprising that asylum seekers make strategic decisions about how to position themselves.

NOTES

1. 18 U.S.C. § 2339B (2000). See https://birdsongslaw.wordpress.com/wp-admin/ - _ftn7 for. Details of the statutes.

CHAPTER 9

Conclusion

In its efforts to differentiate between legitimate and unqualified claimants, the political asylum process employs methods to identify deception and fraud. However, the process sometimes erroneously equates quite different kinds of deception, for example, refusing both applicants who used deception to flee violence and those who lied about their identity. As we have discussed in this book, kinds of deception differ in scale, from minor inconsistencies in an application form to the use of false identity documents, to fraudulent applications. Deception does not always indicate fraud.

As a legal process, in which the central tenet is the search for truth, the political asylum process is complicated by the difficulty of differentiating between strategic lies used to survive and escape persecution and lies that indicate fraud. As we have discussed, many people fleeing persecution out of necessity use false passports, false identity cards, and other forms of deception. In fact, the most legitimate claimant might be one who has had to escape without legitimate documents and who had to use illegal strategies. Some forms of deception can be understood as knowing how to "use the system," for example, the use of bribery and false documents. We believe that the asylum hearing officials are well aware of the necessity of duplicity and even the use of false documents.

In an effort to address the difficulty of determining who is a legitimate asylum seeker, the authorities have introduced new technologies for assessing authenticity, and although more scientific methods of assessing the facts may offer a sense of security, they are often insufficient, both because

C. Bohmer, A. Shuman, *Political Asylum Deceptions*, https://doi.org/10.1007/978-3-319-67404-9_9

the methods are not necessarily reliable and because the results they provide are misused or misinterpreted.

In turn, the underground networks have responded with new kinds of fraud. In this conclusion, we review the confusion, deliberate or not, in considering a claimant who uses false documents as not credible and therefore not entitled to asylum. The stakes for evaluating the authentic asylum seeker have intensified with concerns about terrorism; as we have argued, the kinds of deception most often examined by the authorities have little or nothing to do with terrorism. The discourse of potential terrorist asylum seekers clouds the process.

HISTORICAL CHANGES IN ASYLUM POLICY AND POLITICS

Asylum law is based on the idea of protecting people from persecution, but recent discourses express more concern with protecting the receiving country from dangerous migrants. As we complete this book, the discourses of anxiety about admitting economic migrants who purport to be victims of persecution have shifted into a discourse about international security and the fear of terrorism. In part precipitated by 9/11, and terrorist acts in Europe, the focus on security can neglect the obligations stipulated by international law.

The populations to whom we grant asylum have changed substantially since the 1951 enactment of international asylum policy. In particular, refugees from the Cold War have been regarded differently from those fleeing present civil wars. As Gil Loescher wrote, observing shifts in the situation of refugees in 1993, "The basic international instruments of refugee protection offer neither a comprehensive nor a sufficiently flexible response to the diverse forced population movements taking place today" (1993: 164). Loescher argued that protection needs to encompass not only those able to demonstrate a "well-founded fear of persecution" but also "forced migrants who cannot prove that they are refugees" (1993: 164). As we write, in 2017, the categories of people seeking asylum have expanded to include new social groups, and the suspicions of them have also changed and grown. When Loescher wrote, asylum seekers primarily were suspected of being economic migrants. During World War II, before the establishment of the 1951 Convention, some refugees were suspected of being spies. Today, in addition to the suspicion that economic migrants are trying to game the system by posing as asylum seekers, and despite evidence to the contrary, migrants are suspected of being potential terrorists. One of our larger questions is, when asylum applicants are suspected of being fraudulent, what is it they are presumed to be? Are they presumed to be spies, smugglers, terrorists, economic migrants, or other opportunists attempting to game the system?

Throughout this book, we have regarded the political asylum process as a dynamic interaction among multiple participants. Suspicion is part of this dynamic, driven not only by what asylum applicants say or what documents they produce during the process, but also by larger institutional frameworks, each with its own history, culture, and politics. Political asylum policies change (or don't) in response to changing social conditions of persecution.

Border control includes the seemingly different practices of deporting immigrants convicted of crimes, assessing whether asylum applicants participated in violent activities in their home countries, differentiating between victims and persecutors, using new technologies of surveillance to investigate the veracity of asylum claims, viewing asylum applicants as possible terrorists, and detaining people who cross borders without documents or with false documents. All of these practices are connected to discourses of suspicion that criminalize migrants. The criminalization of asylum seekers has roots in earlier asylum policies but is intensified in present practices, resulting in vastly different portrayals of asylum applicants either as innocent victims of persecution or as opportunists and potential terrorists.

The receiving country's perception of and relationship with the asylum seeker's home country plays a significant role in shaping suspicion. Documents are not trusted from countries with weak or nonexistent governments, such as Somalia. Cameroonians are perceived as "particularly adept at filing faked asylum claims" (Terretta 2015: 59). Although refugees from wars in Rwanda and the former Yugoslavia might have been suspected of being perpetrators rather than victims, they did not always face greater scrutiny. Instead, their complex situations prompted a more general suspicion of asylum seekers. Refugees from Syria face another shift in the asylum process, as they are increasingly suspected of terrorism. Each of these perceptual shifts has resulted not only in new forms of suspicion but also in the erasure of the idea of the deserving asylum seeker. The suspicions are not limited to questions of the inadequacy of documentation or the ability to prove a well-founded fear. Instead, asylum seekers from Islamic countries are generally under suspicion as possible terrorists.

What Makes the Truth Elusive?

In earlier work, we argued that the political asylum process produces both knowledge and ignorance (Bohmer and Shuman 2007). The primary goal of hearings is to discern the truth and to differentiate between legitimate and fraudulent applicants, but some forms of inquiry, especially those designed to identify minor discrepancies in an application, can obfuscate rather than clarify. As we observed in our discussion of successful applicants who were later discovered to be fraudulent (Chapter 7), legitimate asylum seekers are not always able to produce a coherent account of the persecution they experienced, and fraudulent applicants can take advantage of the system by producing exactly the kind of seamless, coherent account that the officials will accept.

The relationship between truth and evidence is always complicated, but it is additionally complex in the political asylum process, which has to manage both the validity of an individual's claim and the question of whether the situation described warrants asylum. The asylum process is designed to identify particular kinds of truth, primarily focused on whether applicants are who they say they are, but the truth of the violence they say they experienced is always part of the assessment. Because the documentary evidence is so limited, the inquiry often focuses more on who the applicants are rather than on the experiences they describe. As Fassin argues, inquiry does not only identify truth but also produces it (2013: 20). Further, the asylum process is always to some extent an exercise in assessing sincerity as well as facts. Describing the asylum process, Fassin writes:

> Yet, this data can also be called into question: is it not forged? and even if authentic, what proof does it provide? In the end, establishing the correspondence between what is being told and what has happened or could still occur supposes a certain level of adhesion to or belief in the story: in the deliberations I attended, the last word was rarely that facts were undoubtedly established. Most of the time, the decision relied on personal conviction. (2013: 23)

Often, asylum inquiries are not able to address the most salient issues, and, for example, fail to differentiate between perpetrators and victims. Applicants might be able to successfully convince the immigration officers that they are who they claim to be, and their documents might support their claim. As we have seen in some of the celebrated cases of people like Beatrice Munyenyezi, who gained asylum but later was accused of being a perpetrator, the deception might not be in the use of false documents.

KINDS OF DECEPTION

Many people fleeing persecution use deceptive means to leave and to cross borders. These deceptions are not indicators of the validity of their asylum claims, and, if anything, the many reports of escape are evidence of deception as a frequent and necessary tool used by legitimate asylum seekers. As we discussed in the introduction to this book, the lies Carol's father told to gain entry into New Zealand did not contradict his status as a victim of persecution. Displaced people tell a great variety of lies, from the strategic lie that stretches or embellishes the truth without compromising the fundamental facts of the case to the deceptions used by perpetrators claiming to be victims.

The categories of persecutor/victim, economic migrant/asylum seeker, or choosing to leave/needing to leave are not always clear. The question of who is the persecutor and who the victim in civil wars depends on an assessment of legitimate forms of defense against someone perceived to be an aggressor. Many asylum seekers are also economic migrants, hoping for the chance for a better life. Since people make decisions not only for themselves but also for their families, their choices about when to leave can be complicated. Each of these categories requires and depends on different sorts of evidence, and each raises different sorts of suspicion.

As we said earlier, we are interested in the question of what supposedly fraudulent asylum seekers are presumed to be. Presuming that asylum seekers are actually economic migrants is quite different than presuming they are terrorists. To disprove the first, asylum seekers narrate their experiences of persecution and their fear of returning to additional persecution targeted specifically at them. Disproving the second can be surprisingly more difficult. Legitimate applicants, fleeing terrorists, are unprepared to be accused of *being* terrorists. In any case, the potential terrorist has become an undifferentiated category, potentially applicable to any displaced person, and thus difficult to refute.

With legal advice, asylum applicants learn the requirements of political asylum policies and learn how to shape their stories to emphasize persecution, torture, and violence rather than, for example, poverty that might be a result of the persecution. Shaping the story might be a matter of describing the persecutor rather than only the suffering. How applicants represent themselves matters enormously, but a coherent narrative does not necessarily avoid suspicion.

The problem may be also the difference between big lies and small lies and what is in between. The big lie is the person masquerading as an asylum seeker who is in fact not a victim of persecution, or worse, is a persecutor. A small lie can be seen as a strategic use of the system. A big lie is an abuse of the system. Too many small lies, in the case of the Chinese applicants discussed in Chapter 7, can add up to a big lie. Small lies can be attributed to inadvertent contradictions. Big lies are viewed as intention to commit fraud. Deception falls somewhere in between, and the difference is often the measure of moral outrage. Many people believe that a child soldier can be redeemed but not Demnaniuk.

In asylum hearings, a small contradiction can be regarded with the same significance as a major form of corruption. Some immigration authorities base their rejection of a case on a failure to include a particular detail or on a minor inconsistency (see Chapter 2). These minor errors cast suspicion on the credibility of the applicant. Similarly, an applicant who describes bribing a border guard can be disqualified as dishonest. Both minor inconsistencies and bribery are usually easily explained, but they are nonetheless used as rationales for denying a case.

KINDS OF SUSPICION

Suspicion in political asylum policy differs not only with regard to country of origin and forms of violence but also with regard to PSGs. As we observed in our discussion of people fleeing gang violence in Central America and people fleeing persecution as sexual minorities in Chapter 5, both the technologies of surveillance and the kinds of suspicion differ for PSGs. Persecution by gangs and violence against sexual minorities have quite different histories and are part of different cultural contexts, but considering them together, as part of contemporary political asylum policies, can tell us something about the discourses of suspicion related to the category of PSGs.

People fleeing gang violence in Central America are not suspected of deception. Instead, they face the difficulty of proving that they qualify under the category of persecuted social groups. The immigration authorities may not doubt that they are telling the truth about fearing the gangs; they are not necessarily suspected of being economic migrants, though their arrival as large groups of young impoverished people has undoubtedly provided a motivation for the refusal of their claims. Immigration officials have not recognized "youths who refuse to join a gang" as a PSG.[1] Applicants fleeing gang violence need to prove that they were specifically targeted by a gang, that they did not participate in violence, and that they are not former gang members. They have had almost no success gaining asylum.

In contrast to the people who are persecuted for refusing to join a gang in Central America, sexual minorities and victims of female genital mutilation have had some success gaining asylum. Like the victims of gangs, sexual minorities are a relatively new group falling under the category PSG. As we discussed in Chapter 5, sexual minorities have been required to prove that they are gay and, until policies were recently changed, were sometimes told to return to their home countries and be more discreet to avoid persecution. The persecution of gang members and of sexual minorities are both cases in which governments have failed to protect individuals from harm. To some extent, in the public discourse, people are more sympathetic to the people fleeing gang membership than to the sexual minorities, though attitudes toward sexual minorities are changing in the West. Both kinds of persecution are part of the ongoing dialogue of who is deserving of the protection asylum affords, and both are evidence of the larger institutional frameworks that motivate forms of surveillance and suspicions of deception.

As part of larger public discourses about human-rights obligations toward people displaced by war, violence, and persecution, suspicion is attached not only to individual cases but also to the question of whether people will bring unrest with them, and whether they will be a burden on the receiving countries and to humanitarianism more generally. As far as we are able determine, the 1951 Convention, on which current asylum law is still based, did not consider possible refugees to be a threat to the receiving country, even though, as we discussed, World War II refugees were accused of possibly being spies. Suspicion that is driven by the undifferentiated categories of victim, imposter, or possible threat is the most difficult to address.

THE PROBLEM WITH DOCUMENTS: STAYING ONE STEP AHEAD OF THE FORGERS

At its inception, asylum law did not require documentary evidence (and legally still does not), but in practice, it is difficult to get asylum without it. As John Torpey observed, the use of identity documents itself suggests that authorities are suspicious that people are not who they say they are (2000: 166). Andreas Fahrmeir discusses how the introduction of the passport paved the way for fraudulent manipulation of identity documents (2001: 230). Not only individuals, but also countries are evaluated as legitimate or corrupt based on the perception of their management of identity documents. In the asylum process, where ascertaining identity is central, the combined industries of producing fraudulent documents and developing technologies for detecting them go hand in hand.

All identity documents have complex political histories, and although birth certificates and passports are regarded as legal proof of identity in the West, we know that they circulate differently in other places, and that, for example, their legitimate use depends on the literacy skills of the population that uses them (2016). As we discussed in Chapter 3, forged passports are relatively easy to obtain. According to a US Homeland Security Intelligence Report, for example, ISIS likely acquired Syrian machines for creating legitimate passports (Varandani 2015). Although the use of fake passports among asylum seekers is well-documented and once was easily explained by the fact that refugees have difficulty obtaining passports and/or may have had to discard them as a measure of safety, today fake passports are marks of deception, and deception is regarded differently.

Although immigration agents at national borders demand to see documents, political asylum applicants continue to arrive without them. That is not to say that asylum cases aren't well-documented. As we discussed in Chapter 3, the production of fraudulent identity documents has accompanied the production of legitimate identity documents from the beginning. Further, forgeries need to be understood within the larger context of the production of fraudulent documents in other realms, especially finance. Beatrice Hibou writes, "Forged documents and forgeries of all descriptions are, so to speak, common currency. In recent years the explosion of forged documents has been staggering" (1999: 107). Further, in an essay on the use of various sorts of deception in Africa, she writes, "False documents are a Nigerian specialty, although forgeries are to be found throughout Africa, in such quantity that banks will no longer accept property title deeds as loan guarantees, while European immigration services routinely suspect African passports of being forged, including (or perhaps especially) diplomatic passports" (ibid.). Although discoveries of forgeries are newsworthy, they are not necessarily new.

In the film *Well-founded Fear*, an immigration officer points to stacks of paper supporting the case of a Chinese asylum applicant and says that, in general, mounds of supporting evidence, from human-rights organizations and other sources, make a case more convincing. In *Rejecting Refugees*, we discussed the asylum cases of individuals who had extensive paperwork to support their cases and individuals with little or no supporting evidence. Although we agree that supporting evidence can be helpful, it is not necessarily sufficient.

An asylum seeker's credibility is not the same as the question of whether the case is legitimate. Many asylum seekers use fake passports because they cannot get legitimate ones, for various reasons; a legitimate Syrian asylum seeker, for example, may use a fake Syrian passport simply because acquiring an actual passport is so difficult. As Ewa Moncure, a spokeswoman for Frontex, reported in an interview, "Most fraudulent Syrian passports are used by Syrians for the variety of reasons. They are not able or not able (sic) to obtain true Syrian passports, so they are using fraudulent passports. But then when their identity if verified, it's clear that they are citizens of Syria" (Siegel 2015).

The Vetting Process

In recent years, with increasing anxiety about terrorism, the stakes have changed in assessing the legitimacy of asylum applications. The question of whether applicants have been properly vetted to exclude possible terrorists is different than the question of whether someone is credible as an asylum seeker fearing return. Responding to concern about a lack of scrutiny of asylum cases, in a National Press Club in 2014, Michael Knowles describes the scrutiny given to asylum cases:

> We give very, very intensive scrutiny to each case. I think I would like to say we're probably one of the most rigorous vetting processes in the entire Immigration Service. And indeed, looking at our consular services abroad, we have an individualized personal interview with each applicant that lasts anywhere from an hour, or in cases of people like Michael Knowles maybe two or three hours. I personally checked, you know, eight to 10 different national criminal and security databases. They get fingerprinted, photographed, registered into the law enforcement and immigration system, which is also a significant side benefit of the asylum program where people are coming out of the shadows and getting registered into the system.
>
> And then I have to do a personalized written assessment of their claim, assessing their credibility, looking at the country conditions, applying the applicable law and making a very difficult decision, very subjective. There is

a lot of fraud. There's a lot of fraud in all immigration programs, and I think Mr. Cadman articulated many of the – you know, the potential pitfalls. But we – you know, I just have to speak again as an individual and for my colleagues. We take fraud very seriously. In fact, under our new performance work plans that were just issued, we were told that 60 percent of the weight of my performance review was going to be how well I did on fraud detection and national security.

In my own asylum office, where we fluctuate between 30 to 40 officers in this office that's responsible for the mid-Atlantic states, four of us are dedicated fraud detection and national security officers. That's all they do, those four officers. And we are constantly flagging not only individual cases but bringing to their attention some of the patterns so that they can not only help us adjudicate the cases but feed that information back into what I think is a pretty robust fraud detection and national security unit, notwithstanding all of the challenges that Dan very carefully articulated. (Griffith 2014: np)

As Gary Trudeau's cartoon illustrates, the asylum process includes extensive scrutiny. The misplaced anxiety about asylum as a means of entry for terrorists is probably best understood as a different anxiety, based on the tension between protecting refugees and protecting borders, but motivated more by propaganda than by evidence.

Toward More Accurate Outcomes

Narrative remains the cornerstone of political asylum cases, and although immigration officials might increasingly require identity documents and most probably will increasingly rely on technologies that provide supplementary information to confirm or question a case, assessments will continue to rely on the personal accounts applicants provide to substantiate their fear of returning to their homelands. The analysis of applicants' narratives is most often superficial, attending to discrepancies in minor details or refusing to accept what appear to the immigration officials to be implausible logics. A more careful narrative analysis would understand the difference between background details (including the failure to provide them), the difficulty of retelling traumatic events, and the ways that narrative is shaped (and usually altered) by question/answer formats in the context of a hearing.

Cellular phones present a new terrain for political asylum assessments, as we have seen in Chapter 4. In some cases, cell phones can replace the missing documents and provide proof of where an applicant has been and who they have associated with (Toor 2017). However, just as applicants sometimes deliberately discard documents, whether to provide anonymity for an escape or to change their identity, they also discard cell phones, a practice that has become even more prevalent as awareness grows that cell phones are often confiscated at the border as part of identity checks.

The use of new technologies, especially language assessments, must take into account the complexity of dialect and language use as a means of determining country of origin. For decades, linguists and anthropologists have demonstrated that nationality does not correlate with language use. Similarly, although images on Google Earth can be helpful, they do not provide definitive information. For the most part, new technologies have been used as short cuts, as means of quickly confirming or disproving information in an application, but often, the situations applicants are fleeing are complex and changing, not yielding easy answers. The more we understand the limits of the technologies available, including their limitations, the more useful they will be in producing more accurate outcomes.

Upon Reflection: The Deception Becomes Heroic

Political asylum is a response to persecution and state violence. As part of other responses to war, genocide, and state violence, including reconciliation, political asylum was designed as a remedy for people displaced by violence. Current discourse, especially following the war in Syria, includes not only how to properly vet applicants to determine their legitimacy but also how to limit the number of people who are accepted. To some extent, assessments of deception, even strategic deception (however minor) used to survive, are a rationale for denying asylum applications. The new intensified fear of terrorism places additional burdens on applicants.

We write at a time when some immigration courts have been described as "asylum free zones," where "asylum seekers are systematically denied protection," regardless of the dangers they're fleeing. According to David Baluarte, professor of law at Washington and Lee University, and director of Immigrant Rights Clinic, the judges' actions in these asylum-free zones are not just an abrogation of our country's moral duty to take in those fleeing for their lives—they also constitute a "violation of international human-rights obligations" (Washington 2017).

Deception is not always viewed negatively. People who forged documents to save victims of the Holocaust are now considered heroes. Of course, history is now on their side, but in any case, their heroism does not translate to the contemporary situation in which deception, especially the forgery of documents, is an affront to government. With enough passage of time and changes in attitudes, however, deception can be and has been understood as a strategy for survival and is not only accepted but also praised as courageous.

The greatest challenge faced by the political asylum process is to recognize the ideological discourses that shape it and that constitute the difficult relationship between protection of refugees and protection of borders.[2] The more the system is seen as reliable and comprehensive, the greater the trust in its ability to differentiate between fraudulent and legitimate asylum seekers. Greater use of technologies might enhance perception of the system's reliability, but when the reliance on technology is a response to the culture of suspicion, based on rumor and supposition, rather than evidence, it can be deployed carelessly and lead to inaccurate assessments. In an anonymously published essay, a recently retired immigration official in the UK described the inadequate staffing, the high public service ethos of most of the people working in the Home Office, the high rate of burnout, and the challenges in trying to assess an applicant's credibility. The author says, "At the Home Office we're moulded to be sceptical and work to unrealistic targets" (Anonymous 2017). The essay ends, "If we don't start taking this seriously...the people who suffer most will be those who have turned to us for help in their darkest hour" (Anonymous 2017). Our research leads us to the conclusion that systemic suspicion and skepticism can get in the way of careful, legitimate, and accurate assessments of individual applicants. The question is, to what extent is suspicion and skepticism motivated by the desire to identify deception, and to what extent is it motivated by a system that values protection of borders over protection of those fleeing persecution?

Notes

1. Amar Sebastian, et al. "Seeking Asylum from Gang-Based Violence in Central America: A Resource Manual." 2007. p. 8 http://www.unhcr.org/uk/585a96a34.pdf
2. Societal and political context is concerned with preventing irregular immigration and ensuring that the asylum system is not abused by persons fabri-

cating evidence. Some determining authorities are located in government departments that have the objective to prevent irregular immigration. This may influence the mind-set of decision makers and make it more challenging to implement an institutional culture in asylum procedures that is adequately human rights- and protection-oriented.

BIBLIOGRAPHY

Affidavit of Chan Aye (2005). May 3.

Affidavit of Dieudionne (2004). July 10.

Age Assessment Practice in Europe. (2013). EASO (European Asylum Support Office) December.

Ahluwalia, Navtej. (2005). Personal Interview, London, November 25.

Ahluwalia, Navtej. (2008). Personal Interview, London, October 8.

Ahmed, Beenish. (2015). "America Turned Away Refugees Because Some Were Feared to Be Nazi Agents." *Think Progress*, November 19. https://thinkprogress.org/america-turned-away-jewish-refugees-because-some-were-feared-to-be-nazi-agents-b3f3524b182d#.1vufe2b3j

Ajana, Btihaj. (2013). "Asylum, Identity Management and Biometric Control." *Journal of Refugee Studies* 26(4): 576–595.

Alpes, Maybritt Jill. (2015). "Airport Casualties: Non-Admission and Return Risks at Times of Internalized/Externalized Border Controls." *Social Science* 4(3): 742–757.

Amery, J. (1980). *At the Mind's Limits. Contemplations by a Survivor on Auschwitz and Its Realities*. Bloomington, IN: Indiana University Press.

Amicus Invitation (Material Support Bar). (2016). http://go.usa.gov/x9nvb

Amnesty International. (2016). "Refugees Welcome Index Shows Government Refugee Policies Out of Touch with Public Opinion." https://www.amnesty.org/en/latest/news/2016/05/refugees-welcome-index-shows-government-refugee-policies-out-of-touch/

Anonymous. (2017). "I Worry Asylum Caseworkers Are Failing People in Their Darkest Hour." *The Guardian*, April 8. https://www.theguardian.com/public-leaders-network/2017/apr/08/asylum-caseworkers-home-office-cuts-syria-war

© The Author(s) 2018   171
C. Bohmer, A. Shuman, *Political Asylum Deceptions*,
https://doi.org/10.1007/978-3-319-67404-9

APA. (2004). "The Truth About Lie Detectors (aka Polygraph Tests)." *American Psychology Association*, August 5. http://www.apa.org/research/action/polygraph.aspx. Accessed January 5, 2017.

Asencio, Karen Mercado. (2012). "The Under-Registration of Births in Mexico: Consequences for Children, Adults, and Migrants." *Migration Information Source, Migration Policy Institute*, April 12. http://www.migrationpolicy.org/article/under-registration-births-mexico-consequences-children-adults-and-migrants

Asylum Aid. (1999). "Still No Reason at All: Home Office Decisions on Asylum Claims." *Asylum Aid*, May. http://www.asylumaid.org.uk/wp-content/uploads/2013/02/Still_No_Reason_At_All.pdf

Bachmann, Chaka L. (2016). *No Safe Refuge: Experiences of LGBT Asylum Seekers in Detention*. London: UK Lesbian and Gay Immigration Group.

Baker, Mona. (2006). *Translation and Conflict: A Narrative Account*. New York: Routledge.

BBC Today. (2013). "Asylum Seeker: 'I Had to Prove I'm Gay'." *BBC Radio 4 Today*. BBC Programme. Broadcast February 13.

Becker, Andrew and Patrick J. McDonnell. (2017). "Mexico's Drug War Creates New Class of Refugees." *Los Angeles Times*, May 15. http://www.latimes.com/world/mexico-americas/la-na-asylum4-2009mar04-story.html

Beneduce, Roberto. (2015). "The Moral Economy of Lying: Subjectcraft, Narrative Capital, and Uncertainty in the Politics of Asylum." *Medical Anthropology* 34(6): 551–571.

Benjamin, Ilil. (2015). "Mixed Migration and the Humanitarian Encounter: Legal Aid for Sudanese and Eritrean Asylum Seekers in Israel." Paper presented at Political Asylum and the Politics of Suspicion Symposium, The Ohio State University, March 23.

Bennett, Claire and Felicity Thomas. (2013). "Seeking Asylum in the UK: Lesbian Perspectives." *Forced Migration Review* 42: 25–28.

Benotman, Noman and Nikita Malik. (2016). *The Children of Islamic State*. London, UK: Quilliam Foundation.

Berg, Laurie and Jenni Millbank. (2009). "Constructing the Personal Narratives of Lesbian, Gay and Bisexual Asylum Claimants." *Journal of Refugee Studies* 22(2): 195–223.

Berger, Daniel. (2016). Personal Communication, August 12.

Berger, Daniel. (2015). Personal Email, December 30.

Betts, Alexander. (2013). *Survival Migration: Failed Governance and the Crisis of Displacement*. Ithaca and London: Cornell University Press.

Berger, Iris, Tricia Redeker Hepner, Benjamin N. Lawrance, Joanna Tague, and Meredith Terretta, eds. (2015). *African Asylum at a Crossroads: Activism, Expert Testimony, and Refugee Rights*. Athens, OH: Ohio University Press.

Bianchini, Katia. (2016). Personal Interview, May 19.

Biometrics in Large Scale IT. (2015). *European Agency for the Operational Management of Large-Scale IT Systems in the Area of Freedom, Security and*

Justice   (eu-LISA).   http://www.eulisa.europa.eu/Publications/Reports/
Biometrics%20in%20Large-Scale%20IT.pdf

Blitz, Brad. (2017). "Another Story: What Public Opinion Data Tell Us About Refugee and Humanitarian Policy." *Journal on Migration and Human Security JMHS* 5(2): 379–400.

Blommaert, Jan. (2001). "Investigating Narrative Inequality: African Asylum Seekers' Stories in Belgium." *Discourse & Society* 12(4): 413–449.

Boakaye-Yiadom, Nana and Dionne Searcey. (2017). "Britain Accuses Ghana Lawmakers of Visa Fraud." *New York Times*, April 27. https://www.nytimes.com/2017/04/27/world/africa/ghana-visa-fraud-parliament.html?_r=1

Bohmer, Carol and Amy Shuman. (2007). *Rejecting Refugees: Political Asylum in the 21st Century*. New York: Routledge.

Bohmer, Carol and Amy Shuman. (2010). "Contradictory Discourses of Protection and Control in Transnational Asylum Law." *Journal of Legal Anthropology* 1(2): 212–229.

Bohmer, Carol and Amy Shuman. (2013, August). "Narrating Atrocity: Obstacles to Proving Credibility in Asylum Claims," *Refugee Law Initiative Working Paper Series*. No. 7.

Bohmer, Carol and Amy Shuman. (2015). "Cultural Silences As an Excuse for Injustice: The Problems of Documentary Proof." In Iris Berger, Tricia Redeker Hepner, Benjamin N. Lawrance, Joanna Tague, and Meredith Terretta (eds.), *African Asylum at a Crossroads: Activism, Expert Testimony, and Refugee Rights*. Athens, OH: Ohio University Press, 41–162.

Bremond, Claude. (1980). "The Logic of Narrative Possibilities," trans. Elaine D. Cancalon. *New Literary History* 11: 387–411.

British Dental Association. (2015). "X-Rays for Young Asylum Seekers: Inaccurate and Unethical." November 23. https://www.bda.org/news-centre/latest-news-articles/Pages/Xrays-for-young-asylum-seekers-inaccurate-and-unethical.aspx

Cabot, Heath. (2012). "The Governance of Things: Documenting Limbo in the Greek Asylum Procedure." *PoLAR: Political and Legal Anthropology Review* 35(1): 11–29.

Cabot, J. Anna. (2014). "Problems Faced by Mexican Asylum Seekers in the United States." *Journal on Migration and Human Security* 2(4): 361–377.

Calabresi, G. and P. Bobbit (1978). *Tragic Choices. The Conflicts Society Confronts in the Allocation of Tragically Scarce Resources*. New York: Norton.

Campbell, John. (2013). "Language Analysis in the United Kingdom's Refugee Status Determination System: Seeing Through Policy Claims About 'Expert Knowledge'." *Ethnic and Racial Studies* 36(4): 670–690.

Campbell, John. (2017). *Bureaucracy, Law and Dystopia in the United Kingdom's Asylum System*. London: Routledge.

Carney, Jordain. (2015). "GOPer: Subject Refugees to Lie Detector Tests." *Agora Dialogue*. http://agora-dialogue.com/2015/12/30/goper-subject-refugees-to-lie-detector-tests/

Centre for Forensic Neuroscience. (2016). http://forensic-centre.com/polygraph-testing/. Accessed June 8.

Chang, Cindy and Kate Linthicum. (2013). "U.S. Seeing a Surge in Central American Asylum Seekers." *Los Angeles Times*, December 15. http://articles.latimes.com/2013/dec/15/local/la-me-ff-asylum-20131215

Chappell, Bill. (2017). "Bogus 'Bowling Green Massacre' Claim Snarls Trump Adviser Conway." February 3. http://www.npr.org/sections/thetwo-way/2017/02/03/513222852/bogus-bowling-green-massacre-claim-snarls-trump-adviser-conway

Chelvan, S. (2014). "C-148/13, C-149/13 and C-150/13, A, B and C v Staatssecretaris van Veiligheid en Justitie: Stop Filming and Start Listening—A Judicial Black List for Gay Asylum Claims." *European Law Blog*. http://europeanlawblog.eu/?p=2622

Chicago Tribune. (2015). "Judge: Croatian Woman Can Be Extradited on War Crime Charges." *Tribune Wire Reports*, July 10.

Cianciarulo, Marisa Silenzi. (2006). "Terrorism and Asylum Seekers: Why the Real ID Act Is a False Promise." *Harvard Journal on Legislation* 43(1): 101–143.

Conference on Plenipotentiaries on the Status of Refugees and Stateless Persons, Summary Record of the Twenty-Third Meeting, U.N. Doc. A/CONF.2/SR.23. (1951).

Conlan, Sue, Sharon Waters, and Kajsa Berg. (2012). "Difficult to Believe: The Assessment of Asylum Claims in Ireland." *Irish Refugee Council*.

Consolidated Appropriations Act, 2008, Pub. L. No. 110-161, § 691, 121 Stat. 1844. (2007).

Coram Children's Legal Centre. (2013). *Happy Birthday: Disputing the Age of Children in the Immigration System*. London.

Corbaci, Christina. (2016). Personal Email Communication, August 22.

Coutin, S.B. (2001). "The Oppressed, the Suspect, and the Citizen. Subjectivity in Competing Accounts of Political Violence." *Law and Social Inquiry* 26(1): 63–94.

Coutin, Susan Bibler. (2003). *Legalizing Moves: Salvadoran Immigrants' Struggle for US Residency*. University of Michigan Press.

CUFI (Christians United for Israel). (2016). "Belgian Minister Compares Hidden Terrorists to Jews During Holocaust." April 15. http://www.cufi.org.uk/news/belgian-minister-compares-hidden-terrorists-to-jews-during-holocaust/

Daily Telegraph. (2014). "Review Ordered into Questioning Over-Intrusive Questioning of Gay Asylum Seekers." March 28.

Daniel, V. and J. Knudsen, eds. (1995). *Mistrusting Refugees*. Berkeley: University of California Press.

Dawson, Jasmine. (2016a). "Protection Struggles: Australia's Approach to LGBTIQ Asylum Seekers and Refugees." *Asylum Insight: Fact and Analysis*, November. http://www.asyluminsight.com/jasmine-dawson#.WIHcY_P4Paa

Dawson, Jasmine. (2016b). "Is Australia Breaching Human Rights in the Way It Assesses Claims for Asylum Based on Sexual Orientation or Gender Identity?" *Australian Journal of Administrative Law* 23(2): 71–75.

Dernbach, Andrea. (2015; updated 2016). Translated by Erika Korner. "Eurodac Fingerprint Database Under fire by Human Rights Activists." *Der Taggespiegel*, July 15. http://www.euractiv.com/section/justice-home-affairs/news/eurodac-fingerprint-database-under-fire-by-human-rights-activists/

Des Forges, Alison Liebhafsky. (1999). "Human Rights Watch, and International Federation of Human Rights." *Leave None to Tell the Story: Genocide in Rwanda* 3169(189). New York: Human Rights Watch.

Dolnick, Sam. (2011). "Immigrants May Be Fed False Stories to Bolster Asylum Pleas." *New York Times*, July 11. http://www.nytimes.com/2011/07/12/nyregion/immigrants-may-be-fed-false-stories-to-bolster-asylum-pleas.html

Dolnick, Sam. (2012). "Immigrants May Be Fed False Stories to Bolster Asylum Pleas." *New York Times*, July 11.

Douglas, Walton. (2005). "Deceptive Arguments Containing Persuasive Language and Persuasive Definitions." *Argumentation* 19: 159–186.

Dove, Edward S. (2013). "Back to Blood: The Sociopolitics and Law of Compulsory DNA Testing of Refugees." *University of Massachusetts Law Review* 8: 466–530.

Driver, Rolf. (2011). "Asylum Claims Made in Bad Faith Under the Refugees Convention-The Australian Experience." *Refugee Survey Quarterly* 30(2): 96–109.

Druckerman, Pamela. (2016) "'If I Sleep for an Hour, 30 People Will Die.'" *New York Times Sunday Review*, October 2.

Dunt, Ian. (2016a). "Disaster for Theresa May as Legal Ruling Brings Student Deportations to a Halt." *Politics.co.uk*, March 23. http://www.politics.co.uk/blogs/2016/03/23/disaster-for-theresa-may-as-legal-ruling-brings-student-depo?utm_source=Editorial+newsletter&utm_campaign=74e6aff1ca-Newsletter_March_233_23_2016&utm_medium=email&utm_term=0_cb6d3a8c9c-74e6aff1ca-184935381&mc_cid=74e6aff1ca&mc_eid=dc9b93464b

Dunt, Ian. (2016b). "May's Student Deportation Programme in Tatters as Legal Appeal Falls Apart." *Politics.co.uk.* http://www.politics.co.uk/news/2016/10/25/may-s-student-deportation-programme-in-tatters-as-legal-appe

Dzubow, Jason. (2015). "Asylum Case Delayed Forever? Here Are Some Possible Reasons." *The Asylumist* Blog, October 20. http://www.asylumist.com/2015/10/20/asylum-case-delayed-forever-here-are-some-possible-reasons/

Dzubow, Jason. (2017). "An Open Letter to My Friends at DHS and DOJ." *Green Card, Published by the Immigration Law Section of the Federal Bar Association.* Spring.

Eastomond, Marita. (2007). "Stories As Lived Experience: Narratives in Forced Migration Research." *Journal of Refugee Studies* 20(2): 248–264.

Eddy, Melissa. (2017). "German Soldier Posed As Syrian Refugee to Plan Attack, Officials Say." *New York Times*, April 27.

Einhorn, Bruce. (2009). "Consistency, Credibility, and Culture." In Jaya Ramji-Nogaes, Andrew I. Schoenholtz, and Philip G. Schrag (eds.), *Refugee Roulette: Disparities in Asylum Adjudication and Proposals for Reform*. New York: New York University Press. 187–201.

Ekman, Paul and Wallace V. Friesen. (2003). *Unmasking the Face: A Guide to Recognizing Emotions from Facial Clues*. Los Gatos, CA: Ishk/Malor Books.

Ekman, Paul, Maureen O'Sullivan and Mark G. Frank. (1999). "A Few Can Catch a Liar." *Psychological Science* 10(3): 263–266.

Ellison, Jesse. (2011). "Why the DSK Maid Lied." *The Daily Beast*. http://www.thedailybeast.com/articles/2011/07/07/dominique-strauss-kahn-accuser-why-lying-on-asylum-filing-doesn-t-mean-she-s-a-liar.html

Emanuel, Gabrielle. (2016). "A Friendly Café Owner in Michigan...or A Militant from Turkey." *National Public Radio*, March 11. http://www.npr.org/sections/parallels/2016/03/11/468732559/a-friendly-cafe-owner-in-michigan-or-a-militant-from-turkey

Erlinder, C. Peter. (2008). "When 'Fear of Persecution ...' Requires Deportation: 'Catch-22' False-Document Prosecutions After a Grant of Asylum." *William Mitchell Law Review* 35(1): 226–246.

Fahrmeir, Andreas. (2001). "Governments and Forgers: Passports in Nineteenth Century Europe." In Jane Caplan and John Torpey (eds.), *Documenting Individual Identity: The Development of State Practices in the Modern World*. Princeton: Princeton University Press, 218–234.

"Failing The Grade: Home Office Initial Decisions on Lesbian and Gay Claims for Asylum." (2010). *UK Lesbian and Gay Immigration Group (UKLGIG)*. http://www.uklgig.org.uk/docs/Failing%20the%20Grade%20UKLGIG%20April%202010.pdf

Faiola, Anthony and Souad Mekhennet. (2016). "Tracing the Path of Four Terrorists to Europe by the Islamic State." *Washington Post*, April 22. www.washingtonpost.com/world/national-security/how-europes-migrant-crisis-became-an-opportunity-for-isis/2016/04/21/ec8a7231-062d-4185-bb27-cc7295d35415_story.html?utm_term=.284590e2c2d5

Fantz, Ashley and Ben Brumfield. (2015). "More than Half the Nation's Governors Say Syrian Refugees Not Welcome." *CNN*, November 19. http://edition.cnn.com/2015/11/16/world/paris-attacks-syrian-refugees-backlash/

Fassin, Didier. (2013). "The Precarious Truth of Asylum." *Public Culture* 25(1): 39–63.

Fassin, D. and E. d'Halluin (2005). The Truth from the Body. Medical Certificates As Ultimate Evidence for Asylum Seekers. *American Anthropologist* 107(4): 597–608.

Fazel, Mina, Jeremy Wheeler, and John Danesh. (2005). "Prevalence of Serious Mental Disorder in 7000 Refugees Resettled in Western Countries: A Systematic Review." *Lancet* 365: 1309–1314.

Feal, Sophie. (2016). Personal Interview, August 23.

Fernandez, Manny. (2015). "Immigrants Fight Texas' Birth Certificate Rules." *New York Times*, September 17.

Foucault, Michel. (1977). *Discipline and Punish: The Birth of the Prison*. Trans. A. Sheridan. New York: Vintage.

Foucault, Michel. Governmentality. In Graham Burchell, Colin Gordon, and Peter Miller (eds.), *The Foucault Effect: Studies in Governmentality*. Chicago: University of Chicago Press. Security, Territory, Population: Lecturesatthe Collègede France 1977–1978. 87–105. Trans. Graham Burchell. New York: Picador.

Foucault, Michel. (2012). *The Archaeology of Knowledge:* Trans. A. Sheridan Smith. New York: Pantheon Books (1972).

Fraser, Helen. (2009). "The Role of Educated Native Speakers in Providing Language Analysis for the Determination of the Origin of Asylum Seekers." *International Journal of Speech, Language and the Law* 16(1): 113–138.

Free Movement. (2009). "Albanian/Kosovar Deprived of British Citizenship by Presenting Officer." October 5. https://www.freemovement.org.uk/albaniankosovar-deprived-of-british-citizenship-by-presenting-officer/

Friedman, Max Paul. (2003). *Nazis and Good Neighbors: The United States Campaign Against the Germans of Latin America in World War II*. Cambridge University Press.

Gallagher, Anna Marie and Shane Dizon. (2010). 2 Immigration Law Service. § 10:138 (2d ed. West).

Gay, Malcolm. (2011). "Dark Past in Balkan War Intrudes on New Life." *New York Times*, April 3.

Gessen, Masha. (2017). "Don't Fight Their Lies With of Your Own." *New York Times*, March 25. https://www.nytimes.com/2017/03/25/opinion/sunday/dont-fight-their-lies-with-lies-of-your-own.html

Gilbert, Geoff. (2003). "Current Issues in the Application of the Exclusion Clauses." In E. Feller, V. Turk, and F. Nicholson (eds.), *Refugee Protection in International Law*. Cambridge, 429–432, at: http://www.unhcr.org/refworld/docid/470a33bc0.html

Gilbert, Geoff. (2017). *Email on Migration Law*. January 19. MIGRATIONLAW@jiscmail.ac.uk

Goldman, Francisco. (2016). "Escape to New York." *The New Yorker*, August 9. http://www.newyorker.com/news/news-desk/escape-to-new-york

Goldstein, Joseph and Kirk Semple. (2012) "Law Firm Are Accused of Aiding Chinese Immigrants' False Asylum Claims." *New York Times*, December 18.

Goodman, Sarah R. (2013). "Asking for Too Much: The Role of Corroborating Evidence in Asylum Proceedings in the United States and United Kingdom." *Fordham Int'l LJ* 36: 1733.

Goodwin-Gill, Guy and Jane McAdam. (2007) *The Refugee in International Law* (3rd Edition). Oxford: Clarendon.

Gordillo, Gaston. (2006). "The Crucible of Citizenship: I.D. Paper Fetishism in the Argentinean Chaco." *American Ethnologist* 33(2): 162–176.

Gov.uk. (2014). Language Analysis, Report. August 13. *AI_Public_v19.pdf.*

Grahl-Madsen, Atle. (1966). *The Status of Refugees in International Law:* Volume 1.

Granhag, Pär Anders, Leif A. Strömwall, and Maria Hartwig. (2005). "Granting Asylum or Not? Migration Board Personnel's Beliefs About Deception." *Journal of Ethnic and Migration Studies* 31(1): 29–50.

Gray, Richard. (2011). "Lies, Liars and Lie Detection." *Federal Probation* 75(3 December): 31–36.

Green, Chris. (2014). "Home Office Quietly Ditches Swedish Firm Contracted to Process Asylum-Seekers." *The Independent,* November 14. http://www.independent.co.uk/news/uk/politics/home-office-quietly-ditches-swedish-firm-contracted-to-process-asylum-seekers-9862182.html

Greenberg, Richard, Adam Ciralsky, and Stone Phillips. (2007). "Enemies at the Gate." *NBC News,* December 28. http//www.nbcnews.com/id/22419963/ns/dateline_nbc-international/#.Ux4275HS_k

Griffith, Bryan, et al. (2014). "Panel Video: A Generous Asylum System Riddled with Fraud." *Center for Immigration Studies.* http://cis.org/Videos/Asylum-Panel-043014

Griffiths, Melanie. (2012). "Vile Liars, and Truth Distorters: Truth, Trust and the Asylum System." *Anthropology Today* 28(5): 8–12.

Griswold, Eliza. (2016). "Why Is It So Difficult for Syrian Refugees to Get into the U.S.?" *New York Times,* January 20. http://www.nytimes.com/2016/01/24/magazine/why-is-it-so-difficult-for-syrian-refugees-to-get-into-the-us.html?action=click&pgtype=Homepage&version=Moth-Visible&moduleDetail=inside-nyt-region-5&module=inside-nyt-region&region=inside-nyt-region&WT.nav=inside-nyt-region

Hallowell, Nina, et al. (2003). "Balancing Autonomy and Responsibility: The Ethics of Generating and Disclosing Genetic Information." *Journal of Medical Ethics* 29(2): 74–79.

Hartwig, M., P.A. Granhag, L.A. Stromwall, and A. Vrij. (2004). "'Police Officers' Lie Detection Accuracy: Interrogating Freely Versus Observing Video." *Police Quarterly* 7(4): 429–456.

Hathaway, James C. and Michelle Foster. (2014). *The Law of Refugee Status.* Cambridge: Cambridge University Press.

Hathaway, James C. (1990). "A Reconsideration of the Underlying Premise of Refugee Law." *Harvard International Law Journal* 31(1): 129–147.

Hauser, Christine. (2016). "Donald Trump Jr. Compares Syrian Refugees to Skittles That 'Would Kill You'." *New York Times,* September 20.

Haviland, John. "'A Politics of Protection' Aimed at Tzotzil (Mayan) Migrants in the US." In Bridget Haas and Amy Shuman (eds.), *Technologies of Suspicion and the Ethics of Obligation in Political Asylum,* forthcoming.

Helen, Ilpo and Anna-Maria Tapaninen. (2013). "Closer to the Truth: DNA Profiling for Family Reunification and the Rationales of Immigration Policy in Finland." *Nordic Journal of Migration Research* 3(3): 153–161.

Helton, Arthur C. (1983). "Persecution on Account of Membership in a Social Group As a Basis for Refugee Status." *Columbia Human Rights Law Review* 15: 39–67

Henderson, Mark and Alison Pickup. (2012). *Analysing the Refusal Letter: Best Practice Guide to Asylum and Human Rights Appeals.* Electronic Immigration Network.

Herlihy, J. and S. Turner (2006). "Should Discrepant Accounts Given by Asylum Seekers be Taken As Proof of Deceit?" *Torture* 16(2): 81–92.

Herlihy, Jane, Laura Jobson, and Stuart Turner. (2012). "Just Tell Us What Happened to You: Autobiographical Memory and Seeking Asylum." *Applied Cognitive Psychology* 26(5): 661–676.

Herman, David. (2004). *Story Logic: Problems and Possibilities of Narrative.* University of Nebraska Press.

Hibou, Beatrice. (1999). "The 'Social Capital' of the State As an Agent of Deception or the Ruses of Economic Intelligence." In Jean-Francois Bayart, Stephen Ellis, and Beatrice Hibou (eds.), *The Criminalization of the State in Africa.* Bloomington: Indiana University Press.

Homans, Charles. (2015). "The Boy on the Beach." September 3. www.nytimes.com/2015/09/03/magazine/the-boy-on-the-beach.html

Home Office Asylum Policy Instruction. (2015). "Sexual Identity Issues in the Asylum Claim." Version 5.0 11/02/15.

Home Office Asylum Policy Instructions. (2016). "Sexual Orientation in Asylum Claims" Version 6.0. August 3.

Human Rights First Report. (2006). "Abandoning the Persecuted: Victims of Terrorism and Oppression Barred from Asylum." *Human Rights First.* New York, NY.

Human Rights Watch. (2005). "Call for Action Against the Use of Diplomatic Assurances in Transfers to Risk of Torture and Ill-Treatment." http://hrw.org/english/docs/2005/05/12/eca10660_txt.htm. Accessed March 8, 2008.

Hutchings, Kate and David Weir. (2006). "Understanding Networking in China and the Arab World: Lessons for International Managers." *Journal of European Industrial Training* 30(4): 272–290.

Iacono, W.G. and D.T. Lykken. (1997). "The Validity of the Lie Detector: Two Surveys of Scientific Opinion." *Journal of Applied Psychology* 82(3), June: 426–433.

ITV News. (2013). "Asylum Seekers Pressured into 'Proving' Sexuality." October 11.

Jacobsen, Erin. (2016). Personal Interview, June 7.

Jacquemet, M. (2005). "Transidiomatic Practices: Language and Power in the Age of Globalization." *Language and Communication* 25: 257–277.

Jacquemet, M. (2016a). "TRANSIDIOMA." *Revista da Anpoll* 1(40): 19–32.

Jacquemet, M. (2016b). "Sociolinguistic Diversity and Asylum." *Tilburg Papers in Culture Studies* #171. https://www.tilburguniversity.edu/upload/044f1c13-9381-4d74-af3d-8813d9fa64f3_TPCS_171_Jacquemet.pdf

Johns, Leigh and Mirko Bagaric. (2002). "Bribery and Networking: Is There a Difference." *Deakin Law Review* 7(1): 159–171.

Johnson, Kevin R. (2007). *Opening the Floodgates: Why America Needs to Rethink Its Borders and Immigration Laws.* New York, NY: New York University Press.

Johnson, Toni A.M. (2011). "On Silence, Sexuality and Skeletons: Reconceptualizing Narrative in Asylum Hearings." *Social & Legal Studies* 20(1): 57–78.

Jordan, Miriam. (2017). "Los Angeles Raids Target Investor Green Card Fraud." *Los Angeles Times*, April 5. https://www.nytimes.com/2017/04/05/us/eb5-visa-investigation.html?hp&action=click&pgtype=Homepage&clickSource=story-heading&module=second-column-region&region=top-news&WT.nav=top-news&_r=0

Jubany, Olga. (2011). "Constructing Truths in a Culture of Disbelief Understanding Asylum Screening from Within." *International Sociology* 26(1): 74–94.

Juss, Satvinder Singh. (2012). "Terrorism and the Exclusion of Refugee Status in the UK." *Journal of Conflict and Security Law* 17: 465–499.

Kan, Paul Rexton. (2011). *Mexico's 'Narco-Refugees': The Looming Challenge for U.S. National Security.* U.S. Army War College Strategic Studies Institute. http://oai.dtic.mil/oai/oai?verb=getRecord&metadataPrefix=html&identifier=ADA552113

Kassindja, Fauziya. (1998). *Do They Hear You When You Cry?* New York, NY: Delta (published by Dell).

Kayihura, Edouard and Kerry Zukus. (2014). *Inside the Hotel Rwanda: The Surprising True Story … and Why It Matters Today* (BenBella).

Kelly, Tobias. (2012). "Sympathy and Suspicion: Torture, Asylum, and Humanity." *Journal of the Royal Anthropological Institute (N.S.)* 18: 753–768.

Kezwer, Gil. (1998). "Bone Scans Can Support Asylum Seekers' Claims of Torture." *Canadian Medical Association Journal* 59(10): 1237.

Kidane, Won. (2009–2010). "The Terrorism Bar to Asylum in Australia, Canada, the United Kingdom, and the United States: Transporting Best Practices."

Kludt, Megan. (2015) Personal Email Communication, December 1.

Knudsen, John Chr. (1995). "When Trust Is on Trial: Negotiating Refugee Narratives." In E. Valentine Daniel and John Chr. Knudsen (eds.), *Mistrusting Refugees.* Berkeley: University of California Press, 13–35.

Kolken, Matthew. (2016). Personal Interview, August 22.

Kurylo, Anastacia. (2013) "Stereotypes, the Cultural Defense and Genetic Mutilation." *The Communicated Stereotype Blog*, January 2.

Lakhani, Nina. (2016). "Mexico Tortures Migrants—and Citizens—In Effort to Slow Central American Surge." *The Guardian*, April 4.

Lewin, Tamar. (2015) "Conflict Between Turkey and Kurds Clouds the Life of a Michigan Cafe Owner." *New York Times*, December 23. www.nytimes.com/2015/12/24/us/conflict-in-turkey-follows-michigan-cafe-owner.html?_r=0

Lewis, Rachel A. (2013). "Deportable Subjects: Lesbians and Political Asylum." *Feminist Formations* 25(2): 174–194.

Lewis, Rachel A. (2014). "Gay? Prove It": The Politics of Queer Anti-Deportation Activism." *Sexualities* 17(8): 958–975.

Liberatore, Angela. (2007). "Balancing Security and Democracy, and the Role of Expertise: Biometrics Politics in the European Union." *European Journal on Criminal Policy and Research* 13(1–2): 109–137.

Lichtblau, Eric. (2015). "U.S. Seeks to Deport Bosnians over War Crimes." *New York Times*. https://www.nytimes.com/2015/03/01/world/us-seeks-to-deport-bosnians-over-war-crimes.html?_r=0

Lipman, Jennifer. (2012). "British Spy Who Saved German Jews Honoured." *The Jewish Chronicle*, July 12. https://www.thejc.com/news/uk-news/british-spy-frank-foley-who-saved-german-jews-honoured-1.34315

Loescher, Gil. (1993). *Beyond Charity: International Cooperation and the Global Refugee Crisis*. Oxford: Oxford University Press.

Longman, Timothy. (2001). "Identity Cards, Ethnic Self-Perception, and Genocide in Rwanda." In Jane Caplan and John Torpey (eds.), *Documenting Individual Identity: The Development of State Practices in the Modern World*. Princeton, NJ: Princeton University Press. 345–357.

MacIntyre, Jess. (2016a). Director of Reachout, Leeds, "Supporting LGBT Refugees and Asylum Seekers." *Training*, March 21.

MacIntyre, Jess. (2016b). Personal Email, August 3.

Macklin, Audrey. (2006). "The Truth About Credibility." *International Association for Study of Forced Migration*.

Macklin, Audrey. (1998). *Truth and Consequences: Credibility Determination in the Refugee Context*. International Association of Refugee Law Judges, 134–140.

Mahler, Jonathan, Ravi Somaiya, and Emily Steel. (2015). "With an Apology Brian Williams Digs Himself Deeper in Copter Tale." *New York Times*, February 5.

Mail Online. (2007). "Crackdown on Albanians Who Lied About Fleeing Kosovo War." June 15. http://www.dailymail.co.uk/news/article-462118/Crackdown-Albanians-lied-fleeing-Kosovo-war.html

Malkki, Liisa. (2007). "The Politics of Trauma and Asylum: Universals and Their Effects." *Ethos* 35(3): 336–343.

Margulies, Peter. (1993). "Difference and Distrust in Asylum Law: Haitian and Holocaust Refugee Narratives." *St. Thomas Law. Review* 6: 135–152.

Marks, Simon. (2014). "Somaly Mam: The Holy Saint (and Sinner) of Sex Trafficking." *Newsweek*, May 21, 2014. http://www.newsweek.com/2014/05/30/somaly-mam-holy-saint-and-sinner-sex-trafficking-251642.html

Marszalkowski, Michael. (2016). Personal Interview, August 24.

Martin, David A. (2005). "Adelaide Abankwah, Fauziya Kasinga, and the Dilemmas of Political Asylum." *University of Virginia Law School Public Law and Legal Theory Working Paper Series* 28. https://www.google.co.uk/search?q=Martin, +David+A.+(2005).+%E2%80%9CAdelaide+Abankwah,+Fauziya+Kasinga,+an d+the+Dilemmas+of+Political+Asylum.%E2%80%9D+University+of+Virginia+ Law+School+Public+Law+and+Legal+Theory+Working+Paper+Series+28.&ie =utf-8&oe=utf-8&gws_rd=cr&dcr=0&ei=q4H5WYSUM4PyaOD8j8AH

Maryns, K. (2006). *The Asylum Speaker: Language in the Belgian Asylum Procedure.* Manchester: St. Jerome

Maryns, Katrijn and Jan Blommaert. (2001). "Stylistic and Thematic Shifting As a Narrative Resource: Assessing Asylum Seekers' Repertoires." 61–84.

Massey, Hugh. (2010). "UNHCR and *de facto* Statelessness." *UNHCR Legal and Protection Policy Research Series.* http://www.refworld.org/pdfid/4bbf387d2. pdf. Accessed August 31, 2013.

Mauss, Marcel. (1954). *The Gift: Forms and Functions of Exchange in Archiac Societies.* Routledge.

McAdam, Jane. (2014). "Conceptualizing 'Crisis Migration': A Theoretical Perspective." In Susan F. Martin, Sanjula Weerasinghe, and Abbie Taylor (eds.), *Humanitarian Crises and Migration: Causes, Consequences and Responses.* London and New York: Routledge. 28–49.

McConnell, John. (2011). Letter from the New York District Attorney's Office Reprinted in the *New York Times,* July 1. http://www.nytimes.com/interac- tive/2011/07/01/nyregion/20110701-Strauss-Kahn-letter.html?hp&_ r=1&cFadden

McDougall, E. Ann. (2015). "'The Immigration People Know the Stories, There's One for Each Country': The Case of Mauritania." In Berger, et al. (eds.), *African Asylum at a Crossroads: Activism, Expert Testimony, and Refugee Rights.* Athens, OH: Ohio University Press. 121–140.

McFadden, Robert D. (2012). "John Demjanjuk, 91, Dogged by Charges of Atrocities as Nazi Camp Guard, Dies." *New York Times,* March 17. http:// www.nytimes.com/2012/03/18/world/europe/john-demjanjuk-nazi- guard-dies-at-91.html

McFadden, John. (2015). "Nicholas Winton, Rescuer of 669 Children from Holocaust Dies at 106." *New York Times,* July 1. http://www.nytimes. com/2015/07/02/world/europe/nicholas-winton-is-dead-at-106-saved- children-from-the-holocaust.html

McKie, R. (2009). 'Eureka Moment That Led to the Discovery of DNA Fingerprinting'. *The Observer,* May 24: 160.

McPhee, Michele. (2015). "The Monster Next Door." *Boston Magazine,* April. http://www.bostonmagazine.com/news/article/2015/03/24/rwandan- genocide/5/

McPhee, Michele and Brian Ross. (2015). "US Intel: ISIS May Have Passport Printing Machine, Blank Passports." *ABC News*, December 10. http://abc-news.go.com/International/us-intel-isis-passport-printing-machine-blank-passports/story?id=35700681

McVeigh, Karen. (2011). "Gay Asylum Claims Not Being Counted Despite Pledge, Admit Ministers." *The Guardian*, May 1. http://www.theguardian.com/uk/2011/may/01/gay-asylum-claims-not-being-counted

Meikle, James. (2012). "Border Agency Halts X-Ray Programme for Child Asylum Seekers." *Guardian*, April 27.

Menchú, R. (1984). *I Rigoberta Menchú: An Indian Woman in Guatemala.* (ed.) Elisabeth Burgos Debray; (Trans.) Ann Wright. London: Verso.

Merrill, Jamie. (2016). "Theresa May Faces Parliamentary Investigation over Flimsy Basis for Student Deportations." *The Independent*, March 23. http://www.independent.co.uk/news/uk/politics/theresa-may-faces-parliamentary-investigation-over-flimsy-basis-for-student-deportations-a6948796.html

Metha, Suketa. (2011). "The Asylum Seeker." *The New Yorker*, August 1: 32.

Migrantionsverket. (2015). "Record Number of Unaccompanied Minors Arrived in Sweden in June." 10 July. http://www.migrationsverket.se/English/About-the-Migration-Agency/News-archive/News-archive-2015/2015-07-10-Record-number-of-unaccompanied-minors-arrived-in-Sweden-in-June.html

Minzer, Max. (2007–2008). "Detecting Lies Using Demeanor, Bias and Context." *Cardozo Law Review* 29: 2557–2581.

Mitchell, Michele and Nick Louvel. (2015). *The Uncondemned* (film).

Modecki, Kathryn Lynn. (2008). "Addressing Gaps in the Maturity of Judgment Literature: Age Differences and Delinquency." *Law and Human Behavior* 32(1): 88.

Moncure, Ewa. (2015) Interview with Robert Siegel, NPR Radio. http://www.npr.org/2015/09/10/439246957/why-syrians-are-entering-europe-with-fake-passports

Montoya, Celeste. (2016). "Exploits and Exploitations: A Micro and Macro Analysis of the 'DSK Affair'." In Alicia A. Hozic and Jacqui True (eds.), *Scandalous Economics: Gender and the Politics of Financial Crisis.* Oxford University Press. 145–164.

Moore, Anne Elizabeth. (2014). "Here's Why It Matters When a Human Rights Crusader Builds Her Advocacy on Lies." *Salon*, May 28. http://www.salon.com/2014/05/28/heres_why_it_matters_when_a_human_rights_crusader_builds_her_advocacy_on_lies/

Moorehead, Caroline. (2005). *Human Cargo.* New York, NY: Henry Holt & Co.

Muir, Hugh. (2016). "As a Nation, Would We Ever Sink so Low As to Check Refugees' Teeth." *Guardian*, October 19.

Muller, Benjamin J. (2011). "Risking It All at the Biometric Border: Mobility, Limits, and the Persistence of Securitisation 1." *Geopolitics* 16(1): 91–106.

Murray, Dean E. (2000). "I.N.S Says Woman Used Fraud in a Bid for Asylum." *New York Times*, December 21.

Nagourney, Adam, Ian Lovett, and Richard Perez Pena. (2015). "San Bernardino Shooting Kills at Least 14; Two Suspects Are Dead." *New York Times*, December 2.

Naik, Sonali. (2016). Personal Interview, London, April 28.

Nesbit, Mark. (2016). Personal Interview, August 31, Columbus, OH.

Neuffer, Elizabeth. (2001). *The Key to My Neighbor's House: Seeking Justice in Bosnia and Rwanda*. New York, NY: Picador.

Neumayer, E. (2005). Bogus Refugees? The Determinants of Asylum Migration to Western Europe, *International Studies Quarterly* 49(3): 389–410.

Neumayer, E. (2006). "Unequal Access to Foreign Spaces: How States Use Visa Restrictions to Regulate Mobility in a Globalized World." *Transactions of the Institute of British Geographers* 31(1): 72–84.

New York Times. (2015). "Paris Attacks: The Violence, Its Victims and How the Investigation Unfolded." November 17. http://www.nytimes.com/live/paris-attacks-live-updates/syrian-passport-reportedly-was-stolen-or-fake

Note. (2010). "A Chance for Redemption; Revising the "Persecutor Bar" and "Material Support Bar" in the Case of Child Soldiers." *Vanderbilt Journal of Transnational Law* 43: 191–222.

Nowrasteh, Alex. (2016). "Terrorism and Immigration: A Risk Analysis." Policy Analysis No. 798. September 13. Cato Institute. www.cato.org/publications/policy-analysis/terrorism-immigration-risk-analysis#cite-11

O'Neill, William, Bonaventure Rutinwa, and Guglielmo Verdirame. (2000). "The Great Lakes: A Survey of the Application of the Exclusion Clauses in the Central African Republic and Tanzania." *International Refugee LJ* 12: 135–170.

OHCHR. (2004). *Professional Training Series No. 8/Rev.1. Manual on the Effective Investigation and Documentation of Torture and Other Cruel, Inhuman or Degrading Treatment or Punishment.* New York and Geneva: UNHCR.

Oltermann, Philip and Jon Henley (2016). "German Proposals Could See Refugees' Phones Searched by Police." *The Guardian*, August 11.

Osnos, Evan. (2015). "The Wasteful Case Against Ibrahim Parlak." *The New Yorker.* http://www.newyorker.com/news/news-desk/the-wasteful-case-against-ibrahim-parlak.

Ossa, Charles. (2003). *The Accra Daily Mail*, January 22.

Pardo, Italo. (2004). *Between Morality and the Law: Corruption, Anthropology and Comparative Society.* Ashgate Publishing.

Park, Rebekah and Janus Oomen. (2010). "Context, Evidence and Attitude: The Case for Photography in Medical Examinations of Asylum Seekers in the Netherlands." *Social Science & Medicine* 71: 228–235.

Passarlay, Gulwali and Homa Khaleeli. (2016). "When I Fled to the UK, No One Believed I Was 13. Ten Years on, Nothing's Changed." *The Guardian*, October 21.

Patrick, Peter L. (2016). "The Impact of Sociolinguistics on Refugee Status Determination." In Robert Lawson and Dave Sayers (eds.), *Sociolinguistic Research: Application and Impact*. Routledge.

Peel, M.R. (1996). "Effects on Asylum Seekers of Ill-Treatment in Zaire." *British Medical Journal* 312(3 February): 293–294.

Pesta, Abigail. (2014). "Somaly Mam's Story: 'I Didn't Lie." *Marie Claire*. http://www.marieclaire.com/culture/news/a6620/somalys-story/

Pogatchnik, Shawn. (2012). *Greek 'Language Test' Protester Wins Free Flights*. Associated Press, March 12.

Polese, Abel. (2008). "'If I Receive It, It Is a Gift; If I Demand It, then It Is a Bribe': On the Local Meaning of Economic Transactions in Post-Soviet Ukraine." *Anthropology in Action* 15(3): 47–60.

Portelli, Alessandro. (1991). *The Death of Luigi Trastulli and Other Stories: Form and Meaning in Oral History*. Binghamton, NY: Suny Press.

Preston, Julia (2016). "Lawsuit Forces Texas to Make It Easier for Immigrants to Get Birth Certificates for Children." *New York Times*, July 24.

Puhl, Jan. (2010). "'Erotic Lie Detector' Used on Gay Asylum Seekers." *ABC News*, December 16.

Ramji-Nogales, Jaya, Andrew I. Schoenholtz, and Philip G. Schrag. (2009). *Refugee Roulette: Disparities in Asylum Adjudication and Proposals for Reform*. New York: New York University Press.

Rankin, Jennifer. (2016). "EU Strikes Deal with Turkey to Send Back Refugees." *The Guardian*, March 18.

Refugee Council. (2016). "Home Office Policy on Age Assessment 'Unlawful'." http://www.refugeecouncil.org.uk/latest/news/4660_home_office_policy_on_age_assessment_unlawful?utm_source=Refugee%20Council&utm_medium=email&utm_campaign=7268024_Age%20Dispute%20Detention%20Success%20&utm_content=Age%20Dispute%20Success%20Link&dm_i=I6P,4BS1K,31R2HG,FUP2D,1

Reijven, Joke and Joris van Wijk. (2014). "Caught in Limbo: How Alleged Perpetrators of International Crimes Who Applied for Asylum in the Netherlands Are Affected by a Fundamental System Error in International Law." *International Journal of Refugee Law* 26(2): 1–24.

Reitano, Tuesday and Peter Tinti. (2015). "Survive and Advance: The Economics of Smuggling Refugees and Migrants into Europe." *Institute for Security Studies* ISS Paper 289.

Report of the Panel to Evaluate the U.S. Standard Certificates, National Center for Health Certificates, (2000, addenda 2001).

Right to Remain. (2017). "A History of Providing Sanctuary? LGBT+ Asylum Claims in the UK." February 28.

Riles, Annelise, ed. (2006) *Documents: Artifacts of Modern Knowledge*. Ann Arbor: University of Michigan Press.

Ring, Wilson. (2015). "Man in Bosnian War Crimes Case Gives Up Citizenship, Leaving." *Associated Press* in *New York Times*, December 16.

Robinson, Catherine. (2016). Personal Interview, London, May 17.

Roeper, Burkhardt. (1998). "Germany Approves DNA Tests for Visas." *Nature*: 723–723.

Rogers, Hannah, Simone Fox, and Jane Herlihy. (2014). "The Importance of Looking Credible: The Impact of the Behavioural Sequelae of Post-Traumatic Stress Disorder on the Credibility of Asylum Seekers." *Psychology, Crime & Law*: 1–17. https://doi.org/10.1080/1068316X.2014.951643

Rome Statute of the International Criminal Court, article 8. http://www.prevent-genocide.org/law/icc/statute/part-a.htm, Accessed January 21, 2017.

Rothstein, Bo and Davide Torsello. (2013). "Is Corruption Understood Differently in Different Cultures?" *Quality of Government Institute Working Paper Series* 2013.55: 1–27.

Rousseau, Cecile and Patricia Foxen. (2005). "Constructing and Deconstructing the Myth of the Lying Refugee." In Els Van Dongen and Sylvie Fainzang (eds.), *Lying and Health: Power and Performance*. Amsterdam, The Netherlands: Het Spinhuis. 56–91.

Royal College of Paediatrics and Child Health. (1999). The Health of Refugee Children: Guidelines for Paediatricians, para. 5.6.

Ruoff, David. (2014). Personal interview, Manchester, NH. August 7.

Sadiq, Kamal. (2009). *Paper Citizens: How Illegal Immigrants Acquire Citizenship in Developing Countries*. New York: Oxford University Press.

Schoenholtz, Andrew I., Philip G. Schrag, and Jaya Ramji-Nogales. (2014). *Lives in the Balance*. New York, NY: New York University Press.

Scroggins, Deborah. (2012). *Wanted Women: Faith, Lies and the War on Terrorism: The Lives of Ayaan Hirsi Ali and Aafia Siddiqui*. New York, NY: Harper, HarperCollins.

Seamark, Michael and Tamara Cohen. (2011). "Asylum Seeker Who Claimed to Have Been Gang-Raped and Witnessed Family's Murder in Somalia Exposed as As £250k Benefit Fraudster." *Daily Mail*, January 10.

Sebastian, Catherine. (2007). "The Second Decade: What Can We Do About the Adolescent Brain?" 2 *Opticon* 1826, 1, 2.

Shaw, J. and R. Witkin (2004). *Get It Right. How Home Office Decision Making Fails Refugees. A Report from Amnesty International UK*. London: Amnesty International United Kingdom.

Sherwood, Harriet and Philip Oltermann. (2016). "Churches Say Growing Flock of Muslim Refugees Are Converting." *The Guardian*, June 5.

Showler, Peter. (2006). *Refugee Sandwich: Stories of Exiles and Asylum*. McGill: Queens University.

Shuman, Amy. (1986). *Storytelling Rights: The Uses of Oral and Written Texts by Urban Adolescents*. Cambridge University Press.

Shuman, Amy and Carol Bohmer. (2004). "Representing Trauma: Political Asylum Narrative." *Journal of American Folklore* 117(466): 394–414.

Shuman, Amy and Carol Bohmer. (2007). "Trauma and Forgetting: Producing Epistemologies of Ignorance in the Political Asylum Process." *Identities* 14: 1–27.

Shuman, Amy, and Carol Bohmer. (2012). "The Stigmatized Vernacular: Political Asylum and the Politics of Visibility/Recognition." *Journal of Folklore Research* 48 (2): 199–226.

Shuman, Amy and Carol Bohmer. (2016). "The Uncomfortable Meeting Grounds of Different Vulnerabilities: Disability and the Political Asylum Process." *Feminist Formations* 28 (1 Spring): 121–145.

Sigmond, Helene. (2017). Personal Communication, January 11.

Silverman, Carol. (2012). *Romani Routes: Cultural Politics and Balkan Music in Diaspora*. Oxford University Press.

Siman, Farzad. (2016). Personal Interview, August 1.

Singer, Sarah. (2015). *Terrorism and Exclusion from Refugee Status in the UK*. Leiden: Brill Nijhoff.

Singer, Sarah. (2016). Personal Interview, February 16.

Smith, Sidonie. (2017). "Human Rights and Comics: Autobiographical Avatars, Crisis Witnessing, and Transnational Rescue Networks." In *Life Writing in the Long Run: A Smith & Watson Autobiography Studies Reader* in Sidonie Smith and Julia Watson University of Michigan Press. http://quod.lib.umich.edu/m/maize/mpub9739969/1:21/--life-writing-in-the-long-run-a-smith-watson-autobiography?rgn=div1;view=fulltext

Stapinski, Helen. (2017). "The Lost Footage of Marilyn Monroe." *New York Times*, January 13. https://www.nytimes.com/2017/01/13/nyregion/marilyn-monroe-skirt-blowing-new-york-film.html

Steidlmeier, Paul. (1999). "Gift Giving, Bribery and Corruption: Ethical Management of Business Relationships in China." *Journal of Business Ethics* 20(2): 121–132.

Stromwall, L.A. and P.A. Granhag (2003). "How to Detect Deception? Arresting the Beliefs of Police Officers, Prosecutors and Judges." *Psychology, Crime and Law* 9(1): 19–36.

Swarns, Rachel L. (2006). "Provision of Antiterror Law Delays Entry of Refugees." *New York Times*, March 8.

Sweeney, James A. (2009). "Credibility, Proof and Refugee Law." *International Journal of Refugee Law* 21(4): 700–726.

Taormina, Robert J. and Jennifer H. Gao. (2010). "A Research Model for Guanxi Behavior: Antecedents, Measures, and Outcomes of Chinese Social Networking." *Social Science Research* 39(6): 1195–1212.

Taylor, Jerome. (2016). "'Gay? Prove It Then—Have You Read Any Oscar Wilde?': JUDGES Accused of Asking Lesbian Asylum Seekers Inappropriate Questions." *The Independent*, April 3.

Terretta, Meredith. (2015). "The Evolving Refuge Definition." In Iris Berger, Tricia Redeker Hepner, Benjamin N. Lawrance, Joanna T. Tague, and Meredith

Terretta (eds.), *African Asylum at a Crossroads: Activism, Expert Testimony, and Refugee Rights*. Athens, OH: Ohio University Press. 58–74.

Thiessen, Marc. (2016). "How ISIS Smuggles Terrorists Among Syrian Refugees." *Newsweek*, April 27. http://www.newsweek.com/how-isis-smuggles-terrorists-among-syrian-refugees-453039

Thomas, Maria Achton. (2013). "Malice Supplies the Age? Assessing the Culpability of Adolescent Soldiers." *California Western International Law Journal* 44: 1–38.

Tinti, Peter and Tuesday Reitano. (2016). *Migrant, Refugee, Smuggler, Savior.* London, UK: Hurst Publications.

Toor, Amar. (2017). "Germany Moves to Seize Phone and Laptop Data from People Seeking Asylum." *The Verge*. https://www.theverge.com/2017/3/3/14803852/germany-refugee-phone-data-law-privacy

Torpey, John. (2000). *The Invention of the Passport: Surveillance, Citizenship, and the State.* Cambridge: Cambridge University Press.

Townsend, Mark. (2010). "Front: UK 'Ignoring Evidence of Torture' Among Asylum Seekers: Reports of Abuse 'Routinely Ignored': Charities Attack 'Systemic Problem'." *The Observer*, March 14: 1.

Townsend, Mark. (2016). "Revealed: Immigration Officers Allowed to Hack Phones." *The Observer*, April 10.

Transparency International Annual Report. (2012). https://www.transparency.org/annualreport/2012

Trueman, Trevor. (2008). "Reasons for Refusal: An Audit of 200 Refusals of Ethiopian Asylum-Seekers in England." *Medical Justice Foundation*. https://www.medicaljustice.org.uk/images/stories/reports/reasons%20for%20refusal%20jianl%20draft8.pdf

Tuohy, Dan. (2010) "Prosecutors: Refugee's Inspiring Story May Be Fiction." *The Union Leader* (Manchester, NH), June 29: 2.

Tuohy, Lynne. (2013). "Beatrice Munyenyezi Sentenced in Rwanda Genocide Fraud Case." *Huffington Post,* July 15.

Tutton, Richard, Christine Hauskeller, and Steve Sturdy. (2014). "Suspect Technologies: Forensic Testing of Asylum Seekers at the UK Border." *Ethnic and Racial Studies* 37(5): 738–752.

UNHCR. (1997). "Note on the Exclusion Clause: EC/47/SC/CRP.29." May 30. http://www.unhcr.org/en-us/excom/standcom/3ae68cf68/note-exclusion-clauses.html

UNHCR. (2009). U.N. High Commissioner for Refugees, Guidelines on International Protection: Child Asylum Claims Under Articles 1(A)2 and 1(F) of the 1951 Convention and/or 1967 Protocol Relating to the Status of Refugees, ¶64, U.N. Doc. HCR/GIP/09/08. Dec. 22.

UNICEF. (2016). "Birth Registration: Current Status." https://data.unicef.org/topic/child-protection/birth-registration/. Accessed November 2, 2017.

Van der Ploeg, Irma. (2003). "Biometrics and the Body As Information." In David Lyon (ed.), *Surveillance As Social Sorting: Privacy, Risk and Digital Discrimination.* London: Routledge, 57–73.

Van Wassenhove, Luk N. and Othman Boufaied (2015). "Europe Can Find Better Ways to Get Refugees in Workforces." *Harvard Business Review*, October 4. https://hbr.org/2015/10/europe-can-find-better-ways-to-get-refugees-into-workforces

Varandani, Suman. (2015). "Does ISIS Have a Passport Printing Machine? Group's Supporters May Have Entered US With Authentic-Looking Passports." *International Business Times*, 12/11/15. http://www.ibtimes.com/does-isis-have-passport-printing-machine-groups-supporters-may-have-entered-us-2221337

Viera, Kate. (2016). *American By Paper: How Documents Matter in Immigrant Literacy.* Minneapolis: University of Minnesota Press.

Vrij, Aldert. (2008). *Detecting Lies and Deceit: Pitfalls and Opportunity* (2nd Edition). Chichester, England: John Wiley and Sons.

Washington, John. (2017). "These Jurisdictions Have Become 'Asylum Free Zones'." *The Nation*, January 18. https://www.thenation.com/article/these-jurisdictions-have-become-asylum-free-zones/

Wenski, Thomas G. (2007). "Fix Glitches That Lock Out Deserving Refugees; Bishop Wenski: Laws' Unintended Effect Denies the Innocent a Home." *Orlando Sentinel*, January 22.

White, Hayden. (1973). "Interpretation in History." *New Literary History*, 4(2): 281–314.

Wiebe, Virgil and Serena Parker (2001–2). "Asking for a Note from Your Torturer: Corroboration and Authentication Requirements in Asylum, Withholding and Torture Convention Claims." *Immigration and Naturalization Handbook.* Volume 1. Washington, DC: AILA, 414–435.

WOAI News Radio. (2015). "Lie Detector Test Proposed for Syrians Who Want to Come to Texas." *Posted*, December 16.

Wolin, Richard. (2016). "Our Prophet of Deceit." *Chronicle of Higher Education*, October 30. http://www.chronicle.com/article/Our-Prophet-of-Deceit/238176?cid=cp60

Wood, Elisabeth Jean. (2008). "The Social Processes of Civil War: The Wartime Transformation of Social Networks." *Annual Review of Political Science* 11: 539–561.

Yale-Loehr, Stephen. (2016). Phone Interview, July 22.

Yee, Vivian. (2013). "Candidate for Brooklyn Prosecutor Drew Criticism for Signature Case." *New York Times*, August 20. http://www.nytimes.com/2013/08/21/nyregion/candidate-for-brooklyn-prosecutor-drew-criticism-for-case-that-made-his-name.html?rref=collection%2Ftimestopic%2FDiallo%2C%20Nafissatou&action=click&contentCollection=timestopics&region=stream&module=stream_unit&version=latest&contentPlacement=3&pgtype=collection

Yeo, Colin. (2015). "Sir Nicholas Winton and the Bygone Tradition of Refugee Welcome." *Free Movement*, July 2. https://www.frjulaeemovement.org.uk/sir-nicholas-winton-and-the-bygone-tradition-of-refugee-welcome

Yeung, Peter. (2017). "Wrongly Classifying Child Asylum-Seekers As Adults Has Cost UK Millions of Pounds." *Buzzfeed*, Posted, January 18. https://www.buzzfeed.com/peteryeung/wrongly-classifying-child-asylum-seekers-as-adults-has-cost?utm_term=.goLRvODMD#.xs1elj

Zabell, Sandy L. (2005). "Fingerprint Evidence." *Journal of Law and Policy* (Brooklyn College Law School): 143–177.

Zetter, R. (2007). "More Labels, Less Refugees: Remaking the Refugee Label in an Era of Globalization." *Journal of Refugee Studies* 20(2): 172–192. 28

CASES

Flores v. Reno (1997) Case No CV 85-4544 RJK (Px) Filed Jan 17. https://www.aclu.org/files/pdfs/immigrants/flores_v_meese_agreement.pdf

Fornah UKHL, 2006

In the Matter of ****, 2011. Redacted copy available from http://louisetrauma.weebly.com/domestic-violence.html

Islam v. Sec'y of State for the Home Dep't (Shah), [1999] UKHL 20, [1999] 2 A.C. 629, 643 (appeal taken from Eng. & Wales C.A.) 2018

M.A.B.N. and K.A.S.Y. v. Adv. Gen. for Scotland 2013.

Maslenjak v. U.S., (2017). case number 16-309, in the Supreme Court of the United States.

Matter of A-R-C-G, 26 I&N Dec. 388, 388-389 (BIA 2014).

Matter of Acosta 191 I & N. Dec. 211 (BIA 1985).

Miranda Alvarado v. Gonzales 441 F.3d 750; 2006 U.S. App. LEXIS 6902. MT (Article 1F (a)—aiding and abetting) Zimbabwe [2012] UKUT 00015(IAC)

R (A) v Camden [2010] EWHC 2882 (Admin), para. 46).

R (AA) v Secretary of State for the Home Department [2016] EWHC 1453 (Admin)

R.B. [Somalia] v. S.S.H.D. [2012] EWCA Civ 277, [2012] WLR(D) 77.

RE HB (1994). Refugee Status Appeals Authority, New Zealand, Refugee Appeal NO. 2254/94

Re J, C.R.D.D. T93-04176 et al., Dec. 7, 1993 (Can.), summat available at http://www.refworld.org/pdfid/4713831e2.pdf

Rivera-Barrientos v. Holder 666 F.3d 641 (10th Circuit, 2012)

Secretary of State for the Home Department (Appellant) v MN and KY (Respondent) [2014] UKSC 30.

United States of America v. Edin SAKOC, 2015 WL 3970514. www.refworld.org/pdfid/4713831e2.pdf

Index[1]

[1]Note: Page numbers followed by 'n' refers to notes.

© The Author(s) 2018
C. Bohmer, A. Shuman, *Political Asylum Deceptions*,
https://doi.org/10.1007/978-3-319-67404-9

191

CPSIA information can be obtained
at www.ICGtesting.com
Printed in the USA
LVHW080140061221
705387LV00009B/606